# TURF WARS

# TURF
# WARS

## THE FIGHT FOR THE SOUL OF AMERICA'S GAME

## DeMAURICE SMITH

RANDOM HOUSE

NEW YORK

Random House
An imprint and division of Penguin Random House LLC
1745 Broadway, New York, NY 10019
randomhousebooks.com
penguinrandomhouse.com

Hardback ISBN 978-0-593-72942-7
Ebook ISBN 978-0-593-72943-4

Printed in the United States of America on acid-free paper

2 4 6 8 9 7 5 3 1


FIRST EDITION

BOOK TEAM:
Production editor: Luke Epplin • Managing editor: Rebecca Berlant •
Production manager: Mark Maguire • Copy editor: Muriel Jorgensen •
Proofreaders: Liz Carbonell, J. J. Evans, Kevin Clift

*Book design by Mary A. Wirth*

The authorized representative in the EU for product safety and compliance is Penguin Random House Ireland, Morrison Chambers, 32 Nassau Street, Dublin D02 YH68, Ireland. https://eu-contact.penguin.ie.

*To the Bravest Generation.*

*My parents and my four centennial ancestors who
were a part of a noble generation of Americans who were
told to "watch their step" but nonetheless chose to stride
forward fearlessly with hope, duty, and courage.*

Until the lion learns how to write, every story will glorify the hunter.

—Chinua Achebe, *Things Fall Apart*

# CONTENTS

# TURF WARS

# IN A HEARTBEAT

My name is DeMaurice Fitzgerald Smith, and for fourteen years I was executive director of the National Football League Players Association, representing the human beings who suited up for your favorite teams. I worked for neither the franchises nor the cabal of greedy billionaires who control the league, which makes them some of the lever pullers of our larger society.

I worked for players.

The men whose uniform included an NFL helmet and pads, whose workplace was one of the league's training facilities or stadiums, who bled or cracked ribs or "got their bell rung"—they were my bosses. And my job as the leader of their union was to fight for them, go to war for them, always against their own bosses and the league's commissioner, Roger Goodell. The men who run the NFL are the same kinds of people who have traditionally accumulated power in the United States: rich, narcissistic, insecure. But rather than pursue political office, where their more devious impulses might play out in public view and be subject to reelection campaigns, these megalomaniacal capitalists have found and exploited a loophole.

In 2017, when President Donald Trump wanted an ally as he publicly attacked San Francisco 49ers quarterback Colin Kaepernick, whose on-field protests of police violence transcended sports and captured the nation's attention, it wasn't just Trump's cabinet or top advisers he contacted. It was Jerry Jones, who owns the Dallas Cowboys. When Trump was making his first run for the White House in 2016, his confidants included Robert Kraft, the owner of the New England Patriots, who has claimed to have known Trump since the 1990s. Jerry and Kraft are the most powerful people in the NFL and are therefore some of the most influential people in the country.

Be they in the Oval Office or a stadium's owner's suite, these men do not see the general public as human. They are voters and customers and fans. NFL owners view their own teams' players not as people with families, aspirations, or pride. They are laborers and commodities, nothing more, an army of soldier ants who can and will be replaced by one of the thousands of cheaper options in college football or lower-tier leagues. Owners only pretend to care about a player's remarkable journey from youth football to college and the pros, the sacrifices that must be made to reach the highest peak in American sports, or how many physical and socioeconomic hurdles must be crossed to reach this point.

They don't ache for the aging men whose careers end with chronic pain in their shoulders and hips. They don't worry for those who fear that football may have damaged their brains.

If someone's performance dips or they question authority or, God forbid, publicly challenge the league? Owners band together, emboldened by the full might of the NFL league office, and stop at nothing to squash this ant and send a message to the remaining army. Because, to them, a rogue is a threat to their business model, which centers on playing games, and no threat can or will be tolerated.

How could I make such callous suggestions? Because they've told me that this is what they think.

I spent fourteen years with a front-row seat, and again and again, owners showed me with their actions by choosing the almighty dollar over humanity and compassion and fairness every single time. It didn't matter if you were Zak DeOssie or Tom Brady.

Of the roughly 341 million people who live in the United States, about eight hundred are billionaires. That translates to about 0.0002 percent of the American population. But those eight hundred people hold more than half of the entire nation's wealth. According to Oxfam, which studies economic inequality, for every dollar an average American earns, each billionaire earns $1.7 million. And no amount is ever enough. While the rest of us were struggling during the coronavirus pandemic, be it financially or physically or emotionally, the superrich never stopped looking for ways not only to exploit the worst public health emergency in a century but to make the rest of us a little worse off. While 99 percent of the population has had to pinch pennies amid rising inflation and increasingly expensive essentials, billionaires weren't just insulated from this strain. They got richer—*way* richer: The Institute for Policy Studies reported that, in the eighteen months between March 2020 and August 2021, these eight hundred people—most of them white men—added $1.8 *trillion* to their combined portfolios.

Is it any wonder why lawmakers and the White House never send a billionaire to voicemail? That the mega-rich can sway legislation, send ripples through the economy, manipulate our wallets and habits and opinions?

Politicians may be the ones signing off on the rules governing our society, but it's that small percentage of the ultra-wealthy who decides on those rules.

There is no greater concentration of American billionaires than the NFL. The city of Green Bay, Wisconsin, owns the Packers, but the other thirty-one clubs have a principal owner. Each one has a net worth somewhere north of ten figures, and as of this writing, the combined net worth of these individuals and families is estimated at $280 billion. The median household income in the United States is $75,000, which means an average American family could work for twenty-eight thousand years and still not be as rich as Cincinnati Bengals owner Mike Brown, who, at $4 billion, is the poorest guy in the room during the twice-a-year league meetings.

More than a century ago, industry titans such as J. P. Morgan,

William Vanderbilt, and John D. Rockefeller belonged to a private organization called the Jekyll Island Club—something of a secret society. More than a century ago, some of their peers met off the coast of Georgia to unilaterally create the Federal Reserve of the United States. Today that club's equivalent is the National Football League. Like the men of Jekyll Island, NFL owners decide how the rest of us live, work, and interact.

The cohorts of Morgan, Vanderbilt, and Rockefeller did this via manipulating our banking, transportation, and education systems. Jerry, Kraft, and their cohorts use football, one of the most addictive, powerful, and profitable drugs in American culture, to influence elections and bully competitors as they ruthlessly pursue an ever-higher percentage of wealth. The most diabolical part? We have no idea that they're doing it. We think we're just watching a game or going to a Super Bowl party. So strong is the league's hold on us that, in 2024, businesses spent an average of $7 million for each thirty-second advertisement during the Super Bowl. Of the hundred most-watched television broadcasts in 2023, ninety-three were NFL games.

We're conditioned to think the individuals who run this financial and cultural behemoth are well-mannered titans of industry. They are, in fact, insecure and petulant—men who sneak partially nude photos of their own cheerleaders, destroy suites in other owners' stadiums, flip each other the bird, and fling drinks on fans. They regularly welch on their own contracts with one another.

If it's to the advantage of one or more owners, they sow division and stoke controversy. Believing they are all-powerful and untouchable, they operate only in self-interest and, for the most part, with impunity.

There's almost no government or legal oversight, and not because the NFL is protected in any way from investigation. In 2012, a prominent owner sent me a spreadsheet that practically confessed that the league had broken federal antitrust laws by coming to a secret handshake agreement that, two years earlier, had denied players millions of dollars they were contractually entitled to. This person was so sure that he and the other owners would face neither charges nor a government inquiry that he actually sent me an email with written evidence of this crime.

And he was right. Neither the Justice Department nor a state attorney general so much as opened a case file despite my meeting with all of them, email in hand.

Why? Because it's sports—supposedly the last bastion of innocence and unity in our country, the one thing we can all agree on, because Sundays in our nation are sacred. The bleachers are where fans can supposedly set aside their differences for just a few hours each week and escape the ongoing culture war, political division, and historic societal ills.

There's a problem with that notion, though, and it becomes increasingly clear when you have the view I did. The NFL isn't a distraction from the country's problems. It is a mirror image of them: economic disparity driven by corporate greed, an out-of-touch ruling class reluctant to modernize its thinking or its demographics, a baked-in racism that separates the power from the labor on our playing fields as much as in our boardrooms.

It's not *just sports*. It is, on the other hand, the most accurate look at how our nation was built, a microcosm of how the haves and have-nots stay that way, because even now, much of the NFL is run or influenced by segregationists or their sons. The NFL is the largest, most successful unregulated socialist system in America, its very existence based on a crime. If you could break the law, get rich, and face no consequences, would you? I know thirty-one guys who said yes, who *keep* saying yes, and they generally lack the moral core that divides right from wrong. They claim to police themselves, or have the league and its commissioner do so for them, but that's just another smoke screen.

They refuse to be policed, controlled, even challenged, because they have spent decades and billions engineering a system that keeps outsiders from knowing the truth, ridding themselves of competitors and anyone willing to stand up to these men, tell them no, and keep them from doing what the Jekyll Island Club did: build a structure whose hubris overpowered its wealth, ultimately leading to a crash.

The only organization that stands in the league's way is the NFLPA, and for the most eye-opening, stressful, and rewarding period of my life, I was its leader. My responsibilities included making players' working conditions safer and better, and usually that involved me being a thorn in owners' sides. Almost nothing, including the most basic acts of decency, came without a battle.

I fought for my guys, and at the same time I tried like hell to convince the owners that the game we all love, whose week-in, week-out symphony is so intoxicating, is in mortal danger. It, too, may be headed for catastrophe.

But I believed, and still believe, that football can be saved, or at least made more sustainable. And the basis of my task, time and again, seemed so simple: Just get the owners and Roger to see (and treat) players as equals, or at the very least as human beings.

■   ■   ■

ON THE EVENING of January 2, 2023, an NFL player collapsed on the field during a nationally televised game. Twenty million people watched as Damar Hamlin's heart stopped following what appeared to be a routine hit—something that happens a hundred times a game.

I don't usually watch NFL games. That may seem strange, considering that my job was protecting the interests and safety of NFL players. And the league and my critics like to paint me as someone who hates football and would like to oversee its ruin. To be fair, this job can be brutal, and the end of my tenure saw me get beaten down and deeply disillusioned, though not about the game itself. The truth is, I *love* football. Always have, and some of my favorite childhood memories were going to RFK Stadium to watch my hometown Washington Redskins alongside my dad. John Riggins, Brig Owens, Charley Taylor: Those are the guys I remember, the players I wanted to be when I grew up.

That's about as clearly as I can sum it up: I do love football. It just so happens that I love the players more. If I have to fight the league on behalf of its participants, I don't feel even a moment of hesitation.

My tasks at the NFLPA were largely performed away from the field, in the days and hours when nobody was watching. It's not unlike when I was a prosecutor in the U.S. Attorney's Office in Washington, D.C. The trial may be the show, but the real work occurs long before the judge bangs the gavel. I prepare to the verge of obsession, which isn't always good for your marriage or mental health, but what made me good as a lawyer and union leader was my willingness to contemplate every possible outcome to every possible scenario. It's game strategy. If my opponent does *this,* then I'll do *that.* Chess, not checkers, as they say.

To me, NFL games are the trial: the culmination of so much work. Coaches build and adjust their game plans; players practice and study film. Sundays are a nationwide stage production, broadcast to millions, and every time, say, the Kansas City Chiefs and Baltimore Ravens line up against each other, a million tiny boxes had to have been checked.

So by the time kickoff happens, I usually want to watch anything *but* a football game.

For reasons I don't remember, my wife, Karen, and I happened to tune into ESPN on that January night: *Monday Night Football.* Buffalo Bills at Cincinnati Bengals. Playoff implications and star power galore. We were cleaning up after dinner as, out of the corner of my eye, I saw Cincinnati receiver Tee Higgins catch a pass before colliding with Damar, a twenty-four-year-old Bills safety.

As hard as we work to make players' jobs safer, there's no denying that these are some of the world's biggest, fastest, strongest athletes slamming into one another at full speed. Their bodies are intricate vessels running on complex, rhythmic networks. Injuries will happen, and the way they play the game, with a reckless and indefatigable abandon beyond what most of us can imagine, makes it our job—*my* job—to mitigate their exposure to those injuries.

In America, it is every employer's duty to keep its workers safe. The NFL has long tried to skirt this responsibility, and players have unwittingly assisted with that narrative by thinking of themselves as gladiators charging into the arena or claiming that they "signed up" knowing the risks. To paraphrase my friend and longtime colleague Don Davis, who's maybe the most empathetic and emotionally intelligent person I've ever known, I wish those players would just go somewhere and sit down.

Translation: *Stop saying what the owners* want *you to say.*

At first I thought Damar had suffered a concussion or neck injury, and the ESPN crew cut to commercial. When the broadcast returned, the young man remained on the turf, not moving. Players, desensitized to on-field violence, were panicking. Tears streamed down shocked faces; teammates joined arm in arm as they prayed. An ambulance crept hauntingly onto the field, and one of the broadcasters reported that a defibrillator had been used to shock Damar back to life.

My phone started buzzing. A veteran NFL player was calling from one of the locker rooms.

"I saw blood," he said, his voice trembling. "We all did. Coming out of his mouth."

I assured the player that everything that could be done to help Damar was being done. He was on the way to the hospital and would receive top-notch care. Other than a hospital, the safest place you can be during a health crisis is an NFL field. With specialists on the sidelines and world-class instruments just out of sight, it's true.

My mind nonetheless pondered which boxes *hadn't* been checked, including post-trauma resources for players. In the blink of an eye, some of the toughest men in America had witnessed something that forced them to question both their physical fragility and their mortality.

As I spoke to the player in Cincinnati, ESPN's Joe Buck insinuated that Damar had been stabilized and that the NFL was pushing for the game to resume. Cameras cut to Bengals quarterback Joe Burrow, starting to loosen up on the sidelines.

"We shouldn't be playing, De," the player told me. I agreed.

I ended the call and immediately tapped the contact for Roger Goodell. I have twenty-two hundred bosses, but the NFL commissioner has thirty-one. All control freaks, all tone-deaf masters of their own fiefdoms. Nobody outside that ambulance had any idea if Damar Hamlin was alive or dead. But in that moment, as a national audience held its breath, owners plotted to remind us how devoid of compassion they are.

Advertising dollars were on the line, after all, and if this game were suspended or postponed, they saw it only through the prism of someday weakening the league's position at the negotiating table.

"I don't know anything yet," Roger said, sounding exasperated.

He said the league's chief football administrator was at the stadium. She was huddling with the teams' coaches as they discussed when and if the game would resume. They would also seek player input. Did he think this would reassure me? Players have spent lifetimes being told to play through anything, to silence the alarms of their bodies and minds while lining up for the next snap.

I implored Roger to end the game, to take the decision out of players' and coaches' hands as the league and union came together to issue a joint statement about doing the right thing.

He stalled. This is typical of Roger, who never agrees to anything in the moment. The league paints this as deliberate contemplation. I've been reminded many times what really drives it.

I could hear in Roger's voice that he was worried about Damar. I don't have the power to stop a game—no union can halt a business's production, short of calling a strike or judicial intervention—and neither does the NFL's commissioner. Not without permission from his bosses.

It was clear I needed to press onward, and I pleaded with him one last time before ending the call.

"Roger," I said, "this game needs to be *over*."

■  ■  ■

**FIFTEEN MONTHS EARLIER,** I was exhausted after a dozen years on the job. Countless fights had come and gone—from a grueling work stoppage when owners locked out players in 2011, to Bountygate and then Deflategate, to defending the rights of Ray Rice after he knocked his fiancée out cold and Kaepernick's divisive protests of police brutality toward Black Americans.

There were enemies inside my own building, with my own right-
hand man and Pro Bowl players trying to cut my throat. I had been
on the front lines of so many battles, drawing the ire of everyone from
Trump and Rush Limbaugh to Aaron Rodgers and Richard Sherman.
After the league's mishandling of return-to-play protocols during the
coronavirus pandemic, I could feel myself physically and psychologically breaking apart.

Then, in October 2021, a reporter from *The Wall Street Journal*
called. He had obtained an old email chain between Jon Gruden, the
Super Bowl–winning former coach of the Tampa Bay Buccaneers and
longtime ESPN broadcaster, an executive with another NFL team,
and, of all people, the co-founder of Hooters.

"And?" I asked the reporter.

Coaches, after all, have no union.

"Well," he said, "the email is about you."

*Dumboriss Smith has lips the size of michellin tires.*

If I had ever met Gruden, I didn't remember. I shrugged off the
language to the reporter, joked about it in our office, told myself that
any job in pro sports requires thick skin, particularly when that skin
has dark pigmentation.

Then again, it also requires denial. I took this job in 2009, just
months after Barack Obama was elected as our nation's first Black
president. This had briefly fooled many of us into thinking we had
entered a "post-racial" society, when racism would no longer exist in
real life, living on only in our imaginations and memories. That the
fissures of our economy may have been exposed during the Great
Recession, but at least we were entering a period of unprecedented
social unity and equality.

Denial is a hell of a drug.

And a useful tool, especially when, for me, denial can be used to
suppress my deepest insecurities, worries, and fears. Why would I

care what some coach thinks? Especially "Chucky," whose cartoonishly angry expressions on the sideline had earned him popularity and fame in the NFL ecosystem.

Hours turned to days and then weeks, and the longer I ruminated on Gruden's words, the angrier I became. In just nine words, he had confirmed every suspicion I had ever had about the plantation mentality that exists not only in the NFL but in the C-suites of every business, law firm, and capitol building in America. There is a ruling elite, in the league's case the owners and commissioner and coaches, overseeing the labor class beneath them. The majority of NFL players are Black, and while every player is well compensated, contracts aren't guaranteed. Meaning that, in the case of injury or a decrease in productivity or even the changing economic winds, teams can reduce what they owe and cancel a player's contract without recourse. Major League Baseball, the National Basketball Association, and the National Hockey League guarantee every dollar of every player's contract and can void it only with cause.

The NFL? Coaches and executives, few of whom identify as minorities, receive guaranteed compensation, but players do not. It's impossible to ignore the historical parallels, even as the league's public relations apparatus works tirelessly to deny them.

Gruden happened to say the quiet part out loud, unmasking a pettiness rooted in race, gender, nepotism, or class. Or all of the above.

But aren't sports the only corner of our society truly built on competition and merit? Doesn't everyone have an equal chance?

Sports leagues and the NCAA (National Collegiate Athletic Association) spend tens of millions to convince you of that. It's a fairy tale. In 2022, two-thirds of NFL players identified as Black or multiethnic. Of the league's thirty-two clubs, four—or slightly more than 10 percent—had a Black head coach, resulting from a hiring structure that provides fewer paths for coaches of color to reach top positions and achieve maximum earning potential. The numbers weren't much better for top executives, and no principal owner identifies as Black.

The bosses, in other words, are white. The workforce is Black.

And while researching an article for the *Yale Law & Policy Review,* I found that 90 percent of all coaches of color believe that the league and its owners ignore federal statutes against discrimination.

The league went so far in 2017 as to agree to pay Black retired players less because of its longtime reliance on "race-norming." That little-known neuropsychological practice assumes that Black people are born with lower cognitive potential than whites, meaning the NFL could withhold money from a Black retiree with neurological damage because that individual couldn't have been that smart to begin with.

"While racial barriers have been eroded in many areas . . . (the NFL) lives in a time of the past," lawyers for Brian Flores, the Black former head coach of the Miami Dolphins, wrote in a landmark 2022 discrimination suit against the league. "Over the years, the NFL and its 32-member organizations have been given every chance to do the right thing. Rules have been implemented, promises made—but nothing has changed."

I had somehow convinced myself I was an exception. Surely, those in and around the league didn't see *me* this way. I had gone to a top law school, obtained a coveted position in the U.S. Attorney's Office, held partnerships at two of the best firms in the world. Denial, though, has been part of my life since childhood. When my sister and I went swimming at a hotel pool during a family vacation in the early 1970s, our parents didn't tell us until much later that all of the white people had immediately fled the pool. Their vision was that we would grow up believing not that we were different or "less than," but that we were just as deserving of an education, opportunity, and time in the pool as anyone.

Gruden, therefore, saw me as I had never been allowed to see myself: the so-called Angry Black Man, hired because of his skin color, who bites the hand that feeds him by fighting every battle and suing the NFL for sport. And it's true that I engaged in public combat with the league, exchanged rough language with owners, cursed them (as they did me) as dogs. I didn't *want* to be part of their club, I told myself, which was the only explanation for why they couldn't see me as a peer.

Many fans just accepted the league's characterization of me, as an impediment to the Sunday escape. The NFL works hard to protect that comfort because, in actuality, they're not selling football. Their product is escape and, by speaking up, I was a threat to their business model.

That was the only way to get owners' attention. There's no reasoning with these people on a moral or intellectual level. In their minds, they know everything. In the micro-societies they create for themselves, there is no one to stand up to, or challenge them, or, God forbid, flatly tell them no. They believe they own not only the franchises and brands but everything and every*one* involved in the sport. Billionaires resist any ethical imperative, so you have no choice but to publicly shame them. They detest condemnation, so you must haul them into court or use the bully pulpit in the media because those are the only kinds of leverage you have.

The fact that it was a Black man doing all this? It drove them crazy.

Gruden, like so many mediocre men of his ilk, felt comfortable being openly racist with his buddies. He is part of the ruling class, after all, strutting about as if on top of the food chain. That's only as true as it is allowed to be, but the NFL is exceptionally good at shaping the contours of public opinion. A few days after *The Wall Street Journal* published its story, Mike Tirico, Tony Dungy, and James Brown appeared on national television. All three men are Black, and their achievements and platforms made them untouchable.

Brown and I grew up together in Prince George's County, Maryland, a predominantly Black community just outside Washington, D.C. I assume he, Dungy, and Tirico have family stories not unlike mine. My dad was a sharecropper, two generations removed from slavery, and his earliest memories include running his fingers across the skin bumps on his grandmother's back, physical reminders of her enslaver's whip—proof that scars are passed through the generations.

My mother and her twin brother fled Atlanta as teenagers to track down their father, who had abandoned the family, justification for escaping the brutality of the Jim Crow South. She became a nurse in Washington, D.C.'s segregated Freedmen's Hospital, where she met my dad, married, started a family, and decided on a parenting strategy that made *me* possible.

So imagine my disappointment when neither Tirico, Dungy, nor Brown came to my defense. They instead backed Gruden, an avatar for the league, presumably because their bosses instructed them to. Millions of fans, therefore, were assured that there was nothing to see here, folks, so let's get on with the games.

"I'm not going to chalk everything up to racism," Dungy said on NBC. "I think we accept his apology, move forward, and move on."

Tirico insisted he'd never heard Gruden use racist language in their time together in the *Monday Night Football* booth.

"I'm not here to judge anybody," Brown said.

It was as cowardly as it was reasonable. Even as much as I wanted to fire back publicly at Gruden, to verbally slam his head into the floor as I did the high school teammate who'd called me the N-word, I couldn't. Or at least I didn't. America, not unlike its favorite sports league, discourages people of color from speaking out.

We live by an additional set of commandments because centuries of trauma have conditioned us to keep criticisms to ourselves. Thou shalt not show anger, for this makes the powerful uncomfortable and potentially dangerous. Thou shalt work twice as hard for half as much success. And thou shalt, at all times, remind our overseers that we are just happy to be here, thankful for opportunity and nourishment, thrilled with even a moment inside the plantation house.

In the satirical film *The American Society of Magical Negroes*, one of the young characters is given supernatural powers in exchange for appeasing white people.

"We're showing the client the parts of ourselves that make them feel good," this character is told, "and nothing more."

That is how the NFL traditionally runs. Tirico, Dungy, and Brown may be happy to retain their jobs to keep their overseers comfortable.

Gruden's email, and how quickly the league made the controversy disappear, led me to make two decisions. The first was that my mom and dad, after all they had been through, deserved to hear about this not in the media but directly from their son. So I drove to Kensington, Maryland, rehearsing how I would explain this to them.

As I pulled into their driveway, my phone rang with a Tampa area code. It was Gruden, who I sent to voicemail.

"I'm really sorry about what's being written out there," he said in a file I haven't deleted. "I'd love to talk."

No thanks.

A few minutes later, ESPN reporter Chris Mortensen, whom I considered a friend, called me to ask for comment on Gruden's apology. The mighty NFL messaging apparatus, far more sophisticated than that of any political campaign, was already hard at work to deflect and obscure.

This led me to the second decision. After so many years of public losses, court cases, and backstabbings from my own side, I decided that I was done. Just before walking into my parents' house, I accepted that the time had come for me to leave this arena and, in effect, give back my magic.

To keep staying silent in the name of entertainment? To keep the league's secrets? To carry on, even a little bit, showing billionaires and their cronies the parts of me that make them feel good?

Fuck that.

■ ■ ■

ON THE NIGHT Damar Hamlin collapsed, I waited for the NFL commissioner to return my call. For years I had known Roger was driven by twin fears, both paralyzing. One was the possibility of a player dying on the field, a dread made more acute by science that brings to bear the damage football causes on the human body, in particular the brain.

That worry seemed to be playing out in real time.

Roger's other fear is that his bosses, in particular Jerry Jones and

Robert Kraft, may be disappointed in him. The league relies on smoke and mirrors, and among the NFL's truths is that Roger is nowhere near as omnipotent as he and the owners want you to believe. He presides over the NFL, yes, but far more optically than in actuality. Owners, not Roger, make decisions. He is merely their mouthpiece, even if he is personally conflicted by what has been decided.

For a long time, this confounded me. Roger is a politician, far more gifted and devoted than most elected officials, even more than his own father, a former U.S. senator. Roger doesn't have to answer to an electorate or the fourth estate. He never has to run for reelection or face a referendum. His caucus consists of the NFL's thirty-one owners, and the commissioner's job isn't to do what's right for football. It is to keep his bosses happy.

Want to understand the NFL? Don't be ashamed if you don't. Most coaches and general managers don't fully comprehend the operational dynamics of their own league, as evidenced by top executives calling *me* to get information about the salary cap or the outcome of some battle between the union and league.

The NFL is *Game of Thrones* or, to be more precise about it, a feudal society with sovereign castles scattered throughout the land. And, oh yeah: The lords all hate one another.

Every NFL owner thinks the others are idiots, liars, and con men. (In my experience, some happen to check all three boxes.) For instance, Jerry detests Kraft's power; Kraft can't stand how selfish Jerry is. They're constantly trying to humiliate and get the better of each other. It may seem odd that billionaires, these supposed titans of industry and the captains of the world's most exclusive boys' club, are so insecure. But it's the one thing they have in common.

These aren't the Vanderbilts or Rockefellers of today. They didn't start Google or Amazon or Tesla. These guys made their fortunes in hedge funds (the Carolina Panthers' David Tepper), manufacturing car bumpers (the Jacksonville Jaguars' Shahid Khan), and running truck stops (the Cleveland Browns' Jimmy Haslam)—businesses that aren't exactly shaping American life or driving the national conversation.

What NFL owners lack individually in the national zeitgeist, they try to make up for collectively by being the puppet masters of a national obsession. Jerry (oil and gas speculation) and Kraft (paper products) are by far the most powerful of them and, for the most part, they're the only owners who care about shaping league policy. Roger may only want to talk to the Baltimore Ravens' Steve Bisciotti (staffing firms) or the Buffalo Bills' Terry Pegula (fracking) when he has to, instead focusing his energy on managing the egos of the second- or third-tier owners who matter: the New York Giants' John Mara, the Pittsburgh Steelers' Arthur Rooney II, and the Kansas City Chiefs' Clark Hunt (their daddies).

Owners aren't stupid—morons on occasion, but not stupid. They realized long ago that a single massive army is more powerful than thirty-two regional ones, especially while fending off an attack. The NFL's league office, based in New York, is the capital of the kingdom, the mega-powerful force that exists only to protect the league's image and fight its wars.

Roger Goodell, then, is Prince Valiant, hired and paid $63.9 million per year to clean up the owners' messes, do public battle, and further enrich the collective. His job is to ride out on a black horse, take the arrows, and be the face of an organization whose actual leaders prefer to remain in the shadows. When Ray Rice slugs his fiancée in a casino elevator, for instance, or yet another NFL player dies and is found to have had the degenerative brain disease chronic traumatic encephalopathy, or CTE, in rides Roger to clumsily explain or deny, deny, deny.

Yes, Prince Valiant gets shot up occasionally, bloodied and impaled as he's knocked off his horse, but that's what the owners are buying for their $64 million. Because *they* split a $13 billion-a-year pie. Roger keeps getting up, limping and caked with grime, to head back into battle again and again. Why? So no owner ever has to take an arrow. So they aren't the ones explaining their antiquated views on racial injustice or trying to explain the league's domestic abuse policy or pretending concussions aren't turning some players' brains to mush.

Roger does it for them. You see him and no one else because that's who the league wants you to see. Don't believe me? Who is the chair-

man of the NFL's governing board? Don't know? You're not supposed to.

Everybody hates Roger, from fans to players, a visceral disgust.
The fact that there's so much venom is evidence of how well the system actually works. You detest Roger, so you never even think about
the Philadelphia Eagles' Jeffrey Lurie (old movie theater money), the
Houston Texans' McNair family (power plants), or the Tampa Bay
Buccaneers' Glazer family (trailer parks) until they're doing something they want you to see.

Owners keep Roger on call twenty-four hours a day, seven days a
week, and he lives in constant fear of letting them down.

When I called Roger after Damar Hamlin collapsed, demanding
he cancel a prime-time game just months after the league signed a
broadcasting rights deal worth $110 billion, he and I were 250 miles
apart. But I could almost see the blood vessel in his throat start to
pulse. That's what happens when Roger gets angry, scared, or cornered.

With Damar on the way to a Cincinnati hospital, I had no idea
what Roger would decide. The right thing for the sport or what his
soulless bosses wanted? I had a hunch, though.

"Looks like we're going out," a player wrote in a text. The NFL
was ready to pretend nothing had ever happened.

No. We couldn't allow that. *I* couldn't allow it.

I wanted to get to Cincinnati, but after 9:00 P.M., there were no
commercial flights available from any of Washington, D.C.'s three
airports. Nothing to Dayton, Louisville, or Indianapolis. I called Michael Rubin, a friend of mine with a private jet, but his plane was on
the West Coast. I even tried chartering a helicopter, but bad weather
in the Midwest curtailed that idea.

Thom Mayer, the NFLPA's medical director and my friend, assured me Damar was alive and stable. He'd experienced a rare condition called commotio cordis, or an agitation of the heart. The blow to
Damar's chest had occurred at precisely the worst time, during the
twenty-to-forty-millisecond window between heartbeats. It had knocked
his heart's rhythm offline, and without immediate treatment, 90 per-

cent of patients die. Even with access to a defibrillator, as few as four in ten people survive.

If this young man had been almost anywhere but an NFL field, he would have died. And though the league likes to take credit for that, the men who run it have repeatedly tried to make the game *less* safe because, to them, it's too expensive to protect their labor force.

These are measures *we* passed. Our union forced owners to do what's right.

On this night, the right thing was canceling a football game, something that hadn't been done after 9/11 or the assassination of John F. Kennedy. I reached out to dozens of players, many of them superstars with social media megaphones, to let it be known the NFLPA's position was that the game should end.

"Blame De," I kept saying. "*I* said we shouldn't play."

After what seemed like hours of waiting for Roger to call, my phone lit up. He may have transformed into a hollow automaton, but I wanted to believe there was some humanity left inside that cold, dark void. Would he listen to his conscience and do the right thing?

"I've decided to call the game," he told me.

Relief washed over me. Our players wouldn't be forced back onto the field. They wouldn't have to go on competing, as if one of their brothers wasn't clinging to life. Roger, at long last, had opted for the greater good. He'd been a true leader and put principle ahead of greed.

Except . . . that's bullshit.

That's the kind of fairy tale the NFL fed you that night—has been feeding you for years—but I'm here to tell you the truth about your favorite sports league. I'm finished holding my tongue about the people and controversies that came to define my tenure as executive director.

And the truth is that, when Roger came face-to-face with a crippling fear, he froze. While he waited on directions from his bosses, actual leadership was playing out inside locker rooms and among the closest band of brothers in any sport. In a moment of crisis, players built a coalition and refused to play.

They chose to neither be compliant nor be appeased and, faced with a revolt, Roger had no choice but to call the men of the plantation and tell them we had forced the league's hand.

I was the villain that night, because that's what our guys needed me to be. They could exhale and start to process, but my role in this nationwide show was just beginning. The next morning, I was on my way to Cincinnati and Damar's bedside. To be with his parents and tell them we actually *had* done everything possible to protect their son, to do what's right for him and every other human being who wears the NFL logo.

It was a frightening week. Exhausting. A little ugly, considering the league's intentions, and for me, just another day in the job. There's a saying in football, and after this latest fight, it felt appropriate.

A win's a win.

# 1

# OUTSIDER

I opened my spiral notebook and took a breath. Nearly two hundred pairs of eyes glared back, and in my mind I wondered if they'd be choosing between voting for me or breaking me in half.

"Gentlemen," I began, "the owners are *not* bluffing. They are ready to lock you out."

March 2009. The Fairmont Kea Lani hotel in Maui. A former Secret Service agent was protecting the door. This was the final stage of the NFLPA's process of selecting an executive director, and each of the final candidates was to give a presentation to a player-representative from every NFL team. Of the four finalists, I was scheduled to go first.

Nobody wanted to hear about a lockout. The league had existed for nearly a century, and owners had never initiated a work stoppage. Why would they? As long as games were played, each franchise at the time stood to pocket between $50 million and $100 million per year. Derailing their own gravy train seemed to make no sense.

But, I explained, this is what I do.

I'm a trial lawyer with an expertise in advanced game theory. I had spent months researching the league's history, finances, employment structure, and relationships. I'd met with Wall Street financiers, labor attorneys, and sports licensing experts to figure out why, a year earlier, the league had made the unprecedented move of opting out of its existing contract with players.

They had tried to remove a federal judge who'd mediated league matters for decades, and owners were publicly bragging about having accumulated a $4 billion rainy-day fund. And the NFL's new commissioner, Roger Goodell, had indicated he had no interest in being a peacetime general.

Players stared toward me. A few rolled their eyes.

It was clear, I said, that the league was gearing up, and I couldn't care less if players took me seriously, as long as they took this threat seriously.

"They *want* a lockout. And if it goes longer than six weeks, you cannot win," I said. "I'm not saying you won't. I'm saying you can't."

■  ■  ■

FOUR MONTHS EARLIER, I was just another partner at Washington, D.C.'s Patton Boggs, the heaviest-hitting legal and lobbying firm on K Street.

And I had a secret.

Barack Obama had been elected president, and this felt like more than just the dawn of a new American idealism. We as a people, especially those of us of color, had made it full circle—from the agony of bondage, the nation's original sin, and the shame of segregation, to the pride and power of the Oval Office. Obama's campaign message had been, "Yes, we can," and that never felt truer than watching the president-elect deliver his victory speech in Chicago's Grant Park.

"If there is anyone out there who still doubts that America is a place where all things are possible; who still wonders if the dream of our founders is alive in our time; who still questions the power of our democracy, tonight is your answer," he said. "Change has come to America."

Obama had already decided to name Eric Holder, Jr., a friend and mentor of mine, to be his attorney general. Eric had arranged for me to do some legal work for the Obama campaign as a side hustle, which opened the door to my joining the transition team. After Inauguration Day, I had the inside track to be appointed United States Attorney for the District of Columbia.

When I entered law school decades earlier, such a position would have been a pipe dream. For my parents? Their ancestors? Impossible. But Obama was right: Regardless of where we start, no matter our skin color, there was no mountain we couldn't climb.

Karen and I started whispering about a possible move from Maryland to Washington, and though she didn't love the idea, she knew this was my dream job and a return to where I had grown into a trial lawyer earlier in my career. This was a position Francis Scott Key, author of "The Star-Spangled Banner," once held. As had Earl Silbert, one of the first prosecutors of the Watergate trials and my first boss out of law school. And, of course, as had Eric.

When almost every prosecutor joins "The Office," as alumni call it, usually the plan is to spend three or four years prosecuting Washington's bad guys before transitioning to a private law firm. I had a different vision, having joined with my close friend Brad Weinsheimer, and remaining there for nearly ten years before Eric summoned me to a job in the Deputy Attorney General's Office. The idea of returning to "The Office" as the top dog felt like a dream.

Then, just days after the election, a former law partner called. A search firm had been reaching out to me. "You haven't returned any of their calls," my friend said.

When you're an attorney in Washington, especially at a prestigious white-shoe firm like Patton Boggs, it feels as if headhunters call you every week. Flattering as it may seem, usually these calls are from desperate people on fishing expeditions. If they broker a job change, the law firm that poaches you gets bragging rights and the search company gets a commission. It's just part of the job's ambient noise.

"No," my friend said, cutting off my spiel about the transition team, the White House, the many irons I had in the fire. "They're interested in you being the executive director of the NFL Players Association."

"Dumbest thing I've ever heard," I said.

As much as I prided myself on being an exceptional trial lawyer, risk strategist, and adviser to chief executives and boards of directors at some of the biggest companies in the world, I was not an NFL agent, nor was I certified to advise athletes. My football career had ended in high school. I had never taken a sports law class, did no legal work for the NFL or any sports league, and had zero experience as a labor attorney. I had gone to NFL games with my dad, but that was the extent of my qualifications.

"Just talk to them," my friend insisted. I agreed, but only as a professional courtesy.

If I suspected this was a waste of time before, my research into the job left no doubt. The search firm, Chicago-based Reilly Partners, had identified more than a hundred preliminary candidates to succeed Gene Upshaw, a legendary former NFL player and executive director of the sport's players union since 1983. The more I read about him, the less qualified I felt. The executive director of a sports union is the direct counterpart of the league's commissioner. They are the parallel and dueling figureheads of the armies at their backs.

As a player and union leader, Gene had led three strikes, forcing owners to adopt such basic workplace benefits as a 401(k) and severance pay, and he oversaw a landmark settlement of star player Reggie White's class-action lawsuit in 1993 that allowed players to become free agents. Until then, players were stuck with the team that drafted them, with little to no control over their own careers.

Working almost entirely behind the scenes, Gene was one of the most consequential figures in American sports history, helping players to break free of the league's almost total control and establish what was essentially a workers' bill of rights. The guy was an absolute *killer*, a soldier for his guys until the end, which had come abruptly and unexpectedly. In August 2008, Gene was diagnosed with pancreatic cancer and died three days later.

Search Firm Guy explained to me that the union's most influential players had requested that any list of possible successors include at least a few names with no connection to or background in sports whatsoever, so I suppose I was qualified in that sense.

In my head, the firm might be looking for a guy like Eric Holder, but he wasn't hirable. Not only had he been tapped to preside over the Justice Department, but he had also worked directly for the NFL after one of its biggest stars, Atlanta Falcons quarterback Michael Vick, was indicted for his involvement in an illegal dogfighting ring. Eric's firm, Covington & Burling, had represented the NFL for decades and the league's longtime commissioner, Paul Tagliabue, had been a successful litigator before owners hired him in 1989. After Vick's conviction, Eric had overseen the league's own investigation into the matter. He couldn't be a candidate.

But me? No such conflict. After I spoke with the search firm, it seemed as if I was seen as "Eric Holder Lite" and that the union was at least interested in someone who knew how to oversee a potentially harsh negotiation and navigate an increasingly fraught political arena. In 2007, with the league drawing unwanted attention from Capitol Hill after a series of news stories outlined the use of performance-enhancing drugs and football's link to a potentially devastating neurological disease, NFL commissioner Roger Goodell had dispatched a top lieutenant to Washington to be a lobbyist on the league's behalf. A year later, the league started the Gridiron PAC, a political action committee designed to cozy up to lawmakers and, let's face it, throw them off the NFL's scent.

My actual connections to the political world were virtually nonexistent, but that evidently wasn't how Search Firm Guy saw it. I had a direct line to Eric, who had the ear of the next president. Still, I wasn't a lobbyist. My job in 2008 was to represent major corporations in massive, potentially ten- and eleven-figure lawsuits. We called these "bet-the-company cases," because they posed huge risks to an organization's overall value, share price, and day-to-day finances, meaning a company had no choice but to hire the best of the best lawyers to defend it.

A guy like me gets called in for one reason: Your company or one of your executives is in a *lot* of trouble, and the firm has agreed to take you on as a client. Once that sequence begins, it's win or die. Luckily for every boss I have ever had, I am a meticulous, possibly obsessive planner who drills through layers of a case like those on a topographical map, inspecting each layer, testing each one for strengths and weaknesses, finally reaching the base before reassembling the entire map in a way that can be understood, manipulated, and organized into a winning argument.

I don't lose. I may not always win, but on "game day" my side doesn't lose.

In 1999, I was at a different firm, Latham & Watkins, when a Ford Motor Company power plant exploded in suburban Detroit. Six workers died and fourteen more were injured. By the time the case reached my desk, the insurance company that covered Ford was refusing to pay for damages in excess of about $1 billion while trying to blame the entire catastrophe on Ford. We represented the automaker in what became a huge case because of the amount of money at stake, as losing was not an option. They hired the partners billing thousands of dollars per hour while also providing me a once-in-a-lifetime perspective on how insurance works.

The meeting was cordial and informal, and what Search Firm Guy described about the union and an approaching negotiation sounded ominous. I told myself the firm was merely checking a box by interviewing me for ninety minutes, and in my mind, there was no path for me to be a serious candidate to succeed Gene Upshaw, the NFLPA's larger-than-life boss.

I was nonetheless asked to remain in the candidate pool, and we agreed to keep our lines of communication open. But that's one more thing you tend to get used to when you practice law at a major firm. To me, the only way this discussion made sense was if the players union might soon be in the market for legal counsel.

We just needed to keep it quiet.

I hadn't told my boss, Thomas Hale Boggs, Jr., about the likelihood that I'd be named U.S. Attorney for the District. Tom was my Upshaw: a legendary figure and storyteller who had started the firm after working for President Lyndon B. Johnson, eventually shaping it into a legal behemoth that, by 2008, was hauling in an astonishing $348 million in annual revenue.

Considering all the scenarios and examining the possible layers, as always, my plan was to use the NFLPA's approach as a way to add to Patton Boggs's earnings—because, I thought, whenever I told Tom that I'd be leaving the firm for my dream job, handing off a potential multimillion-dollar client was a decent way to soften the blow.

■   ■   ■

GOOD TRIAL ATTORNEYS are incurably, possibly compulsively, curious. So it's not as if I could just forget about the NFLPA thing. So, when I returned to my office, I called a meeting with two friends and colleagues who generally saw the world the same way as I did—and, also like me, who enjoyed trying to untie intellectual knots.

Just as important, I knew I could trust Heather McPhee and Ahmad Nassar because they were the only people at Patton Boggs who knew about my future job running "The Office." The three of us had worked together and been a team at Latham & Watkins, where I had become that firm's first Black partner, before the three of us headed over to Patton Boggs. Both are brilliant researchers and tacticians, each a graduate of the prestigious University of Chicago School of Law, but my favorite parts of them were their differences.

Heather is excitable and fluent in the beautiful language of profanity, with an almost supernatural ability to listen, process information, and document facts, a skill that would save our necks time and again. Ahmad is calculating and calm, ruthlessly meticulous with a talent for deconstructing legal principle to apply it in a way that best aids a client—ice, in other words, to Heather's fire.

Our bond was rooted in a shared confidence in the things we knew and an inquisitiveness about what we didn't, which is part of what drove us to begin what became a forensic investigation of the NFL and NFLPA.

This kind of deep dive into a potential client is standard practice at the biggest, most competitive law firms. If a major corporation is thinking of hiring us, for several reasons it's important for us to establish a thorough understanding of the company's legal structure and history, along with its strengths and weaknesses. One reason is that it shows the potential client that we care enough not to just give a damn but, in short order, to learn more about the business than much of its own C-suite knows. It helps us provide a speculative list of solutions to whatever problem that brought the potential client to us in the first place, and it also helps us find out if there's some level of danger the firm should just avoid. We were used to devoting hours to the resulting pitch documents, tens of thousands of dollars' worth of labor hours, for just the hope of being hired.

We spent four days peeling back the layers of the NFL and players union, the historic agreement in 1966 to merge the National Football League with the rival American Football League, the NFL's byzantine power structure, and the team owners who ran roughshod over every federal, state, and local law that would otherwise protect its labor force. Its commissioners were household names, well known in American culture for their power in a sport that seemed to become more popular (and profitable) by the decade. The "league" was in reality the collective alliance of all the franchise owners, with a posh headquarters in Midtown Manhattan. The U.S. government considered the NFL a nonprofit organization, which was confusing because a company that hauled in $8 billion in 2009 had somehow been deemed tax-exempt (it wouldn't relinquish this nonprofit status until 2015).

This wasn't a sports company. It was a massive corporation with a robust legal team whose primary responsibility, it seemed, was keeping the NFL free of governmental checks and balances. This allowed it to collect allies and systematically destroy enemies, serving notice time and again that anyone who wanted to work and exist in this space had better fall in line, keep their mouth shut, and sell off a slice of their soul.

The NFLPA, meanwhile, seemed to merely exist by the thinnest of threads. A coldly brutal monolith, the league shamelessly bullied its

workforce, took a lopsided amount of revenue, and had for generations denied players pensions, meaningful healthcare, and a fair wage.
Even the NFL draft, which the league had developed into a made-
for-TV spectacle, had been installed decades earlier for neither entertainment nor fairness. It was to suppress player wages and strip
players of the freedom to choose not only their workplace but the city
in which they were employed.

Gene Upshaw had been a warrior, but as we dug deeper, I had my
doubts that the cancer in his pancreas was any more responsible for
killing him than the job was. Yes, he had spearheaded three work
stoppages to try to force a more equitable landscape, but the owners
had steamrolled players in every instance—largely because the most
powerful among them, even those with nothing to lose by standing
up to owners, crossed the picket line. Joe Montana, for instance, had
won two Super Bowls at the time and was seen for years as arguably
the greatest quarterback of all time. When 1,585 of his professional
teammates were counting on him during a strike in 1987 for better
pay, more robust benefits, and improved injury protections, Montana
screwed them by siding with owners and going back to work.

Like any labor organization, we learned, the NFLPA represented
members in all matters since declaring itself an independent union in
1968: wages, hours, and working conditions. Its organizational structure was, in a word, confusing. There was an executive director but
also a president, an executive committee but also a board of player
representatives.

So we dug even deeper.

The NFLPA president, in theory the union's most powerful figure,
is a player who must be on an active roster and a union member "in
good standing," according to the union's bylaws, at the time of his
election. The president and ten vice presidents, also players, make up
the executive committee and serve two-year volunteer terms before
running for reelection. Think of this as the Senate of professional
football. The House of Representatives, therefore, is the board of
player reps. Members of each team appoint a player as the union's

eyes and ears in the locker room, along with three alternates—all of whom vote on major decisions. It is a diverse and occasionally un- wieldy group, with each player rep stumping for concerns and wishes unique to the culture of their locker room.

Then there's the executive director. There had been only two in the union's history, Gene Upshaw and Ed Garvey, and this position is the NFLPA's primary advocate, administrator, and public face. Rich- ard Berthelsen, a longtime union lawyer, had been installed as in- terim. The full-time job comes with lots of media scrutiny and pressure but, on paper, the least amount of power. The executive director serves at the pleasure of the executive committee and is elected for three-year terms. The executive director's most important responsibil- ity is representing the union during collective bargaining negotiations, essentially an all-encompassing contract between players and owners that determines everything from how long each NFL team can prac- tice to the share of total revenue each side receives.

And this was a part of the knot that Heather, Ahmad, and I just couldn't untangle. The most recent collective bargaining agreement, a three-hundred-page document ratified in 2006, had been scheduled to last six years. Owners, though, had in May 2008 exercised an arcane clause that allowed either side to terminate the agreement two years early and, at least in theory, return to the negotiating table in 2011 instead of 2013. It's not terribly unusual to have such a clause. It is odd that, after only two years, the league had unanimously voted to deploy it—almost as if that had been their plan all along.

Gene had pushed back, insisting to owners and Roger Goodell that their power move, meant to strike fear into players under the threat of an owner-driven work stoppage, would fail. The NFLPA, he pledged, would cede no ground on the gains they had made in previ- ous collective bargaining agreements.

But then Gene died, and the mystery deepened. Gene's right-hand man in the union, president Troy Vincent, had abruptly quit in March 2008, and media reports suggested this was because Vincent and Gene had a falling-out so cataclysmic that the two didn't speak in the five months before Gene's passing.

Callous as this may seem to the legally uninitiated, the three of us sat in my office and strategized. We determined that NFLPA wasn't just in trouble. With leadership questions and a group of billionaires signaling an approaching war, it seemed to us that—and this being a legal term, of course—players were screwed.

. . .

WEEKS LATER, I was summoned to a hotel meeting room in Dallas. About a dozen NFL players wanted to sit down with me on January 20, 2009. The date of Obama's historic inauguration, when more than two million jubilant supporters would gather on the National Mall to witness and breathe in a pivotal and inspiring moment of social and racial progress.

"Can we not reschedule?" I asked.

Not a chance.

So I promised Karen I'd be back in time for us to toast the First Couple at an inaugural ball and found myself in a car before sunrise, off to the airport. Seven years after 9/11, Washington was the most paranoid place in America. Local and federal law enforcement was scattered throughout the city, access to the skies and rivers had been restricted, and swaths of roads were sealed. I wasn't truly annoyed, though, until I made it to Dallas but my checked bag didn't. My blazer was inside, and the only replacement the airport Brooks Brothers carried was six sizes too big.

I bought it anyway, leaving it unbuttoned in an attempt to look like I *wasn't* wearing a heavy-duty tarp. Tim Christine, the NFLPA's security director, who—being trim and bald—looked every bit like the retired Secret Service special agent he was, drove me to the hotel. Then I waited. And waited. Noon, when I was booked on a flight home, came and went. I called Karen, who advised me to just find her "whenever."

Three hours after the meeting was scheduled to begin, Tim escorted me in, and I immediately scanned the faces. After years of trials, it's almost a habit. Meetings, cocktail parties, even cookouts—all the world's a jury selection, and I'm an expert on body language and social cues. There was Domonique Foxworth, the slim Baltimore defensive back, staring at me with skepticism; Mike Vrabel, the New England linebacker, impassive and looking impatient, like he'd rather be anywhere else in the world; Brian Dawkins, the hard-hitting Philadelphia safety, with his gliding movements, manicured goatee, and pressed blazer making him look a hell of a lot more put-together than me.

"Can I bring you some water?" a man asked.

"Sure, sparkling?" I replied, and he shuffled to a nearby table.

When he returned, offering me a glass, I noticed the man's face: Drew Brees, the New Orleans quarterback.

"To begin," Tennessee Titans offensive lineman Kevin Mawae said, "why don't you explain why you're interested in this job?"

This enormous human was almost scowling.

"I'm *not*," I snapped, by now fully annoyed. "You guys approached me."

Months earlier, he had been elected as Vincent's replacement, and I wouldn't learn until much later why Kevin wasn't in a jovial mood. For the moment, I knew I would have disqualified this guy from any potential jury pool and matched his glare in an act of trial lawyer swagger. It wasn't fake, because I knew their business in a way they did not, so I opened the blue binder I was cradling to prove it. When I did, a white sticker announced the binder's usual purpose: ALEX'S MATH FOLDER.

Karen had given me our son's school binder. It was just that kind of day. I nonetheless launched into the results of the two-hundred-page client report Heather, Ahmad, and I had generated. I started by framing the history and structure of the NFL in the context of labor negotiations, pointing out something I thought was obvious: that a lockout isn't the same as a strike. It's worse. This is the most aggressive measure that management can take against its workers, and in this case, it meant that owners would cut off players' salary, eliminate their health insurance, and adopt a strategy that choked out opposition until the NFLPA accepted a deal that was patently unfair.

Owners viewed players as neither equals nor peers but rather as complaining children who could and would be punished simply for talking back. With little history of successful defiance, given the players' three failed strikes and the spinelessness of some star players, owners held all the cards. Since the advent of free agency in 1993, the bones of every subsequent collective bargaining agreement had been essentially the same. Gene Upshaw and Paul Tagliabue had presided over more than a dozen years of labor peace but, considering that Tagliabue stepped down in 2006 and Gene had passed away, both of them were gone.

The league had spent the previous two years painting Roger, its new commissioner, as a no-nonsense sheriff who would restore order to the league and fix the perception that players had gotten the better of owners in the most recent collective bargaining agreement. I explained that the NFL had hired some of the same lawyers who had represented the National Hockey League in a 2004–05 lockout, squeezing players until they limped back to work, eager to accept pay cuts and robbed of millions of dollars in shared revenue.

Those lawyers had gone so far as to try to remove David S. Doty, the federal district court judge who had refereed disputes between the league and players since 1993. Doty had recently ruled in favor of Michael Vick after the Atlanta Falcons attempted to recoup $16 million in roster bonuses during his dogfighting scandal, and owners were furious that Doty had gone against them.

The Vick saga had been a horrific stain on pro football, and bringing it back up now made several players squirm. It dawned on me then that they thought that if the Falcons had reclaimed that cash, it would have gone back into the pool of money divvied up among players.

The Falcons' owner, Arthur Blank, acted as if he had every right to keep the money. Then again, Vick's contract stipulated that it was still owed to Vick. There was no clause that made good behavior or even avoiding a criminal conviction a condition of his getting paid. That $16 million had been *guaranteed,* Doty had defied a bunch of entitled lords, and now they wanted him nowhere near a new collective bargaining agreement negotiation.

"I've brought more than a hundred cases to trial and probably had another hundred before a judge," I told the players. "Know how many times I tried to remove a federal judge?"

The guys looked at me but said nothing.

"Never," I continued, "because it's courtroom suicide."

I saw Brees smile, and I wondered how many of the men in this meeting understood the stakes they were facing. The owners weren't posturing. They were preparing for an all-out blitz. If it was true that, amid the Great Recession, the league had somehow stashed away $4 billion, as the owners were publicly claiming, the players were in trouble. At most, I said, the NFLPA had $300 million banked. If the league declared war, owners had armed themselves with a howitzer. Financially speaking, players were packing a slingshot.

The thing is, I explained, I was skeptical they actually had the $4 billion they kept bragging about. As thorough as we had been in researching the league and owners in assembling our dossier, this part made no economic sense. The end of 2008 and beginning of 2009 were the worst of the economic crash that would be known as the Great Recession, the worst collapse in nearly a century. The national housing market cratered, with millions of Americans trapped in troublesome subprime mortgage loans, leading to more than three million foreclosures and the loss of $9.8 trillion in wealth. Pressure accumulated on some of the biggest banks, including several previously determined to be "too big to fail," with Bear Stearns, Washington Mutual, and Lehman Brothers eventually going under.

Only a handful of NFL owners had backgrounds in finance, but nearly all of them had financing for stadiums and renovations. Some had large debts tied to prime loans. But somehow they had been immune? *They* had each kicked in an average of nearly $130 million to create this supposed lockout war chest?

Something didn't add up.

Sure, I continued, NFLPA lawyers will recommend that players decertify as a union and file a class-action lawsuit against the league. But this was simple strategy. Boilerplate stuff. Owners and their high-powered attorneys would see this coming. They were ready for it.

And with Obama's predecessor, George W. Bush, flooding the federal judiciary with pro-business judges, I didn't like players' chances in court. Even a win was unlikely to deliver players a fair collective bargaining agreement.

Brandishing my son's blue math folder, I told players my team back in Washington had a different game plan. We believed it was watertight. And it started with suggesting that every player prepare for a war they may never have to fight instead of fighting a battle they didn't believe was coming.

"These guys are out for blood," I said.

No one said a word. Nobody asked a question. Kevin shook his head, and Brian issued a long sigh. After a few silent moments, Drew finally spoke up.

"Would you be willing to give us your blueprint," he said, "even if you don't get the job?"

I chuckled, unsure if he was joking.

"Sorry, guys," I said. "That's not the way this works."

■　■　■

**WHEN I FINALLY** touched down back in Washington, still buzzing hours after Obama's swearing-in, I noticed a voicemail on my phone. I had met George Atallah in 2006, since we were both assigned to help save an evil corporation from ruin—me a lawyer at Latham & Watkins, George a young ace messaging expert for Qorvis Communications. He was young, by no means the most senior person on his side, and he and I may have been the only people in a room of about fifty who thought the corporation's narcissistic chief executive testifying before Congress was an idiotic idea.

We stayed in touch after that meeting, and even before we became friends, I was struck by how he could somehow mix ruthlessness with loyalty. And, through his connections in the media world, he seemed to know the details of a story before it became public. I had asked him to help me think through this overture from the NFLPA.

As the plane taxied, I heard George's voice.

"Just letting you know," he said, "that ESPN is about to release that you're among the final three candidates to be executive director."

This told me a couple of things. First was that the players clearly wanted a fighter in the mix. Next was that my supposed confidentiality agreement with the search firm was over. For reasons I still can't explain, the meeting with players in Dallas had convinced me that I wanted this job. These guys just weren't equipped to fight a war they hadn't even seen coming, and I truly thought I could help them.

If I was going to aggressively pursue it, though, I would need to alert Tom Boggs, my boss, and Eric Holder, set to become my *future* boss. My first call went to Karen, because, as an accountant, she weighs the potential risk in everything.

"Why is *this* the right thing?" she asked.

Short answer? I didn't know. My family is filled with preachers, and when I was an undergraduate at Cedarville College, a Baptist and mostly pre-seminary institution in Ohio, there was a time I felt that the ministry was my calling. I have a strong Christian faith, ingrained and strengthened by my grandfather, Frederick Douglas Smith, who, for as long as anyone could remember, had been a church pastor in the tight-knit rural Virginia community where my family's roots took hold. I could think of no better path than following in this incredible man's footsteps, and Cedarville introduced me to both the pros and the cons of the Baptist Church's teachings. On one hand, Jerry Falwell and his theocratic ilk had used hyper-conservative and isolationist Christianity to strike a fissure in our culture that was as politically useful as it was lucrative.

I preferred the perspectives of Howard Thurman, James Cone, and William Barber, who wrote thoughtfully about salvation theology and loving the sinner instead of shaming or even ostracizing him. This was the backbone of Martin Luther King, Jr.'s teachings, centered on uplifting the meek and fighting for the underprivileged, and over time this pitted the dogmatic beliefs of my youth against those that encourage believers to grow, protect, and seek justice for the wider flock. Considering the ideological gulfs in our present-day society, I figure that experience may not be unique.

But my wife knew that this tension had informed my worldview long after it had prevented me from supposedly feeling guided to the pulpit as if by the hand of God. Pastors talk about this in terms of a spiritual awakening more than the pursuit of a profession. I just never felt it, and I wondered if anyone actually did.

Until now.

"I can't really put my finger on it," I told my wife. "It just feels like a calling."

When I got home, she and I quickly dressed for the Inauguration Day parties and headed toward Patton Boggs to meet good friends Todd Jones, Steve Rau, and their wives. From there it was a short ride to the event hotel, where we would share space with Barack and Michelle on this pivotal day, and where I knew a tough conversation awaited me.

Eric was there, and the impending ESPN report meant that I had to tell him about the last few months: the search firm, the paring down of hundreds of candidates, that I was about to be announced as a finalist. I blurted it all out, including for good measure this feeling in my bones that this was what I was meant to do. He nodded and looked into my eyes.

"So let me get this right," he said. "You have a job to be the U.S. Attorney in January, and you're willing to give that up for a job that you *might* get in March."

Well, when you put it that way . . .

"I just kind of feel like this is the right thing," I told Eric. He wished me luck. I know now that he thinks I made the right decision, underscored by remarks he made after grueling fights I would go on to have with the NFL.

"Well done," which is Eric's way of gushing, may not seem like the most inspiring words. But, knowing Eric's wisdom and the vast expanse of his mind, they meant the world to me.

My final conversation was about to be the hardest. Tom Boggs is a legendary lawyer and political fixer, just a straight-up avatar of the Washington, D.C., badass. Pretty solid pedigree, too.

His dad was the Louisiana congressman Hale Boggs, who happened to rise to power at the same time as the NFL-AFL merger. The fourteen-team NFL had existed since 1920, but the AFL gained traction in the 1960s for signing the biggest college football stars and because its high-scoring games were more appealing to audiences than the traditional defense-wins-championships ethos of the NFL. Eight insurgent team owners, whose enterprise lost so much money that their nickname was "The Foolish Club," nonetheless took on the establishment with franchises in major markets such as New York, Boston, and Oakland.

A television contract with NBC forced the NFL to the negotiating table, because the infusion of cash allowed Kansas City Chiefs owner Lamar Hunt and AFL commissioner Al Davis to outbid for players who had been drafted by the New York Giants, San Francisco 49ers, and Dallas Cowboys. When Alabama quarterback Joe Namath signed in 1965 with the AFL's Jets instead of the NFL's St. Louis Cardinals, a merger was inevitable.

Tom was a young tax lawyer then, but he occasionally spent free time as a congressional runner for his father, who'd risen to House majority whip. The merger required special congressional approval, and Hale Boggs led the lobbying efforts for a new antitrust law that would grant limited immunity for both leagues. The two pillars that govern sports are antitrust and labor law, the latter being the subject of numerous disagreements over whether professional athletes are "employees," thereby entitled to protections such as the forty-hour workweek.

Antitrust law governs monopolies, a direct federal response to robber barons of the nineteenth-century railroad, banking, and steel companies that drove up prices by limiting production while also forcing workers to live in oppressive "company towns." Employees had no choice but to buy food and shelter from the powerful corporations and trusts that employed them, and antitrust laws were designed to rescue workers from this supposed "free" market, though the likes of Cornelius Vanderbilt, J. P. Morgan, and John D. Rockefeller didn't get superrich by being passive. They simply colluded to skirt these laws and keep their machines running, employees working around the clock, children coated in coal dust and railroad dirt.

It wasn't until a group of Colorado mine workers went on strike in 1914, eventually leading to strikebreakers led by the National Guard firing machine guns into a crowd and killing twenty-one workers and injuring dozens more, that public sentiment shifted and compelled the federal government to enact child-labor laws and companies to adopt the eight-hour workday.

Sports leagues can be monopolies, too, and if not for these congressionally approved loopholes—including, notably, that players *are* workers who must be allowed to form a union, with protections agreed on by management—today's NFL would not be allowed to exist.

Anyway, in a story that, I'll admit, may be apocryphal, Hale Boggs asked his son to deliver a handwritten note to NFL commissioner Pete Rozelle. The latter read it, scrawled his own note, and gave it to Tom to bring back to the Capitol. Unable to help himself, the young man stopped and read the note.

### FINE WITH MERGER, CONDITION: LOUISIANA GETS TEAM

And that, as legend has it, was how the New Orleans Saints came to exist. Hale Boggs took his political victory back to Louisiana, cruising to reelection, just months before the first NFL-AFL Championship game. Today this contest is known worldwide as the Super Bowl.

On that early February morning in 2009, I sat down at my desk just before my phone rang. It was Tom's assistant. Tom wanted to see me in his office. Now.

*Dammit.*

I had mentioned my candidacy to Tom the morning after the inauguration, and though he'd been cool about it at the time, a hastily called meeting with the boss is never good news. Tom may have been a mentor, but he wasn't the type to have friends. Especially not those working for him at a ruthless firm that was a lot different from the Latham & Watkins cruise ship. Patton Boggs was more like a pirate ship, its partners and associates mercenaries, its captain a combination of William Bligh and Jack Sparrow.

Tom didn't usually do a sit-down in his office. His preferred meeting space was a center table at The Palm, where he pounded martinis while glad-handing executives, elected officials, and media figures while you tried to go drink for drink, all while trying to stay sober enough to learn how Washington actually works.

I walked in, and Tom was chomping on his morning cigar. His office had the mother of all exhaust systems, which was the only thing keeping me from entering a thick cloud of smoke.

"We have a problem," he boomed.

The NFL had recently approached Patton Boggs, he explained, about retaining the firm as its chief lobbyist. Such an arrangement can be worth millions of dollars per year. I knew Tom and the Saints' owner, Tom Benson, had known each other since they were kids in New Orleans. It had been Benson, in fact, who'd phoned to suggest such an agreement.

"What do you think?" he asked me.

"Obviously it's a great deal," I said with a shrug. I hoped he couldn't hear the crashing sound my insides were surely making.

This was a shrewd act of political chess, I immediately realized, because the league was trying to freeze me out. Any business association with the NFL would represent a conflict of interest and would disqualify me from working with the union. If I wanted to stay in the race, my partnership at Patton Boggs meant I had a fiduciary duty to resign, leaving me out of a job if I lost an election with a bunch of football players who couldn't seem to decide if they liked me or wanted to throw me into rush-hour traffic.

It was a death sentence, and part of me admired that it was as brilliant as it was diabolical.

"I'll step down immediately," I told Tom.

He just stared at me, gnawing on that damn cigar. This was a poker player at the top of his game. I made myself stare back.

"I told Tom Benson to go fuck himself," he said.

I perked up, not sure I had heard him correctly, considering the wave of shock and relief that was washing over me. Tom had declined the league's proposal and its millions.

"The NFL is afraid of you," he said, "which means you better go win that fucking job."

■  ■  ■

BY THE TIME I arrived in Maui for the NFLPA's annual meeting and the election of Gene Upshaw's successor, the process was down to three guys. Trace Armstrong had played fifteen seasons in the NFL, the last eight of which he'd spent as president of the union. Troy Vincent's background was nearly identical: fifteen years as an NFL defensive back, four of them as president.

And me.

I'd been a serviceable high school running back at Riverdale Baptist in Maryland, and five months earlier, I'm not sure I had even *heard* of the NFLPA. If I didn't have imposter syndrome when *New York Times* columnist Bill Rhoden threw his full support behind Vincent, it was in full force when the NFL posted a written endorsement of Troy on its official website—going so far as to suggest that Gene had handpicked his successor more than a year earlier.

"It should be Troy Vincent. It has to be Troy Vincent," the piece read. "Vincent is a man of character and a man of the players. His passion for their lot is genuine. His ability to reach across the aisle among his players and in the league is sturdy. His knowledge about NFLPA affairs is beyond repute."

Sounds like a swell guy. Still, it struck me as odd that the NFL was backing a presumed opposing general.

The election process had been explained to me in terms that felt almost papal. The executive committee and full board of player reps is the conclave, and instead of deliberating and casting votes inside the Sistine Chapel, that would occur inside the sealed-off Fairmont. The operation is secretive, with no one on the outside aware of where the candidates stand or the issues in play, to say nothing of any potential behind-the-scenes alliances and oaths. The Vatican's Swiss Guard is a group assembled by Tim Christine, the NFLPA's security chief whom I had met in Dallas, there more to protect the process itself than the safety of the finalists.

And like a conclave, this process can take as long as it needs to take. I kept joking to Karen that we would learn that an executive director had been chosen only when we saw the unmistakable sight of white smoke wafting from the Fairmont.

The three finalists were forbidden to leave the Marriott until it was our turn to address the group, at which point Tim would knock on our doors before security staff escorted us to the players' hotel. Our first night had been a disaster. Alex had been up most of the night with a stomach bug, and it felt as if every time I sat down to study my PowerPoint slides, he was heaving again. Elizabeth, our daughter, was on a seventh-grade trip to Mexico, so at least Karen and I were able to take turns comforting our son and cleaning up. I'm not a great sleeper in general, but that's especially true when I'm away from home, so I took the late shift while Karen slept. Around midnight, my phone buzzed.

"Hey, De, it's Trace," the voice said. We hadn't met, and everyone seemed to agree that Trace Armstrong was a nice guy. He asked if I was interested in getting coffee the next morning, and I said sure, asking if we could meet up later in the morning considering my son was ill. Bizarrely, Trace said his kid was sick, too.

Whatever. Surely just a coincidence.

By the time Trace and I met in the lobby hours later, I had begun learning about other weird stuff. For one, it seemed that a small army of Troy's friends and loyalists, many of them current NFL players and board members, were busy trying to stack the deck in Troy's favor. They wanted votes to be cast verbally rather than via secret ballot, as stipulated by the NFLPA's constitution. I had learned more about Troy during this process, though my deeper dive into his questionable methods and character wouldn't come until later. Everyone said Troy was likable but persistent to a fault, and he had spent the weeks lead-ing up to the meeting forcing discussions with board members who claimed to be on the fence about their vote. Presumably just to get him off their backs, I had heard, some guys had promised to vote for him, and now Troy's guys were trying to get them to stand in front of everyone and, by announcing their selection, create pressure to stick with Troy.

Kevin Mawae, who a year earlier had narrowly won the NFLPA presidency over Brian Dawkins, refused. The constitution is the con-stitution, and to preserve the vote's integrity, Kevin had hired a well-known accounting firm to count votes.

Back at the Marriott, Trace and I got coffee and formally intro-duced ourselves. I was scheduled to present first, but Trace suggested he and I join forces, similar to how many people wanted Obama and Hillary Clinton to team up to secure victory. Okay, I wondered, but which of us was Hillary and which was Obama? Who'd be the top dog? Trace tried selling me on this, but I declined, saying I was more comfortable just doing my own thing.

I retreated to the biohazard site that was my hotel room, and I was relieved when there was a knock on my door. It was go time. Standing outside a courtroom, just before the doors opened, used to be my favorite part of a trial: heart racing, blood pumping, mind locked on to the story I'd be telling the jury. We climbed aboard a van and headed north on Makena Alanui, with my trusty binder, now having doubled in size, to six inches thick, under my arm.

Tim led me through the rear entrance of the Fairmont, and I spent five grueling hours in three breakout rooms, meeting with players and fielding questions. My approach was similar to what it had been in earlier meetings with the executive committee, painting the owners as thirty-one billionaires who had been born into wealth and who, above all, wanted players to fear them and their plans for a lockout. Players grilled me about having no experience in professional sports or labor law, which was fair and something I had planned for. My lack of ath-leticism was on full display when my whiteboard marker ran dry, one of the players tossed me a fresh one, and it predictably went right through my fingers—embarrassing for me, hilarious to them, but at least it broke the tension.

"Why do you think you're the best candidate?" one of the players asked.

"I don't know that I am," I said. "But you guys need to understand what's ahead."

Unlike in Dallas, I knew now that I wanted this job. Players needed me. Not some ex-jock with a history in the union. *Me.* I understood government, media, the law. More important, I understood the opposition. NFL owners were the robber barons of the day, shaping policy and creating another free market that enriched and protected them while endangering their workforce. Kansas City and Green Bay and Jacksonville were all company towns, and the possibility of standing up to modern-day Vanderbilts and Rockefellers was exciting as hell.

I explained my interpretation of the league's history and told the group that the NFL was a nonprofit organization. Their murmuring suggested that no one had ever pointed this out before, nor were they aware of the decades-old antitrust exemptions that combined for an annual gift from Congress. As clever as the language had been in 1966, when Hale Boggs and his colleagues green-lit the merger, it was outdated by fiscal year 2008, when the league's revenue was $7.6 billion.

I proposed that we educate the public on this antiquated structure, reminding players that I knew the secret handshake to get into the important rooms in Washington, D.C., and tell everyone that the league was likely shrouding billions of dollars by juicing up their expenses and not reporting their profits. Engaging in media and political warfare was among the best ways to defend the union against the league's threatened attacks.

"These guys are trying to engage you in a linear fight," I said, "when it's not actually a linear playing field."

The next morning, Tim again knocked on my door and led me

back to the Fairmont for my final presentation. I took my deep breath, opened the binder, and told the players they were in trouble if they questioned the possibility of a work stoppage.

"How long will you guys last if you're out of work?" I asked. "Owners with money, how long will they last?"

But my presentation wasn't about rubbing players' noses in what might happen. It was about helping them fight back. We needed a robust messaging apparatus to create public pressure, and it had to go deeper than a bunch of millionaires who weren't getting enough money from their billionaire bosses. The public would have no appetite for such a conversation. I believed it *would* respond to risk mitigation and the incongruence of a workforce that takes all the risks and endures all the injuries but doesn't get an equal share of the pie.

"That's our message," I said. "That's our battle plan."

I shut off my PowerPoint, closed my binder, and rode back to a holding room with Tim. He told me to hand over my phone and laptop for security reasons. I wouldn't be allowed to leave the room or contact anyone, my wife included, because the possibility existed that our hotel room had been compromised. Weird, but okay. He at least let me call Karen to check on Alex, who was finally feeling better, and explain that I might be late for the evening's pig roast. Then I handed over my phone, flipped on the TV in the suite, and lay on the sofa.

One hour passed, then two.

I kicked off my shoes and got comfortable. Ordered a room-service sandwich and ate half of it.

Three hours, then four.

I stared at the TV and periodically catnapped. Then, finally, another knock on the door that startled me awake. Looking at my watch, I saw that I had been inside this suite, my waterfront prison cell, for five hours. I opened the door, expecting to again see Tim, hopefully with an update.

But it wasn't him.

It was Kevin Mawae. His eyes were bloodshot.

"You're our leader," he said.

That's all he said. Then he burst into tears and wrapped me in a hug.

. . .

WHEN AMERICANS ELECT a new president, he is immediately briefed on the country's official secrets. Not so much about the existence of aliens or the JFK assassination but operational details of the nation's nuclear weapons program, the locations of spy satellites, and a list of its global enemies.

The stakes are obviously lower for the executive director of the NFLPA, but the process of bringing me up to speed—and acknowledgment of the job's incredible pressures—felt similarly overwhelming.

At the same time Kevin was alerting me that I had won, a security crew was busy packing our things at the Marriott and—against Karen's wishes—moving us to the Fairmont. Kevin and Tim hurried me toward a waiting golf cart, which whisked the three of us to the hotel's service entrance, and we walked through the kitchen as I learned that Cleveland Browns wide receiver Donté Stallworth had fatally struck and killed a pedestrian with his car in Miami, which would eventually lead to a DUI manslaughter charge.

"It's time to meet the men," Kevin said as I was led through a curtain, toward a stage, before the same group I had addressed hours earlier. This time they welcomed me with applause.

I did not make it to the evening pig roast.

Tim did return my phone, warning me to be careful about who I spoke to and about what, and I called Karen followed by my parents. My next call was to George Atallah, who asked me to step out of players' earshot. Somehow he had sources inside the room and knew about my election even before I did. But early media chatter suggested some players were expressing discontent about the voting process. Despite reporting that I had been elected unanimously, George was hearing that some players were insisting Troy nonetheless be added to NFLPA leadership.

Hours later, thoughts about the Stallworth incident kept me awake. I was working at 4:00 A.M., organizing notes for a meeting the next afternoon, when I heard a sheet of paper being slipped under the hotel room door. I opened it and read a typewritten note.

> Tomorrow afternoon at the business meeting, there is going to be a motion for you to name your No. 2 person. If that person isn't Troy Vincent, there's going to be an immediate motion to rethink the Executive Director election.

It was midmorning in Washington, so I again called George. Reporters had already reached out to him, requesting confirmation that Troy was to be elevated. After Tim spooked me about my room potentially being bugged, I conducted this call with the shower running in the bathroom.

"Who the hell *is* this guy?" I asked.

Then I remembered that my new job may not come with nuclear launch codes, but it did entitle me to more information. In lawyer mode, I called individuals in and around the union—people who could explain what was going on, download me on why Troy and Gene had gotten sideways, help me strategize a plan.

A year earlier, I learned, Troy had grown tired of waiting for Gene to retire. So he apparently assembled a small team of confidants to attempt a coup, potentially while trying to make a few extra bucks. Even throughout Troy's playing career, it seemed he always had a side hustle, albeit with dubious success. He was involved in numerous businesses, including a shipping company and several real estate and insurance firms, several of which were dissolved. He'd formed a professional motorcycle drag racing team, and in 2003 a bank sued him for failure to pay back a loan of $832,760 that had been secured to buy a bus. Troy and his wife co-owned a spa that, in 2009, faced litigation after allegedly employing a massage therapist who had been accused of sexually assaulting a client.

I learned from agents and others that Troy's associates included a former NFL agent who served jail time for stealing $150,000 from a player, as well as a beloved but shady league insider named Mike Ornstein, who'd been to prison for fraud and had a second conviction that resulted in probation. According to the head of NFLPA Security and others, while Troy was serving as NFLPA president, he sent confidential information about agents, including their Social Security numbers, to his partner in an insurance and financial services company.

In early 2008, Gene learned that Troy was planning to unseat him. Troy had used his NFLPA email account to leak to prominent NFL reporters that Gene would announce Troy's promotion during a meeting of player reps that fall. In fact, Gene was planning no such announcement. But at that same meeting, Gene was planning to distribute the contents of a file he had been assembling, including emails in which Troy had promised leadership jobs to his business associates.

"I understand we have to wait another year before you can do anything with me," Ornstein wrote to Troy in February 2008, found months later during a cleaning out of Gene's desk. "I just wish I could get started a little sooner."

Gene ultimately exiled Troy, and I imagine that Troy seethed, ruminating on this in the same way Gene had never forgotten where he'd come from. Gene's high school football team, the Robstown Cotton Pickers, had been a bridge from a Texas mill village to the Pro Football Hall of Fame in Ohio, and long after Gene's playing career ended, he kept a tuft of raw cotton in his suit pocket to remind him of this journey.

By the summer of 2008, with cancer growing in his belly, Gene could hold his tongue no longer. He was adding names to his list of enemies.

"One problem," Gene wrote in an email to Ornstein in June 2008, "I am the only one who can hire anyone at the PA. You do not want to be on that list and you are. I don't get mad, I get even."

After Gene died, Troy kept maneuvering. I heard he or someone on his behalf secretly met with members of the Congressional Black Caucus, warning them—and compelling a joint letter to the Department of Labor—that the NFLPA, and specifically Kevin, were conducting a racist search for Gene's successor. Troy also assured them that Gene had privately promised Troy the job, though this ploy led to a congressional inquiry whose findings made it back to Berthelsen, the interim executive director.

Kevin just absorbed the accusations and kept the search process confidential, never even mentioning to investigators that two of the three finalists were Black. In fact, it had been Kevin who'd sniffed out that Troy had been the original source of the congressional letter. I would learn later that the previous year had taken a harsh emotional toll on Kevin, which explained not only his surliness during our initial meeting in Dallas but the reason he hugged me so tightly after telling me the election results.

Because now it was over. Or so he thought.

Hours after I had gotten the note slipped under my door, I headed to the hotel lobby, saw Mike Vrabel, and said hello.

"Are you going to fuck this up?" he asked me. I would eventually learn this was the grizzled linebacker's way of saying congratulations.

Then I noticed the text on my phone.

**Hi DeMaurice this is Troy Vincent, can you give me a call?**

I did, we agreed to meet for lunch, and upon arriving at the restaurant, I saw two men scurry away from Troy's table. He stood and extended his hand, and after we ordered, he grabbed my hand and launched into a long prayer.

"Please give this man strength, God," he said. "Make him into the leader we need, and if I can be a vessel to help him, please let it be known."

Then we opened our eyes, and Troy did most of the talking. He bragged about having a close relationship with Roger Goodell, which I found odd, but I let him continue. A good prosecutor knows when to let a witness carry on. Eventually he arrived at his point.

"So," he said, "have you given any thought to your number two?"

I hemmed and hawed, he nodded, and I kept deflecting during

one of the most awkward lunches of my life. Troy suggested we pray about it.

Then I skittered out of the restaurant, back to the Fairmont, and into the meeting with players. I shared my full analysis of the planned lockout and attempted to explain a confusing but important difference in terminology that Heather, Ahmad, and I had discovered: "Total revenue" was not the same as "all revenue." I could see the players' eyes glazing over, so I wrapped the meeting and invited questions. A hand went up from the back of the room.

"Have you decided on your number two?" asked a player I didn't recognize.

"You know, I'm glad you asked," I told the group. "Because Troy Vincent and I just had lunch, we talked about it, and we agreed that we need to pray about it."

Then I adjourned the meeting, followed Tim Christine like a blocker back to my hotel room, and found Karen packing our stuff. She was ready to go home, and after three unpredictable days, I agreed. In fact, the ten-hour flight back to Washington, a chance to turn off my brain, seemed like bliss. I spoke with the NFLPA's travel coordinator, who confirmed our return flight and told me I had been upgraded to first class. Karen and Alex would be relegated to coach.

When we arrived in Honolulu and boarded the next connecting flight to Denver, I noticed a passenger step on just before the entry door closed. He stowed his things and sat down next to me.

It was Troy.

And he started talking and didn't stop until we landed.

"I can be a help to you," he kept saying, going on about a trove of internal NFL documents that I might be interested in seeing.

Troy claimed that he had been meeting regularly with Roger Goodell, saying he had additional discussions with him already scheduled. I felt like a hostage, and all I could do was pretend this was interesting and might be useful. In my mind, though, it was this incessant pitch and an overall tone of desperation that sealed Troy's fate.

I decided there would not be a no. 2 at all. I would spend time learning who did what at the NFLPA, who was more interested in players' interests than their own ambitions, and eventually install seven lieutenants who'd report to me. There was no place at the NFLPA for Troy Vincent.

After a month of wrapping up my outstanding cases at Patton Boggs, I stepped into my new office near Washington's Dupont Circle. A banker's box of files sat on Gene's desk, a metal Raiders trash can on the floor. The inescapable grief still permeated the staff.

I spoke to my new co-workers, some of whom looked at me with suspicious eyes, some because I wasn't Gene and never would be. Others who resented that I had become executive director and Troy had not. I wasn't of this world, of their world, and months would pass before I felt like anything but an outsider.

Among my first official acts was hiring Heather McPhee and Ahmad Nassar as in-house counsel, then, after a two-month consulting agreement with Qorvis, George Atallah to oversee communications. These were people I could trust, because after Hawaii, my circle had grown small and my paranoia felt high.

One morning as my red-eye flight landed after a week of team meetings, I noticed a few dozen alerts on my phone. The NFLPA's operations officer had called to let me know that the office was on fire, and the blaze had started in my office. My private restroom, in fact.

The sprinkler system had doused the fire, and when I finally walked in, I saw ashes in the restroom's trash bin. Had someone sneaked in and tried smoking me out? Who else had keys to my office?

Maybe just another unfortunate coincidence.

What I do know is that, for weeks, every time I entered my office, a bitter stench greeted me. It was the aroma of change, clinging to the fixtures and walls, impossible to wipe away. The operations staff changed the locks and limited access to my office, but for more than a month, welcoming me to work and lingering until I just learned to ignore it was the unmistakable smell of smoke.

CHAPTER

2

# ACE IN THE HOLE

In opting out of a collective bargaining agreement in 2008 a mere two years after it had been signed, NFL owners had declared war on players. Now, in February 2010, the league was forging alliances, plotting its strategy, and growing its army.

Among the newest soldiers? Troy Vincent, whom the league hired as vice president of player development just months after he lost the executive director job to me.

"The snake finally came out of the grass," Kevin Mawae would say.

For many reasons, this is foul. Troy had spent four years as president of the NFLPA, but no true labor leader—let alone the one who represents men who go to work knowing their job will result in torn ligaments and dislocated joints—would ever work for management.

Knowing what we know? And then joining *their* side? There's no coming back from that.

But the NFL plays dirty, and whatever Troy's "player development" responsibilities may have been, his actual value to the league was an intimate knowledge of the NFLPA's inner workings, its pressure points, and which issues players actually cared about—and might cave on. He could walk into any locker room in America and speak to players in a way I simply never could. He had laced up his cleats just as they did, knew the players who matter and those who might be pliable, along with the issues we might budge on. He was a member of the all-important NFL brotherhood, a stark contrast to me, a fast-talking lawyer. I can't imagine it was lost on owners that their new executive might want to exact revenge on me.

"De Smith is going to lead all of you into an early grave," he said, according to people in those locker rooms.

Just as he had done while running for executive director, Troy was trying, again, to establish a following. He has a very charismatic way. He's very savvy. Which is why he's so dangerous.

I called Roger almost immediately. Sending Troy into our locker rooms was out of bounds, by no means an act of good faith. I doubted Roger or the owners would care, but it's still a call I had to make. Sure enough, he did absolutely nothing, and Troy continued his meetings.

My next move was to meet with people in our office who had discovered the documents Troy had left in the printer years earlier. Gene Upshaw had chased him out of the building so quickly that Troy never had a chance to delete the emails from his NFLPA account, but the union's operations staff had also made a terrible mistake by not immediately cutting off his remote computer access. A forensic analysis and internal investigation had revealed a data breach that had been conducted using Troy's employee credentials, along with emails between Troy and another person who'd requested Troy's login credentials so he could download confidential materials.

Because Troy was no longer an employee, any direct involvement on his part could constitute a crime. We had no idea how this confidential information was being used. So it's possible that someone from our office made a call to the office of the U.S. Attorney for the District of Columbia (Barack Obama had appointed Ronald C. Machen to my dream job), which opened a grand jury investigation into allegations that certain individuals may have engaged in computer fraud, the illegal infiltration of our data system, and possible violations of federal labor law. Troy was the subject of that investigation, and he was also identified in a civil lawsuit in which a former union employee had accused Troy of colluding with the NFL. I knew his deposition testimony would be subpoenaed. Though no charges were ultimately filed, when the NFL later asked that we reimburse the league for Troy's legal fees, we politely declined.

Now armed with this information, I again called Roger.

"Are you really sending a guy who's under federal investigation into locker rooms?" I asked.

This time the league benched him while he dealt with these sudden, and clearly mysterious, legal entanglements. It wouldn't keep him away forever, but the first eight months of 2010 were critical if we were going to educate players about the threat they faced. With him on ice, this allowed me to visit all thirty-two team facilities and personally explain the opponent's personnel and game strategy: that owners were more prepared than we were, that we had no match for the $4 billion war chest they claimed to have, that we believed the league had tried to directly install Troy Vincent as executive director, and that it was about more than a single labor deal—it was about crushing the players' union forever.

But, I told players, none of this meant we were doomed.

Our strategy, after all, was straightforward. And it started with an overhaul of how players thought about "total revenue" versus "all revenue," or the amount of money that was traditionally divided between owners and players. For decades, the "total revenue" model had allowed greedy owners to take a massive portion off the top before splitting whatever amount remained. Think of it not like a nebulous pile of cash, I explained, but like a birthday cake. Every January, my wife gets me a strawberry cheesecake. It's my favorite, and because I am allergic to tree nuts, it has the added benefit that it won't kill me.

But just before she lights the candles, Karen cuts out a big chunk for herself. It's my birthday, so while it stands to reason we'll share, it's still kind of weird that I'm being presented with a hacked-into cake while being told this is my "total" dessert.

It is, by no reasonable measure, *all* of a cheesecake. It's a partial one. And partial anything, be it a cake or revenue share, is bullshit.

In 2006, the collective bargaining agreement entitled players to 57 percent of "total revenue." That percentage may sound high. Lopsided, even. But by 2010, with NFL revenue surpassing $8 billion, owners were allowed to take a *billion* dollars off the top, supposedly to offset working expenses, before players got 57 percent of the remaining $7 billion. And that extra billion? It wasn't enough, which is why they wanted to tear up the existing deal.

So we're done talking about "total revenue," I told players. The only figure that mattered was "all revenue." Owners may have operating expenses, but players are assuming all of the physical risk and just resigning themselves to the reality of lifelong pain and, in many cases, mental incapacitation and premature death. Players just . . . accepted this, claiming it's what they signed up for and the reason why they get paid so much.

No, I told them, they're highly compensated because they are the absolute best in the world at what they do, in an absurdly popular arm of the entertainment industry. And in no other job in America is it okay for an employer to take money away from workers to pay their operating costs. If you work on a construction site, warehouse, or fire station, would you accept your boss removing a portion of your benefits and pay in exchange for a reliable hard hat or working firehouse?

*Hell no.*

In fact, employers are obligated to make the workplace as safe as is reasonably practicable, and they get fined if they refuse to mitigate risk. When injuries happen, workers receive workers' compensation that, in most cases, provides lifetime medical coverage.

NFL players, on the other hand, had been conditioned to think of themselves not as employees but as gladiators in a modern-day Colosseum, just lucky to be given the opportunity to play a schoolyard game. This mindset had to change, and not just because of the approaching negotiation.

Football, we were learning, wasn't just bad for players' shoulders and knees. As much as I couldn't unsee the images of twisted fingers and gnarled faces, it was the damage we couldn't see that haunted me. In 2005, a pathologist named Bennet Omalu published a paper that described an unusual buildup in the brain of Mike Webster, the famed Pittsburgh Steelers center who had died of heart failure at age fifty. This overabundance of tau protein, tiny birds' nests that essentially interrupt the brain's natural circuitry, may have explained why Webster's latter years had been marked by dementia, severe depression, and homelessness.

Omalu's discovery of these proteins would become known as chronic traumatic encephalopathy, or CTE, a disorder that had been previously linked to "punch-drunk" boxers. We didn't realize at the time that CTE would present an existential threat to the NFL or even football itself, but maybe I should have. Because the league was going to extraordinary lengths to block Omalu from publishing his research and, I assumed even then, prevent the public from learning about the burgeoning connection between CTE and the repeated head impacts that are just part of an NFL player's job.

I simply didn't accept this. And in meeting after meeting, in city after city, I urged players to join me in rejecting this narrative as well. It didn't have to be this way, and owners weren't signaling a possible lockout so the game could be made safer. They were doing so for one reason: to squeeze twice as much juice from the battered bodies and shriveled brains of the men who played for them.

It'd be lying if I said these meetings went smoothly. It was clear that many of my 2,500 new bosses were skeptical of me. I wasn't Troy, just as back home I wasn't and would never be Gene. It was up to me to accept that the fact that I wasn't Gene bothered some guys and that I'd have to earn their trust.

Still, if just a few players were open-minded and heard what I was saying, I had to do whatever it took to make an impression, just to get them thinking and, hopefully, chattering with their teammates. This is how an idea spreads and a movement begins. With this in mind, I always ended my presentations by recommending that players begin saving money, because in a war against billionaires, a pool of cash would buy us time. It was our best available shield.

Take, for instance, the cash generated by NFL Players Inc. If you've ever played the Madden NFL video game, you've seen the logo: a colorful outline of a ball carrier, lowering his helmet in antici-pation of a hit. This is the NFLPA's licensing arm, an entity that over-sees any for-profit business that wishes to include players' names, likenesses, or voices in their product. Each year, every single active player is entitled to a royalty check, just one more way for guys to earn their fair share.

In 2010, it was about $10,000 per player, and if players realized they got this check at all, this felt like free money. Not a huge amount, I acknowledged in these meetings, but it was something. And it was enough to start squirreling away as the storm clouds approached.

■ ■ ■

INVARIABLY, THESE MEETINGS at team facilities led to encounters with owners. At the time I was under the impression that everyone—from Indianapolis Colts owner Jim Irsay to the New York Jets' Woody Johnson—has equal influence in shaping how the league operates, widens its portfolio, and negotiates with players. I knew the NFL commissioner works for owners but, considering that he runs the league, they listen to and defer to him.

The league's media partners work overtime to shape these beliefs, bolstered in part by the notion that every franchise's most powerful and well-meaning figure is the owner, often portrayed as the kindly and omnipotent being who, when push comes to shove, will always do the moral and just thing. And if one strays, Roger will herd him back into place.

Jerry Richardson, the founding owner of the Carolina Panthers, was the first owner I met. He invited me to his home outside Char-lotte, North Carolina, and he had a reputation for being a staunch proponent of labor peace, something that made my predecessor, Gene Upshaw, and him longtime allies. In going through Gene's files, I had discovered a handwritten note from Richardson alongside an article about the National Hockey League's 2004–05 lockout, praising Gene for having avoided such a work stoppage for his members.

Richardson had also gotten his start as an NFL player, so with all of this in mind, I brought him a gift: a miniature NFLPA helmet that had been autographed by each of the thirty-two player representatives.

Still, I approached this meeting with hesitation. Richardson had chosen to build Bank of America Stadium, where the Panthers play, on soil that had once supported a thriving Black neighborhood. Not long after the Civil War, newly freed men and women built their homes, sent their kids to school, and had their own hospital. In 1913, a Black man was dragged out of that hospital, attacked by thirty-five white men, and shot dead—the city's first documented lynching. A century later, a small historical marker is the only remaining piece of that history, one that is overshadowed by Richardson's massive stadium.

Years later, Richardson would hastily sell his franchise, after a 2017 *Sports Illustrated* investigation discovered that he had, for years, acted inappropriately toward female employees. He had a "special interest in female grooming," the report detailed, and often commented on the condition of employees' nails and asked if he could shave their legs.

"Well, aren't *we* fancy?" I thought upon entering Richardson's ornately decorated living room and waiting for him to emerge.

When he did, it was carefully. Richardson was seventy-two and had recently undergone a heart transplant, still imposing, though, at six foot three. His voice, a deep baritone, oozed through a thick Southern drawl.

"You should know," he said, "unless we get what we want, I'm no longer in favor of peace."

Fair enough, and though I wanted to tell him where to shove the signed helmet, I consider myself a gentleman and so I thanked him for his time.

When I visited the Oakland Raiders, a team executive interrupted my meeting with players.

"Mr. Davis will see you now," she announced.

Al Davis was among the league's most famous owners, having been a championship coach before he was named commissioner of the rival American Football League and helped to negotiate the merger. He bought up chunks of equity in the Raiders for years, buying or forcing out partners until he owned the entire franchise in 1976.

"After I'm done here," I told the executive.

"He said right now," she replied.

"Hey, just shut the door."

Players looked at me, eyes wide, oohing and aahing as if I had just cursed out the school principal.

"Oh, *shit*!" a few said. "This dude's crazy!"

When the meeting broke, the executive led me upstairs, down a long corridor with flickering bulbs. I had heard that Davis kept his facilities in a state of disrepair, with dripping pipes and peeling paint. This was supposedly a way to keep opponents and even his own players as uncomfortable as possible, with, I assume, the thought being that everyone would play better if they were treated like animals.

The executive opened the door and led me to a huge conference table. There sat John Madden, the legendary Raiders coach and broadcaster, who offered me a Bloody Mary from the pitcher in front of him. I declined, and from the corner of my eye, I saw a gaunt figure approaching as if in slow motion. It was Davis, now in his late eighties, wearing his trademark scowl and connected to an IV bag. He shuffled toward me on a walker, his ninety-pound frame swallowed by his white jumpsuit.

I extended my hand and expressed my admiration for Gene, who had won two Super Bowls with the Raiders. Davis just glowered at me.

"*He* was a great union leader," he snarled. But me? Davis insisted I wasn't up for the job and that a work stoppage was inevitable. "Unless you give us what we want."

"We're not just going to lie down," I said.

"Then we're going to lock you out," he said before turning around and shuffling off.

And that was it. The entire meeting. It was just . . . confusing. Were Richardson and Davis really this dismissive and angry? Neither had dug in his heels on a particular issue or even helped me understand how a lockout could benefit either side. For as many high-level negotiations as I had been part of, none of the preamble had ever been this murky, and the opposing side had never come across as zero-sum.

*Give us what we want!*

Sure. But what are we talking about here, really?

When I visited the Dallas Cowboys, a few of the pieces started clicking into place. Jerry Jones came off as neither angry nor bitter. He took me on a tour of the Cowboys' newly opened stadium, whose construction costs had totaled an unprecedented $1.3 billion. It was Jerry's cathedral, a shrine to America's Team, a monument to himself. He didn't wince at the structure's nickname, "Jerry World," which highlighted it as a symbol of his own ego. He basked in it.

We stopped in a room that felt like a stock brokerage, the pump-and-dump kind you see in the Wall Street movies. Dozens of employees yakked into phones, slammed the receivers into headsets, picked them up again to dial more numbers. There was a tally board at the front of the room. This, Jerry explained, was the Cowboys' nerve center: The team responsible for selling season tickets. He beamed.

"This is what we do," he explained. I knew I was meant to notice how the color of his finely tailored navy suit was a perfect match for the team's iconic star logo. "We sell the Cowboys."

It was almost hard to hear him, with his Arkansas accent, over the din of American commerce. Licensing, merchandise, television. All of it starts right here, he said, by putting asses in the seats of Jerry World.

That's how you turn a business he bought in 1989 for $140 million into one worth nearly $2 billion, the most valuable brand in sports.

"Now what I *don't* like," he continued, "is that some owners don't drive revenue. Not like we do."

Freeloaders, he called them. Bums. The guy in Cincinnati? The old man in Buffalo? The guy in Cleveland? Some owners didn't even

have naming rights for their stadiums, therefore forgoing their obligations to drive revenue and, in Jerry's mind, refusing to pull their
weight as the NFL machine was growing into a behemoth. Everyone
else? Forget about them, he said. Sucklers at the teat of a cash cow, he
said, getting one thirty-second of every dollar Jerry makes.

"We've got to fix it," he said.

The NFL wasn't some monolith. Owners weren't a united front.
They're just guys who had gotten rich their own way, which was the
*wrong* way to everyone else. But unlike competitors in most industries, team owners are also collaborators—awkward bedfellows
forced a few times a year into the same room, expected to get along
in the name of their shared baby, the National Football League. And
to guys like Jerry, no amount of revenue can ever be enough. In a
twisted way, I think that's how the world's best businesspeople think.
Because if Jerry Jones saw a dollar bill on the ground, I truly believe
he'd stop and pick it up.

Not because he needs it. It's because he wants to deny you, me,
and everyone else from getting to it first.

■ ■ ■

HOUSTON, INDIANAPOLIS, TAMPA Bay. On and on it went, week after
week, with my remarks to players the same. Save your money. A lockout is coming. These owners aren't bluffing. Seattle, Kansas City, Arizona.

As different as the settings were, with Super Bowl contenders in-
terspersed with serial losers, I was struck by the consistency of these
meetings—and how, again, they echo our wider society. Regardless of
the team or locker-room culture, there are some locker rooms where
Black players sit apart from white. Within those divisions are smaller
factions, and not just by position group. There's a small number of
players who show an interest in the league's history between management and labor, and those are often the guys who become player reps
or even members of the executive committee.

There's a faction of what I started to view as the ultra conservative; the members who seem to believe they're here by nothing more than their God-given talent and destiny. Those are the guys who are just thankful to play football. They don't give a hoot about where their paycheck comes from, so long as it comes, and a sure way to make guys' eyes glaze over is to suggest a short-term sacrifice for the greater long-term good. These players roll their eyes when a union meeting begins, or sink into their chairs, or fall asleep. Some stay awake by arguing that unions hurt free enterprise and that a strike is an affront to their salary-paying masters.

It's hard to compete with a century-old culture in which players do as they're told or sprint until they puke. Even at the highest level, players are expected to fall into line when their coaches give an order. To challenge the owner, in effect biting the hand that signs their checks, good luck.

The third group is the worst. Not only do they avoid union involvement, they actually side with management and undermine their own teammates because they idolize owners. These are often quarterbacks, though not always, which I rationalized by reminding myself that these guys had been singled out by their physical skills and intellectual superiority since youth football. I heard about Joe Montana and Danny White, both of whom badmouthed and undermined their own union.

St. Louis, Jacksonville, Green Bay.

My first encounter with Packers quarterback Aaron Rodgers, if it even qualified as an encounter, wasn't terribly inspiring. Like so many people, I saw him play on television, and it's easy to create the image of a Greek god. This god is fast and wise. This one is empathetic and kind. But in real life, the god of Cheesehead Nation was isolated and dismissive. He sat in the back row of the meeting room, issuing loud sighs before standing for a dramatic exit. An incredible quarterback, to be sure, but an even more impressive antagonist.

Chicago, Indianapolis, Atlanta.

One offensive lineman, a massive human being, seemed particularly skeptical of me and my intentions. He avoided eye contact and accused me of being secretive with players, indicated that I might be behind a conspiracy, and suggested I was an operative on behalf of shadowy elites. I wasn't even sure what to say to that, but this player hijacked our meeting to such a degree that a teammate stood up and screamed that the lineman was being selfish. A testosterone-fueled battle royale ensued, with teammates getting between them and, at one point, a chair flying across the room.

"These are my people," I remember muttering to myself. Then it was on to Cleveland, Pittsburgh, New England.

George Atallah, who as the NFLPA's messaging expert was quickly becoming one of its most important figures, arranged for the longtime journalist Andrea Kremer to shadow me during my visit to New England. The piece would air on HBO's *Real Sports with Bryant Gumbel,* an in-depth news magazine show that, for nearly three decades, peeled back the curtain on the key figures and issues in American sports.

A producer miked me up in the Gillette Stadium parking lot, and Andrea and a videographer trailed me into the facility. I had no idea where I was going. We kept walking before turning left around a corner, when I saw one of the world's most famous men lounging in a leather chair.

"I'm Tom Brady," he said, standing to greet me.

"De Smith," I said. Or I think I did.

Chiseled jawline, perfect hair, piercing eyes—less Greek god than marble statue. Neither of us could have known this would be the start of a strange and occasionally unpredictable friendship and an adventure that would involve deflated footballs and many dozens of conversations. Tom is a soft talker, not easy to hear, with an unrelenting stare that seems to look into your soul.

"I'm going to walk you into the team room," he said. "Everybody should know that you're our leader."

I followed him inside the Patriots' meeting space and immediately noticed something odd. Players were divided neither by race, position group, nor worldview. Because they weren't divided at all. Tom sat in the front row, right in the middle. I can only assume now that an ability to connect a large and diverse group is among the explanations for how to win seven Super Bowls. He couldn't care less who you are or where you're from. Can you help him win? Yes? Then you're okay by Tom.

Mike Vrabel, the veteran linebacker who I hadn't seen since my election, introduced me and prefaced my address with words of alarm about the coming war with owners. The atmosphere felt strict, perhaps vaguely military, with constant order and professionalism.

After I did my usual spiel, I met with a handful of Patriots assistant coaches, part of a long-term effort by Gene to help coaches unionize. During a forty-minute sit-down, the men stayed almost silent—terrified to be seen commiserating with a union leader. The assistant coaches never voted to unionize despite not having the guaranteed contracts of their boss and horrendous and inconsistent work hours. The funny thing is that, a year later while other coaches were facing discipline without recourse, some of these same individuals requested a meeting with me in the basement of a restaurant in Foxborough, Massachusetts, terrified of angering their head coach.

Then Vrabel escorted me to the executive suites, where I met the Patriots' owner, Robert Kraft. He's a squat man, with a shock of white hair above a square face. He wears sneakers almost everywhere, no matter the occasion, and his office is a shrine to himself. There are dozens of photos of him with Senator Robert Kennedy, President George W. Bush, the Dalai Lama.

Robert is easygoing and charming, almost the polar opposite of Jerry Jones's bluster. He is self-deprecating, with a sly grin that makes you feel in on the joke. He often begins these meetings with his own hardscrabble story of getting an Ivy League education before working at a paper company owned by his father-in-law. Sometimes he tears up while telling it. He went from season ticket holder with the Patriots to the team's owner, by his own telling a kind of Cinderella story.

The full story is a bit more complicated, but we'll get to that later. For now, these up-by-his-bootstraps vignettes were precisely what Robert wanted me to know about him. They're also a vital part of the NFL's machinery. Fans are meant to believe that owners are benevolent, well-meaning people who want to win just like you. They just happen to be billionaires, of course, but mega-wealth is no match for their work ethic, humility, and grace.

By and large, this image naturally obscures their ruthlessness and the many pitfalls that prevent the rest of us from approaching such status, and the truth is that most billionaires are either born rich or marry into it, freeing them to treat people with a level of cruelty that is almost hard to believe. I could tell you they're entitled, but it's easier to show you. After the next Super Bowl, following a grueling season in which players endure adversity and injury, pay attention to the first person to touch the Vince Lombardi Trophy. The game's most valuable player? The winning coach? Nope, Roger hands it to the owner, the message being that his oversight and leadership made this moment possible.

On this day in Robert's office, he had me convinced he was different. He insisted that nothing mattered more than being a good partner to players, and therefore with me. That we ultimately wanted the same things. That he was there to be helpful and that the NFL ecosystem required us to work together.

My takeaway from this conversation was that, of every owner I'd met, Robert was the smartest. Just by looking into his eyes, I could tell his mind was playing high-level chess, analyzing not just the moves but a zillion *possible* moves. He kept referring to the "whole," meaning not just his fiefdom but the NFL at large, and it was clear that he saw himself as a man—if not *the* man—who pulls the league's strings.

I left Patriot Place feeling as if I had an actual ally—that, more than power and money, Robert actually cared about the men who play the game.

Then, weeks later, I watched the *Real Sports* segment. Kremer asked him about me, and that sly grin spread across his cheeks.

"This business can be very cruel and unforgiving at times," he said. "Until you get roughed up a little, you're probably not ready for it."

The implication being that, if I didn't fall into line, Robert and his fellow owners would provide me a harsh initiation.

■ ■ ■

**WITHIN THE NFLPA** offices and among the executive committee, our pre-lockout strategy began coming into focus. Job One: Create leverage, because as it stood, we had virtually none. In every strike in NFL history, owners had crushed players, in large part because they knew that appealing to a few star quarterbacks' ownership fantasies would lure them across the picket line.

I'm not sure I could get players to organize enough to order lunch, let alone mount a convincing threat to withhold services.

So we had to get creative. With the help of Sean Morey, a former NFL player who retired in 2010 after multiple concussions, we formed a committee whose mission was to ruthlessly promote brain injury research and suggest potential rule changes. Bennet Omalu, the pathologist who'd discovered CTE in the brains of former players Terry Long and Andre Waters, was the committee's first member. Considering that the league had ignored and denounced Omalu's research for years, they predictably hated it.

Which meant we were getting somewhere.

This is how leverage works in a negotiation: You do something that makes the other side uncomfortable, keep doing it louder and more publicly until your opponent becomes defensive. Then, after what becomes a relentless assault on this pressure point, they almost beg you to stop. Then you agree—in exchange for something you want. Our plan was to be so loud, so annoying, so ruthless that the league becomes willing to trade money or other considerations just so we'll shut up. Hiring Omalu wasn't enough. So I went to Patton Boggs, my old law firm, and told Tom that I needed his expertise.

His specialty was lobbying, and I needed to convince a few of his associates on Capitol Hill that we needed a hearing to discuss the NFL's failure to address the issue. If a player suffered a concussion on the field, he was evaluated by the team physician and asked if he could return. NFL players being NFL players, they almost always said yes—good for the team, fans, and owners, perhaps, but horrible for a player whose neurological circuitry had been knocked offline.

Until then, the league's answer to brain injuries had been to establish its own group of specialists, called the Mild Traumatic Brain Injury Committee. I'm no doctor, but I know enough that there's no such thing as a *mild* brain injury. A doctor led this group, though Elliot Pellman wasn't a neurologist. The specialist in charge of steering the NFL's response to brain trauma was the former team doctor for the New York Jets, with an expertise in rheumatology, the science of arthritis and treating joint pain.

When we proposed a neutral expert to evaluate players who may have been concussed, Pellman said no, the same response as when we suggested the end to the brutal two-a-day practices that had been glamorized in football lore but, in reality, exponentially increased exposure to brain trauma. We learned, in fact, that the objective of Pellman and his committee was to intimidate or buy off scientists conducting their own CTE studies, including one that suggested that NFL players were nineteen times more likely to get dementia than the general population.

So Tom and I brought out a megaphone. We took hundreds of active players to the Hill for meet-and-greets with members of Congress, having learned about its jurisdiction over the league given the antitrust exemptions granted decades earlier. Arlen Specter, the cantankerous Republican Pennsylvania senator, surprised us not only by being passionate about football and player safety but in expressing a general distrust of the league.

In 2008, the Patriots were busted for illegally videotaping a St. Louis Rams practice, a controversy that became known as Spygate. The league investigated and issued a hefty fine to coach Bill Belichick and the Patriots, but Specter felt this was insufficient. More than that, he was troubled by the fact that the league had destroyed evidence related to its investigation. Specter threatened to revoke the league's antitrust exemption before Kraft called in a favor. He and Specter had a mutual friend, an ambitious and deep-pocketed businessman who liked to throw money at politicians, and this person asked Specter to give Kraft a pass.

The mutual friend's name? Donald J. Trump.

Still, Specter's renewed interest in the league wasn't enough to compel Congress to subpoena the league's audited financial statements, which I suspected would disprove owners' claim that they were losing money and therefore were entitled to a juicier percentage of revenue. But, as 2011 began, it was enough to draw the league to the negotiating table. A lockout still felt inevitable, but it was important nonetheless to show players that we were working toward a compromise.

The actual meetings, though, felt pointless and confusing. Roger Goodell and the league's lawyers seemed unwilling to budge on even simple issues. After forty or so of these sessions, I had a eureka moment: It wasn't that the NFL commissioner wasn't interested in finding common ground. It was that he lacked the authority to negotiate, and he was attending these meetings with the sole purpose of killing time.

On and off the field, the NFL seems to have its own language, from "YAC" (the number of yards gained after a catch) to "Tampa-2" (a defensive coverage with two deep safeties, popularized by the Tampa Bay Buccaneers) to "icing" a kicker (when the opposing team calls a time-out before an important field goal in the hope that the kicker will overthink his responsibility, succumb to the pressure, and miss the kick). It also has its own calendar. The "league year" doesn't end on December 31 or even upon the conclusion of the Super Bowl. Similar to a company's fiscal year, the NFL's year begins and ends each March, and the specific date and time are among the hundreds of things that go into the collective bargaining agreement.

The 2011 league year was scheduled to begin at precisely midnight on March 12, at which point the previous collective bargaining agreement would be null and void, allowing owners to officially lock players out. Even six months before the first game of the season, players wouldn't be allowed to enter team facilities to work out, receive medical treatment, or prepare for the next season on league-managed property. They could assemble on their own, even conduct practices, but there would be no central gathering place. Players wouldn't get paid, and they wouldn't be covered by insurance.

Owners had their $4 billion in savings, enough to survive a months-long pause. But every day would turn the screws on players a little more, a little more, a little more until enough of them panicked and begged me to sign whatever lopsided agreement the owners were proposing. In a word, owners were icing us.

So as March 2011 approached, I started giving interviews in which I pointed out that owners were so hell-bent on a lockout that they weren't even attending negotiating meetings. They didn't even *want* a deal.

Again just to shut me up, a small number of owners agreed to meet, and our next move was to bring players who'd be willing to be aggressive with their billionaire bosses. Most players hated Roger Goodell, but they were conditioned to being submissive to owners. The New York Giants' owner wasn't John Mara, the Patriots' owner not Robert Kraft. They were *Mr.* Mara and *Mr.* Kraft. This is self-defeating in a negotiation, so I reminded our representatives that the league would sure as hell refer to them by their first names, so to avoid falling into a psychological trap, we needed to do the same. I next provided players with dossiers on each owner, an attempt at dispelling the notion that Kraft, Mara, and Jerry Jones were demigods gracing us with their presence.

"These guys have never *given* you anything," I told them. "You earned the right to be where you are, and unlike them, you prove your ability and worth every day."

Shortly before our first scheduled meeting, Roger called. Owners had agreed to reduce their off-the-top "credit" from $2.4 billion to $650 million. Tempting? No, it was telling. These guys would rather cut their demand by two-thirds just to avoid the inconvenience of meeting? I told Roger no and that we looked forward to seeing him soon.

We were to assemble in Washington, D.C., in a grimy 1970s-era building a few blocks from NFLPA headquarters and enlisted a government agency called the Federal Mediation and Conciliation Service to moderate our negotiations: referees, even at the NFL bargaining table. They had no real power to force the owners to do anything, but having learned about how owners think, the FMCS could alert a certain Pennsylvania senator that the league wasn't cooperating.

So in marched Kraft, Mara, and Jerry, followed by Kansas City's Clark Hunt, Carolina's Richardson, and the San Diego Chargers' Dean Spanos. They were huffy and irritable, which I hoped to use to our advantage, and Roger sat between Kraft and Jerry. On our side sat Kevin Mawae, Indianapolis Colts center Jeff Saturday, Denver Broncos safety Brian Dawkins, and Baltimore Ravens defensive back Domonique Foxworth.

Off we went, and it was clear from the outset that owners lacked any real interest in negotiating. Hunt and Spanos sat with their arms crossed, and Roger barely said a word. They left for lunch, kept us waiting for nearly four hours, then informed the mediator that they weren't coming back. This went on for days, with the owners wincing every time Domonique called the Giants' owner *John* and the Chargers' owner *Dean*.

Jerry Jones scolded me for wasting everyone's time, to which Dawkins responded by staring into Jerry's eyes and quietly reminding him that, as executive director, I deserved Jerry's respect. By the afternoon of the fourth day, with our side standing our ground and owners running out of ways to apparently assert their dominance, Jerry had clearly had enough.

"Let me just make sure y'all understand something," he said. "All of us have decided that if you don't agree with us, we're going to have to teach you a lesson."

He bumped his fists together as if addressing a group of insolent children.

"You think this is one immovable force against another immovable force," he continued. "But *we're* the force."

With that, he dramatically stood, announced there was nothing more to discuss, and stomped toward the door. The other owners were nodding, but nobody followed him. They just sat there as Jerry stopped at the open door, awkwardly waiting for the others to join him in this parade of exasperation.

Our guys just looked at him, saying nothing. I believe it finally hit them, as it had me, that owners weren't here to compromise or do what's right. This wasn't even about money. It was about power, control, getting their way.

Players didn't blink. They kept watching, as did everyone else in the room, as Jerry sheepishly closed the door, walked back to the table, and sat in his chair without so much as a word.

■ ■ ■

LATE ON THE evening of March 11, 2011, I made the loneliest decision of my career and signed a legal document that dissolved the NFL Players Association.

A union cannot sue its employer for an antitrust violation, as employees are the victim of this crime, not the entity that represents them. So, months earlier, team representatives had voted unanimously to authorize me to decertify the union in order to seek antitrust relief in federal court as a class action and pursue an injunction that bars owners from collusion. It's one thing to organize a vote for something that feels inevitable. It's another to sit in a chair and, in a series of pen strokes, nullify the very organization I had sworn to protect.

"We're with you," Jeff Saturday told me. Then he wrapped me in a hug.

If there was any consolation, it was that Jeff and Domonique had emerged during our negotiations as ruthless and thoughtful leaders. They attended every meeting for eight days, showing neither fear nor hesitation, acknowledging the terrible but necessary reality that owners were offering them an unfair deal. Kevin and I ground through meeting after mindless meeting, which resulted in our refusing their offer to take $325 million off the top of every year's gross revenue and their turning down our counteroffer of $137.5 million for the first four years before that money went away entirely.

I kept searching for a speck of light in a dark and lonely tunnel, when Jeff, Domonique, and a few other members of the executive committee knocked on the door.

"We're done," Domonique said. Our army, disparate and tentative as it had been, was ready for war.

Upon the league's announcement that players were locked out, I directed NFLPA lawyer Jim Quinn to walk outside, where NFL general counsel and chief bushwhacker Jeff Pash was holding a news conference, and call Pash a liar. Quinn, a consummate gentleman, didn't want to. But he did it anyway because his client asked him to. We held our own news conference the next day, with Drew Brees, Brian Dawkins, and the rest of the executive committee by my side, trying to appear as a unified front.

We reminded the public that the league had been the aggressor and, in attempting to financially suffocate their own workforce, they proved a willingness to deny healthcare to the men who suit up and wear their team logos, yes, but also to any player's wife who was due to give birth during the next few months. Professional athletes have families, too, and many couples try to plan babies to arrive during the offseason. For the foreseeable future, Mom, Dad, and baby were on their own.

I was exhausted, disappointed, and livid because I had recently learned why most of Congress had ignored us. Just a few months earlier, the NFL had hired Kenneth Edmonds, a longtime Washington insider, as the league's chief lobbyist. He'd introduced owners and league office executives to members of the Congressional Black Caucus, a group with whom he had great familiarity as the former chief of staff to Rep. Jesse Jackson, Jr.

Roger had schmoozed with caucus members during a foundation meeting, and the league had set up its own political action committee, named the Gridiron PAC. In 2010, the league spent more than $680,000 to grease the movers and shakers on Capitol Hill, not a lot of money by NFL standards but enough for members to ignore our calls. And enough, apparently, for Edolphus Towns, the New York congressman and chair of the House Oversight and Government Reform Committee, to decline our request to subpoena the league's financial records.

With negotiations tabled, I did what I do when I'm overwhelmed: I escape, and I drink.

An old law partner buddy, David Barrett, and I went to Palm Springs, California, and pounded cocktails and debated how and why the National Hockey League's lockouts had been successful. Yes, we're lawyers, and this is what lawyers do. Players lost hundreds of millions and returned to work with a dramatically worse deal than the one that had been on the table before the lockout. Hockey team owners had no such $4 billion war chest, but players had capitulated anyway.

Speaking of the $4 billion, Dave said, did I buy it? Could they really have bundled *that* much?

I did buy it, actually, and this hit on a suspicion I'd had since before I was elected. Owners had been openly bragging about their rainy-day fund for years, even before the dust had settled following the Great Recession. Banks weren't in a position to lend so much money, and after meeting so many owners, I couldn't imagine that some of those overgrown man-babies had the discipline to save roughly $130 million apiece.

"Would the TV networks give it to them?" Dave asked.

I set down my glass.

"The league has leverage," he continued, "because of how much the networks want the broadcast rights."

*My God.*

That had to be it. When the league negotiates its TV deal with networks (and now streaming services), they gather the top executives in a room, show them a list of the most-watched prime-time shows, and tell them to start bidding. The executives know that they're going to pay more than they did for the previous deal and that they will never recoup their investment in advertising revenue. This has been the case since 1993, when CBS allowed itself to be outbid by $100 million per year by the Fox Network, at the time Rupert Murdoch's upstart TV experiment. *Fox NFL Sunday* was born, and CBS, which had controlled broadcast rights since 1956, predicted it'd lose only about 5 percent of its Sunday audience.

Instead, *60 Minutes* went from the top-rated television show in 1993 to no. 6 in 1994, then no. 9 in 1995, then no. 11 in 1996. Fox changed how NFL games were presented, leaning into the league's entertainment value more than the traditional X's and O's analysis that had defined football coverage. In 1998, CBS paid $500 million per year for the privilege of televising NFL games, more than double what NBC had paid in its previous deal.

The day after Dave and I hit the bars, we nursed our hangovers and I authorized the hiring of a former network executive to advise us on television contracts. We had no access to the league's negotiations, so for the time being, this was nothing more than a way to indulge this theory. I lobbed what felt like a stupid question to the former executive: Could there be a clause in a broadcast rights contract that would pay owners even if games weren't played?

Every contract, this executive explained, includes language about "makegoods," which is essentially a sign that reads: IN CASE OF EMER-GENCY, BREAK GLASS. Say you run a doughnut shop and advertise it on Google. If, for instance, Alphabet's servers get hacked and all of its sites go dark, this is the clause that requires Google to *make good* on the agreement and publish the ad later.

Using similar logic, networks could agree to a deal in which they paid a certain amount of money in the event that games *weren't* played, in exchange for a discount on future payments. Sure enough, as we kept digging, we learned that, just six months after the NFL agreed to its collective bargaining agreement in 2006—the one it'd opt out of in 2008—the league agreed to a nearly $2 billion-a-year broadcast contract with NBC and ESPN.

The expiration of that contract? You guessed it: 2011, the season that owners had long been targeting for a lockout.

If our theory was correct, it was as if the league had taken out an insurance policy from the networks. If they had, it would have been for less money—a potential violation of the league's obligations to players under the collective bargaining agreement. Later, a federal judge made that exact ruling, effectively dismantling the NFL's entire war chest. I had learned about the insurance business while representing Ford Motor Company a dozen years earlier. Insurance is just risk transfer, which is what makes the business world work. You and I pay for a cup of coffee at the time of receipt, but corporations do things differently. So many transactions require millions or even billions of up-front money to finance the infrastructure that allows me to tap my phone or card on a pay terminal and immediately walk away with my pumpkin spice latte. But if there's some problem, the coffee shop's corporate office has invested in so many fail-safes that the operation keeps running. If the pay terminal goes down or the coffee grinder spontaneously combusts, some insurance company covers the cost of repairing or replacing it, so that the next customer barely notices.

Another example is homeowner's insurance, which you pay a monthly premium for, and in the event of a fire or flood or attack of the murder hornets, the insurance company makes you whole. The owners had, in effect, transferred their risk to the TV networks—each of which was hoping to avoid paying for games that wouldn't be played *and* get a discounted future deal.

All of this got me thinking that it sure would be amazing if there were such a thing as lockout insurance. It was a disaster we'd known was coming, and it wasn't as if we were *causing* the lockout. In fact, our players were trying like hell to avoid missing work, so the risk wasn't even ours to transfer.

Still, I wondered, *could* there be such an insurance policy? It was a question worth asking.

A few of us went to work drafting out the parameters of a policy that didn't exist, then finding a company that would underwrite it. Further complicating matters was that no insurer with even the faintest tie to the NFL, any of its owners, or any of the league's business partners would work, because they'd immediately tip off the league.

In between grueling negotiation sessions with owners, staying on top of congressional meetings and various lawsuits, the NFLPA team and I traveled the world trying to explain the NFL to groups of savvy insurers and to convince them to create a policy that never existed. It was a tough sell. Insurers don't want to pay out, considering they're betting there *won't* be a coffee grinder mishap or murder hornet attack, and the forecast for missing NFL games was roughly 100 percent.

Most underwriters politely declined, but Dave Barrett and Heather McPhee worked with an international expert named Duncan Fraser to develop a labyrinthian policy that contained many caveats that would reduce the payout impact. The premium was expensive as hell, and if somehow there were no missed games, the companies would keep that money.

With the pieces in place, I got permission to pursue this as a potential nuclear option in our arsenal. Its ultimate value wasn't the payout. It was the leverage it would create. Because if the policy did pay out, our side could withstand a work stoppage for far longer than the owners believed. Their $4 billion had to cover keeping stadiums and team facilities online, administrative staffs paid, and front-end costs guaranteed. Factoring in players' salaries, this amount suggested they were prepared to miss half the 2011 season as they waited on players to cave.

But if we sprang this insurance policy on owners at the right time, I explained, owners would realize their eight-game strategy was doomed. The insurance payout was $850 million, set to be distributed after two missed regular-season games. It was enough for players to sit out the entire year, and while it might not pay for their full salary, bonuses, and benefits, it was enough to pay each player $200,000 per week—enough that players wouldn't beg me to sign whatever proposal the league put forth.

Now, here was the tricky part: The premium would cost $47 million. Players murmured, knowing the union had only $200 million in its coffers. It was a huge gamble.

I believed that the insurance payout would be enough to protect our men and give them financial security for an entire missed season. For now, we had to keep it quiet. Secrecy was our most important component. But shortly before the season, owners would learn about our plan from the most heartless competitor any of us had ever known.

■  ■  ■

**EVERY UNION ORGANIZATION** has infighting, especially during a work stoppage, but rarely so venomous, public, and damaging as ours. Management was projecting a united front.

Our side? Not so much.

Antonio Cromartie, the talented New York Jets cornerback and ace trash talker, called Tom Brady an "asshole" during a meeting with reporters. "Fuck him," Cromartie added. He later directed similar language to me and members of our executive committee, some of whom didn't exactly smooth things over. Seattle quarterback Matt Hasselbeck posted on Twitter that someone should ask Cromartie if he knew what "CBA" stands for, to which Cromartie would later offer to "smash" Hasselbeck's face in. Another player hijacked a call with player reps to accuse me of being a liberal activist.

"Stop bitching about money. Money ain't nothing. Money can be here and gone," Cromartie told reporters. "Us players, we want to go out and play football."

This played right into the owners' hands. Football players are brainwashed into believing they'd suit up for nothing more than the love of the game. Getting paid is just extra. Which, I kept reminding our guys, is both nonsense and self-defeating. Players were going on the record to announce they were so terrified of losing their paychecks, there was no chance they could be patient enough to mount an effective defense.

During one bargaining session, Baltimore Ravens general manager Ozzie Newsome became the latest in a parade of Black guys the league kept putting in front of me, presumably to talk some sense into me, brother to brother. I took considerable offense at this, not just because of how obviously insulting it is, but also because Newsome and the others had no authority to negotiate. Now, Newsome is a respectable guy, a former NFL tight end who's a member of the Pro Football Hall of Fame, and my problem was never with him. It was that owners were using him as a puppet to undermine us by reinforcing the love-of-the-game narrative.

"I know we're arguing about money, De," he said one day. "But you have to realize what an honor it is to play NFL football."

He happened to catch me in a particularly bad mood, so I fired back at him.

"Are you telling me that, when you were playing, if the owners came in and said, 'Hey, Ozzie, you should play for five thousand dollars less,' what would your answer be?"

"I'd probably say yes," he said.

"Okay," I continued, "what if they said fifteen thousand dollars less? Or fifty thousand dollars less? Or that you should play for free?"

"I'd hear them out," Newsome said.

"Then you know what that makes you?" I said, hoping he received the analogy of someone who worked for no pay. Ozzie is a good man, and, I assumed that he decided he was unwilling to do owners' bidding, because that was the last time he attended a bargaining session.

Rank-and-file players may not listen to me about messaging. That's why it was so important for Jeff Saturday, Domonique Foxworth, and Minnesota offensive lineman Steve Hutchinson to keep guys in line and, for the love of God, stop telling the press that they just wanted to play. Hutchinson was an absolute boss. He educated players and was relentless as he talked to reporters about owners' refusal to negotiate in good faith.

Weeks turned to months, though, and the union was getting nowhere on the bigger issues. Was this Jerry Jones teaching me a lesson? Was Robert Kraft roughing me up? I still knew their offers stank, and shortly after we'd decertified as a union, I sent our $47 million insurance check. Why wait? Because any union has an obligation to disclose certain things in its annual filings to the Department of Labor. Now that we had decertified and were merely an *association,* we could keep this information concealed from owners and their legal teams.

Only twenty people knew about this policy, all of them sworn to secrecy. Somehow, as summer approached, there had been no leaks. Owners never found out. So a group of ten players could move forward with a federal class-action lawsuit, filed in Minneapolis with Judge Susan Richard Nelson presiding. Not for the last time, a clerk of court would file a document with this heading:

BRADY ET AL. VS. NATIONAL FOOTBALL LEAGUE ET AL.

Think of a lawsuit as a formal story that's filed in the hope of a judge or jury writing the ending you want. It's therefore important to title the opening act in a compelling way. Owners knew we were going to sue, as it's a predictable move whenever someone is illegally conspiring against you. Still, it's a legal backstop, and you have the backing of the government if negotiations go awry.

Our argument was simple: The United States bars companies from colluding, especially if there's economic harm to consumers or others. Imagine you're a teacher or nurse. What if you found out that every school district or hospital in your state was conducting back-room meetings to reduce the maximum salary each person can earn? This would stifle your chances of improving your benefits and pay, be it in negotiations with your employer or in discussions with a different school or hospital. In America, this isn't just frowned upon. It's a crime.

Early in 2011, we'd begun asking players to be lead plaintiffs in our case against the NFL. Eight players had sued the league during the war for free agency, and many of those guys were demoted or cut. We nonetheless needed ten or so players to be our leads, and we quickly eliminated anyone who was nearing the end of his career or guys whose contracts had been written in a way that they could be punished. Ideally, we'd get a few top quarterbacks, who are team owners' most prized "possessions" and could undercut us the way Joe Montana did a generation earlier.

In my mind, I wanted the faces of the NFL: Brady, Peyton Manning, and Drew Brees. Our lawyers said I shouldn't hold my breath.

Brees was a lock. He'd been a player rep who, throughout the 2010 season, had worn a Gene Upshaw hat during postgame news conferences. He was the very definition of a union guy, having entered the NFL as an undersized passer out of Purdue and worked his way into being one of the most prolific and popular players in the league. Once he was on board, I asked him to reach out to Peyton and Tom, hoping there was some secret quarterbacks club. There wasn't.

So, as I'm prone to do, I went to work trying to find out every tiny fact about both of them. By meeting me at Patriots headquarters during my first team visit there, I have to believe he had defied the wishes of both Bill Belichick, his maniacally controlling head coach, and Kraft. One of his best friends, Mike Vrabel, had recently been traded to Kansas City, and Tom was livid about it.

We were filing a class action on behalf of all players, but I believed that there was symbolism in featuring certain players as lead plaintiffs. Reggie White, the legendary pass rusher, had been atop the 1993 action that delivered free agency to players. But there's something even more powerful about the lead plaintiffs being superstar quarterbacks, so Brady, Brees, and Manning would send a shock wave to our opponents—alongside a message about how the union was approaching this war.

That same day, my phone rang with a Texas area code. I answered but didn't recognize the gravelly voice on the other end.

"Is this DeMaurice Smith?" he asked.

"It is. Who's speaking?" I responded.

"Von Miller, sir."

A star pass rusher at Texas A&M University, Miller was projected to be one of the first picks of the 2011 draft. Considering the league's use of college football as its unpaid farm system, amateur players were subject to NFL collusion, too. Miller told me he wanted to be among the plaintiffs. I explained how ruthless the owners were, and that by joining the suit, he could be risking the loss of millions if certain owners refused to draft him.

"I want in," he said, so we added him to the document.

Judge Nelson granted us an injunction that legally banned the lockout and allowed our members to immediately go back to work while the case progressed. Owners appealed, reiterating that they weren't interested in fair negotiations so much as asserting their control, and they were granted a stay of the injunction by the Eighth Circuit Court of Appeals. The lockout was continuing, and no appeals court was willing to hear our side as July arrived and training camps were scheduled to begin. Players hadn't been paid and their insurance was cut off. Regardless of pregnancies, children with special needs, or relatives with acute or even terminal illnesses, the NFL left players to fend for themselves.

Thankfully, we still had a card to play.

*Play it!* a few members of our executive committee urged. But the secret insurance policy was our last move, and I still thought it was too early. After the early disharmony, our guys were angry at the owners and holding the line.

I had hired Don Davis in the spring of 2010, adding the former NFL player and coach to our staff as a player director who'd be in charge of the union activity of ten teams. One of the wisest and most emotionally secure people I have ever met, Don lent insight on the minds of players that proved invaluable. Teams were meeting informally on college facilities to practice, and as a lawyer, this seemed like another way to weaken our side.

But Don, with a silky voice that runs counter to an intimidating physical appearance, reminded me that football players *need* to play football. If they don't occasionally hit each other, they get edgy. And an edgy player is an unpredictable player.

Many players had also taken my advice to save money the previous two years, and several high-profile players volunteered additional savings to help fellow players, accumulating nearly $500,000. The bad news was that, without a steady income, some guys were falling on hard times. You may not think guys who supposedly "get paid millions" would have such delicate financial situations. But the overwhelming majority of NFL players never make $1 million, and like many Americans, some people just aren't good with money.

So of that $500,000 our guys had bundled, all but about $50,000 went to reimbursing players for utility bills and food costs. It reinforced my belief that, without our lockout insurance, guys would have caved less than four weeks into a lockout.

We kept meeting with owners, usually in a conference room of a tiny airport that could accommodate their private jets, and it was becoming clear that Roger Goodell's role was that of the bad cop. We'd be cooped up in some meeting space near St. Charles, Illinois, or Hull, Massachusetts, and Roger would offer additional safety protocols for players, then reveal that this was contingent on our agreement to expand the regular season from sixteen games to seventeen.

The previous collective bargaining agreement had given the league unilateral authority to add games and increase the season to twenty-one games, but with everything in flux, I saw this as potential leverage. Players needed the right to approve any season expansion, considering they'd be assuming additional risk and extra work, ostensibly for no additional pay. We commissioned an analysis that found that, year after year, more players were getting injured more often. Forcing them to play more games would surely make it worse.

We were willing to discuss an expanded regular season, just not for free.

The good cops were Jerry Jones, Kraft, and Jerry Richardson. For as combative as Roger Goodell could be, turning red before leaning back in his chair with his arms crossed, not unlike a petulant child, the owners were downright genial. I knew, though, that they were hell-bent on getting the better end of this deal and, if they had their way, crush the union and lock in an economic system that'd tip the balance of power for generations.

It became a source of entertainment in which our side would debate which issue would send Roger into a fury on a given day.

"I bet this is going to get his ass!" Foxworth would announce. A highly intelligent thinker and skilled negotiator, Fox has a flat and deep voice to go along with a quick mind and edgy demeanor.

I confided in him and Kevin Mawae that I wasn't exactly sure when to drop the bomb on owners that we had the secret insurance policy. They understood the stakes better than anyone, and they knew by that July that owners had no interest in reaching a fair resolution. The league wasn't just sweating us for a chunk of revenue and a potentially expanded season. Owners were targeting players' pensions because it placed risk on the league and required owners to continuously fund the accounts.

Fans may believe that current and former players are part of a unified fraternity, an idea bolstered by NFL Films and ESPN. If you once inhabited an NFL locker room, then you'll always be a member of the tribe. It's another of the league's myths. Current players think retired guys are yesterday's news, no more important or relevant than a wily-eyed uncle complaining about modern music. Young players also didn't want to look at ex-players because this was like accepting their own mortality. Retired players were deteriorating at an advanced rate, with bad knees and early-onset dementia, likely caused by CTE.

Owners signaled that they were willing to negotiate on certain issues, especially if it offset the perception that they were indifferent to concussions and brain trauma at a time when they wanted to add more games. They agreed, finally, to budge on two-a-day practices and eliminating certain drills that were particularly dangerous. But they refused to negotiate on the revenue share.

*Play the card!*

By late July, the first preseason games were just weeks away. The possibility of starting the regular season on time was fading. Owners agreed to leave pensions intact and to include more ex-players in the benefits pool, but they were digging in their heels on our demand of a minimum amount spent in salary each year and with their decree that rookie players should receive standardized salaries.

Some players and their agents had publicly spoken about the need for a fixed wage scale, pointing out that it was unfair that an unproven player was paid as much as or more than an accomplished veteran. But this had become the market standard. What these players didn't understand was that it wasn't as if teams' savings from the new salary structure would benefit veterans. It would just go back into owners' pockets.

Every now and then, Jerry Richardson and Jerry Jones liked to hurl thinly veiled insults at each other, apparently a way to assert dominance in their own faction. One day Richardson removed a sheet of paper, wrote something on it, and passed it to Roger to give to Jones.

Jones read it, wrote something, and passed it back to Roger. Richardson read it, pursed his lips, and nodded. The meeting devolved, with Richardson bellowing at me and calling me "uppity," before we agreed to end the day's session. The owners stormed out, off to their luxury jets.

But the note was still on the table. I couldn't help myself.

"You talk too damn much," Richardson had written.

"Shut the fuck up," Jones had replied.

Kraft was the most mature of the league's representatives, and usually he'd stay mostly quiet during our meetings. He wasn't a peacemaker, exactly. He just wasn't interested in the displays of caveman superiority of his cohorts. George Atallah, who had begun joining us for some of the meetings, pointed out that Kraft seemed to go out of his way to convince the public that he was a nice guy—the savvy grandfather who'd built the Patriots out of nothing and was content to let his ornery coach be his organization's bad guy.

It had also become public that Kraft's wife, Myra, was in the final stages of ovarian cancer. To me, Kraft came across as a husband who seemed overwhelmed by his wife's diagnosis but continued to attend negotiation sessions because, left alone, the other owners would tear one another apart. It made me wonder if any path forward, at least one that avoided Armageddon, relied on Kraft.

Roger and Jeff Pash usually did most of the talking while owners—at least those still invited to our negotiating sessions—listened. Mike Brown, the Cincinnati Bengals owner, attended for a while but was banished after an unhinged screed about how players were lucky to have a job in the NFL and should therefore be thankful for anything in the way of compensation. Pash's methodical nature was the counterweight to Roger's tantrums, and being a lawyer who's careful with his words, I wasn't the only one who noticed when Pash repeatedly referred to players receiving a larger share of "incremental revenue" in the 2006 deal. This was gibberish, apparently meant to sound as if our side had been receiving an outsize percentage, and I noticed Kraft perk up as we hammered away at the absurdity of Pash's argument.

Like "total revenue," this "incremental" amount was just another way to refer to the pile of cash left after owners took their preliminary share off the top. Pash wasn't trying to trick us so much as this former member of the Harvard Debate Club was just an expert of massaging language in a way that supported his side. It's a false premise, in other words, used in the hope that we won't catch it.

"Here's the problem, Jeff: No owner should think for a nanosecond that that means players are getting sixty percent of the money," I said one day. "If that's the impression you're going for, you're lying."

Pash started yelling at me. I yelled back. Kraft looked genuinely confused.

"Say that again," he said, "about incremental revenue."

"He wants you to think that sixty percent of all the new money, or what he's calling 'incremental,' is going to the players," I told Kraft. "That's just not true. Players get fifty-three percent of a smaller share."

Kraft just sat there, seeming to absorb the possibility that his own top lawyer had been lying. To us. To them. To everyone, just because it was a handy sound bite and part of the league office's media narrative.

This was a turning point, because the "60 percent" figure disappeared from our talks. Our strategy changed, too, because if the number you've been citing is bullshit, and now you're claiming that the *actual* percentage is unfair, then show us your financial statements and prove it. Pash is far too smart for that.

"Some teams are not doing as well as they should be," he said. He was predictably vague, refusing to name the teams or how underwater they supposedly were, unaware that Jerry Jones had already told me that teams like the Bengals and Bills were forgoing ways to increase revenue in the league.

By late July, training camps were delayed as we reached yet another impasse. I went home but suffered from chronic insomnia, my brain trying to untangle an impossibly large knot. What if I had overplayed my hand such that players lose their pensions? What if they're forced to play two extra games *and* take a pay cut? What happens if we actually go a full year without football?

Sleep-deprived and feeling beaten down, I escaped to Boston to watch my son play in a baseball camp. Alex and I stayed with Heather McPhee's father, Neil, who at the time was head coach at nearby Northeastern University. I coached Alex's team all day, had a great dinner with the McPhees, and got one-on-one time with my son that's priceless under normal circumstances but that I desperately needed now.

One morning as the kids took grounders, my brain finally decompressed enough to see clearly. We had an ace in the hole, and I had known for months who I wanted to deal the cards.

∎ ∎ ∎

I LEARNED THE most about Tom Brady by talking to people who knew him best. Among the most important nuggets I gleaned was that he and Kraft had a special relationship. So it wasn't just important that Kraft learned about the insurance policy. It was who tipped him off. Played the right way, this would give us the most leverage at the bargaining table. So, through back channels, we engaged launch sequence. The next day, my phone rang. It was Kraft.

"Are you up for one more meeting?" he asked.

We met days later at the hangar where Kraft parks his jet, and together we'd fly to New York for a session with key owners and union reps. I had never been on a private plane, and I was busy marveling when Kraft arrived, looking exhausted and older than usual. He told me the end was near for Myra, and he'd spent months sitting at her bedside. I shared that Karen was a breast cancer survivor and that the fear and powerlessness of watching the person you love worn down by a diagnosis and debilitating treatments were feelings I knew well.

This meeting was clearly important enough for Kraft to step away from Myra, and I respected his gumption that day and still do.

I didn't say much on the quick flight to New York. It was my duty to listen. Two guys separated by so many things, lacking virtually anything in common, thrown together by an unusual set of circumstances and bonded by trauma.

"Look," Kraft said as the jet began its descent, "this isn't a time to be hiding stuff. If you guys have more resources, we need to be transparent with each other."

I paused, finally understanding how it feels to have Tom Brady on my team. As he had done for his side so many times, he had gotten us to the goal line.

"Let's just say I took steps to protect our players," I said. "Nobody is going to crumble early."

Kraft sat back in his chair.

We landed and made our way to Proskauer Rose, a law office in Midtown Manhattan not far from NFL headquarters. To this day, it's the only firm I've been to with a floor-to-ceiling wine cabinet just outside their conference room. Union busting is big business, as it turns out.

Kraft disappeared through a door, and I was escorted into a holding room. It was packed. The full executive committee had arrived alongside several player reps, and they sat next to our small army of attorneys. I addressed the group and shared what was about to happen, and how I expected our opposition to react. In my legal career, I had worked for men like these. Gone against them. They're not the type to congratulate you on a successful gambit and just accept defeat with a warm handshake. These guys are used to winning, and on the rare occasions they don't win, their response is to change the rules and punish the opposing side for making them sweat.

As we waited, I mostly felt dread. My brain had produced three possible scenarios, two of them bad. Owners could storm out or call our bluff, effectively a challenge to see who broke first. Players are taught to feel comfort in certainty, so either of those possibilities would break us. The third was that Kraft realized that a civil war was good for no one, that the NFL's business model was impervious to inflation, elections, and geopolitical conflict, invincible to almost everything except greed.

The door finally opened, and we were invited into an initial meeting with just a few participants. On our side, Mawae picked Foxworth, Jeff Saturday, and me. I made eye contact with everyone in the holding room, more than fifty guys, and tried to convey confidence and conceal my anxiety. There's no such thing as a "fearless" leader, and if there were, I can't imagine following them. Any conflict requires self-awareness and the acknowledgment that all of your planning, strategizing, and overthinking could fail. Against some of the most powerful and dangerous men in the world, I was well aware of the odds.

I reminded myself that we were ready. I had prepared for everything, churned through every possibility.

Except one.

Because in walked Tyson Clabo, the Falcons lineman who hated unions and me, not necessarily in that order, and wanted to wring my neck the only time I had met him. The guy who'd kicked off a shouting match that devolved into thrown chairs and hurled expletives. He had traveled to New York to settle the score.

"Where are you guys going?" he asked. "Y'all are really going in there without us? This is a problem, De."

"Tyson, just keep your voice down," I said. "Come with us."

Mawae looked at me, and a shrug was all I could muster. The five of us started down a long hallway and reached the door of a conference room. Before I opened it, I pulled our group aside and looked Tyson in the eye.

"You need to know something before we go in," I told him. "Your player leadership voted nearly two years ago to purchase a secret insurance policy that'll pay everyone six figures every week if we're locked out. It was a secret because owners don't know about it. We're telling them today."

Tyson stared so deep into my eyes that I thought one of us might explode. He looked at Fox, Jeff, and Kevin.

"Is this true?" he asked.

"My balls aren't so big that I'd bluff over billions of dollars," I said.

Tyson's face relaxed.

"That's fucking *awesome*!" he said.

We returned to the conference room door, and I lowered the handle. There sat Roger, Jerry Richardson, Kraft, and Jerry Jones at a round table. To me, every group is a jury, and I try to read their shoulders and eyes. Richardson was fuming; Jones calmer than ice water. We took our seats, and Kraft began the meeting.

"It's important," he said, "that the sides not hide anything."

In the same tone of voice I used for closing arguments in a murder trial, I told everyone about the insurance policy and its details. I paused, allowing the information to sink in. Nobody said a word.

"I'm sure you thought there would be a resolution by week four," I said, "because players would collapse. But we're content to sit out the entire season."

I'm not sure I've ever seen a hatred in someone's eyes like that of Jerry Richardson. Roger turned bright red, the vein in his neck pulsing. Kraft remained silent. Jerry Jones seemed to realize that, in a single sentence, we had destabilized years of planning and maneuvering by the league.

"So let's just wait a minute," he said. "Maybe it's time that we all put our guns away."

Kraft and Richardson looked at him.

"We can just *sliiiide* 'em back into the holster," Jones continued.

In a negotiation, this is what's called the deal point—the moment of truth. Jones recognized it before anyone else, acknowledging that owners were cornered. There would be no player collapse, and there'd be no eight- or ten-game season.

"Why haven't I been told about this?" Roger said. "De, you have to understand that I've set up some things to protect the owners. Things I haven't even told them about."

That's when I knew. It was checkmate.

*Ah, Puddin'*, I remember thinking. *I got you, didn't I?*

Kraft took a long breath and said that we'd given the league some things to discuss. They stood to walk out, and Kraft let the other men exit first. He looked at me and issued the faintest smile, an acknowledgment, finally, that I might actually be worthy of respect.

■  ■  ■

AND JUST LIKE that, with the league's primary leverage gone, owners were motivated to get a deal done. We agreed to some of the economic concessions they wanted, but we got the larger structure we needed. Gone was the one-sided "total revenue" model, and in its place was "all revenue"—the entire strawberry cheesecake, without a chunk removed.

Players would no longer be partially responsible for paying for owners' stadiums, suite upgrades, and jumbo screens. What owners received in return was a rookie wage scale that made it so the highest-risk players wouldn't get the most lucrative contracts, which we could claim as a win for our more proven members because the savings would go to them.

We locked in a mandatory revenue share of 47 percent that had to be spent each year meaning cash actually distributed instead of accounting tricks. Before 2010, teams had a salary cap but never a salary *floor*. If they wanted to underspend and pocket the savings, there was nothing to stop them. Now there was, and players would no longer be paid less because of the specific franchise and owner they happened to work for.

Teams would now be required to spend no less than 89 percent of the cap on a rolling four-year basis. Before the salary floor, Kansas City, Buffalo, and Cincinnati were notoriously cheap. In 2009, the Chiefs spent only 70 percent of the salary cap, the Bills 78 percent, the Bengals 76 percent—all while claiming to make just as much of an effort to win as New England, Dallas, and Baltimore. Forced to spend at least 80 percent of the cap, wouldn't you know it, Kansas City, Buffalo, and Cincinnati became year-after-year contenders.

Player pensions remained in place, with every owner required to match employee 401(k) contributions as much as two-to-one, along with owner-funded health research programs and a transition program that owners would fund but players would oversee.

Among the biggest wins was that we gained control of our work. The NFL would need players' agreement to add new games to the schedule, a symbol of our union regaining strength and a long-term strategy that would act as a structure for future collective bargaining agreements. Roger kept asking if we could agree on moving to an eighteen-game schedule within two years of the new deal.

"Of course!" I said. But I had no intention of going through with it. Not for free, at least.

After months of negotiating and years of posturing, we hammered out the broad strokes of a new ten-year deal within three days, all because our lockout insurance policy meant that owners no longer had players over a barrel.

By the end of July 2011, we faced only one more hurdle. Every story, even the ugly ones, needs a hero—a symbol of the path forward and a palatable way for everyone to move on. It wouldn't be me. It damn sure wouldn't be Roger.

The proposed collective bargaining agreement was put to a team vote, and only the Steelers voted against it. The Steelers' union rep, Ryan Clark, would later explain that his team had voted this way because the proposal allowed Roger to retain full authority over player discipline. It was a fair point, but it also illustrates the difficulty of finalizing these agreements. Owners refused to budge on the commissioner's disciplinary power, so what is the right choice: accept what has been agreed on or risk a work stoppage—and owners removing other important provisions and demanding more money back—in an attempt to get more?

With the proposal's overwhelming passage, we reconstituted the union and set up a lectern on the sidewalk outside the law office.

News cameras pushed in. Kraft stepped to it, thanked Roger and me, and singled out Domonique Foxworth and Jeff Saturday, saying they'd earned his respect during a harsh negotiation.

"You're going to see a very great NFL over the next decade," Kraft said.

Then Kraft stepped aside, allowing Jeff to address the media. Myra Kraft had died five days earlier at age sixty-eight, and a few of us attended the funeral near Boston. Kraft, broken and emotionally wrung out, introduced me to his good friend Trump. I wound up sitting next to Jerry Richardson, who grumbled about it the whole time.

Jeff leaned toward the microphone and spoke softly, crediting Kraft for somehow negotiating a landmark collective bargaining agreement while overcome with unbearable grief.

"Without him," Jeff said, "this deal does not get done. . . . He is a man who helped us save football."

Then he wrapped his arm around Kraft, who leaned in and closed his eyes. Photos of their hug would be displayed on the front pages of almost every major newspaper in America, the video played again and again on highlight shows and news programs.

This was what unity looked like, and that's exactly how our leadership had choreographed it. This was the image that needed to endure—not the bickering, the supposed millionaires battling billionaires, or even owners' greed.

Kraft wanted this moment, knowing its importance to the NFL's mythology, and we knew he'd be willing to trade for it. He was the smartest guy in the room, a guy who many of his peers respected, and as such he was an important piece on the owners' chessboard—and a potentially useful one for us, now that the NFLPA had leaders who knew how to play the game.

# 3

# "KILL THE HEAD"

NFL-NFLPA
Collective Bargaining Agreement
*August 4, 2011*

ARTICLE 2, SECTION 3: The NFL Clubs maintain and reserve the right to manage and direct their operations in any manner whatsoever, except as specifically limited by the provisions of this Agreement.

Before the 2010 season, as I toured every team facility as we geared up for the lockout, I suggested to players that we consider a show of public solidarity. The season-opening Thursday night game between the Minnesota Vikings and New Orleans Saints would be a nationally televised rematch of the previous season's NFC championship game.

The Saints had won that game before going on to claim their first Super Bowl championship, a symbol of incredible rebirth less than five years after Hurricane Katrina leveled New Orleans and put the city's economic and racial disparity on global display.

I thought it would be really powerful if there were some gesture that would show that players were sticking together. The Saints' player representative was Drew Brees, and he recommended that I fly down before the game against Minnesota. He told me a symbolic gesture had been agreed on, but he wouldn't tell me what it'd be.

I arrived, made it to the Superdome through the sea of "Who Dat" faithful, and stood on the sideline as Colbie Caillat performed a stirring version of the national anthem. As much as I love my native Washington, D.C., there's something special about New Orleans. It is America in a city: proud, diverse, a little screwed up. I got goosebumps as Caillat hit the final notes and the crowd roared, remembering that just five years earlier, the Superdome had been repurposed by the city as a "shelter of last resort" for ten thousand displaced locals, many of whom had lost their homes during one of the worst natural disasters in history.

Then players from both teams streamed onto the field and lifted their index fingers. Players were "One Team," the mantra we had adopted in 2009 after my election. As I stood next to Kevin Mawae, the NFLPA president and alumnus of nearby Louisiana State University, and George Atallah, my best friend, it was all I could do to avoid bursting into tears. It was that meaningful, that moving, that cool.

The three of us raised our fingers as well, and I saw Drew, punter Thomas Morstead, and team leader Will Smith making the same salute as Minnesota's Steve Hutchinson, Chad Greenway, and Jared Allen. I noticed that Brett Favre, who had recently joined the Vikings after a dispute with the Green Bay Packers, was the only player not demonstrating.

"Nothing like a labor statement to start the season," NBC play-by-play announcer Al Michaels smugly said. "Let's get to *football* now."

The following Sunday, several other teams followed with this same display, perhaps the strongest and most important show of brotherhood since players voted for a strike three decades earlier.

Even when fans booed, players kept doing the "One Team" gesture, showing they were a singular, united force who wouldn't be bullied by greedy owners. It obviously wasn't enough to scare the league into preventing a lockout, and memorable as that night in New Orleans was, I should've known the warm fuzzies wouldn't last.

A few weeks before the NFLPA's annual meeting of player reps in March 2011, there had been grumblings about something nefarious having allegedly transpired before and during the NFC title game between the Saints and Vikings, then again during the season-opening game I attended in 2010. The league issued a $20,000 fine for New Orleans defensive end Bobby McCray for hits on Favre, and end Anthony Hargrove and linebacker Jonathan Casillas were each fined $5,000 after being penalized for unnecessary roughness. The game is inherently violent, but certain guardrails had been—and would continue to be—formalized to protect our workforce. Others were merely understood, just part of the game's honor code, the most important being that injuries happen, yes, but players don't deliberately hurt an opponent.

*Ever.*

But Brad Childress, the Vikings' coach, had publicly indicated that Saints players had defied the code. They had gone so far, I learned Childress had privately told league officials, that his player Hargrove had heard from a Saints player that the New Orleans defense had cash incentives in place for intentionally hurting opponents and knocking them out of the game.

It is possible that my idealism clouded things back then. I found it hard to believe that men at this level of football, barbaric as the game can seem, would operate a bounty program. Something so heinous just couldn't be.

I called Roger Goodell and told him I had heard about the allegations, suggesting the union and league should come together to conduct a joint investigation.

"I'm outraged," I told him, "and our players are as outraged as you are."

He seemed open to it.

"I'll get back to you," he said. As always, he needed to take the temperature of his overlords.

I never heard back. Weeks turned into months, and amid the day-to-day stress of lockout negotiations, I mostly forgot about it. If I thought about it at all, it was to reassure myself that Childress's reports to the league office were surely exaggerated.

In March 2012, a full year after the whispers began and months after we signed the new collective bargaining agreement, *The New York Times* published a bombshell report as we arrived at rep meetings. After an "extensive investigation" by the NFL, including the supposed review of more than eighteen thousand documents totaling fifty thousand pages, the league had determined that as many as twenty-seven Saints players had financed a bounty system in which $1,500 bonuses were handed out for injuring an opponent so badly that he couldn't play. The team's defensive coordinator, Gregg Williams, had been recorded before one game encouraging players to injure multiple San Francisco 49ers players.

"Kill the head and the body will die," the veteran coach had told his players. "We've got to do everything in the world to make sure we kill Frank Gore's head. We want him running sideways. We want his head sideways."

When talking about knocking quarterback Alex Smith out of the game, Williams rubbed his fingers together to indicate there was extra money waiting.

"Go lay that motherfucker out," he said. "We're going to dominate the line of scrimmage, and we're going to kill the fucking head. Every single one of you, before you get off the pile, affect the head. Early, affect the head. Continue, touch and hit the head."

If an opponent was carted off the field, the report suggested, Saints players would kick in an extra $1,000 to the responsible teammates. The amounts could double or even triple during the postseason.

"We have made significant progress in changing the culture with respect to player safety," Roger was quoted as saying, "and we are not going to relent."

Perhaps just as shocking, the article claimed, Saints general manager Mickey Loomis had ignored owner Tom Benson's instructions to stop this grotesque program. Mike Ornstein, the ex–NFL agent and businessman (and associate of Troy Vincent's) who, despite two fraud convictions, maintained relationships with members of the Saints organization, had sent an email to Saints coach Sean Payton pledging $10,000 for any player who knocked the opposing quarterback out of a playoff game.

It was a hell of a smoking gun.

Awful as the details were, I read everything like a lawyer. I just couldn't shake the notion that the league was going way out on a limb without the safety net that a joint investigation would have provided. And the *Times* dropping its report right as our meeting began? That couldn't have been a coincidence. When I practiced law, opposing counsel gave you the courtesy of a phone call to let you know something big was coming. There's no posturing and rarely any bluffing. Discovery rules allow both sides to take testimony from all witnesses and examine every document.

If the other side plans to slit your throat, in other words, they call and tell you it's coming. The NFL has no such decorum, which pissed me off.

So I called Roger.

"I guess we're not doing that joint investigation, huh?" I said.

• • •

THE FIRST TIME I met Roger was a few weeks after I was elected executive director. He traveled from New York to Washington, and the two of us had lunch at the Caucus Room, an old-fashioned Georgetown brasserie co-owned by my old boss, Tom Boggs.

Roger was there when I arrived, wearing a tailored suit with no tie. There was a pin on his lapel of the NFL's shield logo, and when he stood to greet me, I noticed that, at six foot two, he's taller than I'd expected. I did wear a tie with my suit.

Our lunch was cordial, just two professionals who play the same sport but on opposing teams—not unlike the hundreds of meetings I'd held with rival lawyers before a big case. Television and movies make it seem as if these interactions are high-stakes tugs-of-war, both sides looking for a weakness to exploit, but real life is far less interesting. Usually there's a casual conversation about what each side wants in a potential settlement, though if an agreement is impossible and a trial unavoidable, we wish each other good luck.

Roger isn't a lawyer, but he presents himself as capable, a comfortable member of a class that wields almost unimaginable resources and power. I don't remember much about our actual conversation, but one moment stands out. Near the end of our meal, he unclasped his lapel pin and set it on the table.

"Welcome to the family," he said. Then he slid it toward me.

Looking back, I don't think this was an attempt at intimidating me or some other form of psychological warfare. It was the commissioner trying to be nice, so long as it happens to fit into his worldview. I knew by then that Roger had never worked anywhere but the NFL, an ecosystem and wider universe that, to him, is all connected. To work in pro football is to be in it together as we all "grow the game," expand the business, and share the same objectives as owners. When that's the only perspective you've ever had, it's hard to understand when someone sees it a different way.

So when I slid the pin back to him, he looked at me with confusion. My job isn't to assist the league and make owners richer. It is to protect players, fight their wars, set and enforce boundaries. If my guys are safe and the game grows, that's great. But this is neither an alliance nor a joint venture, and even accepting something as simple as a lapel pin is a signal that I can perhaps be compromised, bought, or ethically pliable.

Maybe it seems petty that I would refuse Roger's token, but to any good union leader whose membership faces real danger, the job must sometimes be zero-sum.

Roger and I had our first big disagreement about something called StarCaps, a relatively obscure weight-loss drug that had found a market among athletes trying to drop pounds. Some players' contracts require them to make regular weigh-ins, a layer of protection for clubs worried one or more players may balloon during the mostly sedentary months of the offseason.

The league had spent the last few years coming down hard on performance-enhancing substances, an attempt at avoiding the same steroid-related catastrophe that had befallen Major League Baseball in the late 1990s and early 2000s. It was also a way for Roger to establish himself as a strict disciplinarian and the league as a bastion for integrity on and off the field. Roger's predecessor as commissioner, Paul Tagliabue, was a longtime lawyer who was seen in and around sports as a thoughtful pragmatist. Whether in dealing with the union and Gene Upshaw or with players, Tagliabue sought solutions that were fair to everyone. Nobody wanted a sideshow, Tagliabue determined, and anything that occurred away from the field threatened to distract fans, deflect attention from the game, and muffle the influx of advertising dollars and television revenue that was flooding into the league office.

But that's not what owners wanted out of Roger. When he replaced Tagliabue in 2006, he made it immediately clear that he was the law-and-order commissioner and was the only voice that mattered when it came to matters of personal conduct. Tennessee Titans defensive back Adam "Pacman" Jones got suspended without pay for the entire 2007 season for a series of incidents involving the police, and Cincinnati's Chris Henry and Chicago's Tank Johnson were banned eight games after each was arrested. Henry and Johnson hadn't been convicted of a crime (Jones had pleaded no contest to an unrelated misdemeanor in 2007), and despite public cries that Roger was going too far, it was obvious this was precisely what owners wanted him to do.

"I hope this sends a message to people in our league for how to conduct themselves," Robert Kraft said at the time. "We have to be careful. People in America can't relate to overindulged athletes not acting responsibly."

To further rein in misbehavior, the NFL updated its list of banned chemicals, among them a diuretic called bumetanide (Bumex), which can be used to mask traces of previous steroid use in a urine test.

The league and teams claimed to conduct these tests at random, and getting popped with one of the banned substances led to an immediate four-game suspension. With the NFLPA's blessing, the NFL even set up a hotline so players could call with questions about a particular supplement or medication to ask a pharmaceutical expert if one of the ingredients ran afoul of the doping policy.

In 2008, the year before I joined the union, six players called the hotline to ask about an over-the-counter diuretic labeled StarCaps. It was safe, the six players were assured, but what neither the league nor the players knew was that StarCaps had recently added bumetanide to its formula without updating its ingredient label. All six players—the Saints' Charles Grant, Deuce McAllister, and Will Smith; Minnesota defensive linemen Kevin Williams and Pat Williams; and Houston long snapper Bryan Pittman—tested positive for a banned substance.

Each of those guys got suspended four games. The players appealed, a court sided with them, but Roger didn't stop. He went before Congress to ask them to change federal labor laws.

In another instance, an Indianapolis Colts player found out that a close relative had a terminal illness. He and his wife visited a fertility clinic in an attempt at having a child before the relative's death, and the player asked the doctor if any of the proposed treatments contained an ingredient found on the league's list of banned substances. The doctor assured both of them that the treatments were safe, but after the player took the medication, he failed a drug test. The doctor offered to write a letter on the player's behalf to take responsibility, but Roger didn't care.

He suspended the player for the full four games, and though by then I was leading the NFLPA and advocated for the guy, Roger refused to decrease the punishment.

"Hey, what are we doing here?" I asked Roger in one of our early meetings. The league's drug-enforcement hotline kept records, so there was no question that the players had done what they were supposed to do.

"Every player is responsible for what goes into their body," Roger told me.

I argued that this undercut the entire system and would discourage anyone from calling the hotline ever again. It was a trap.

"The suspensions are going to stand," he said.

It made no sense, either from a legal or from a moral perspective. So, for the first time, I sued the National Football League in federal court, the league refused to back down or even work with us toward an amicable resolution, and back and forth this idiotic case went for years. By the time the case was resolved, most of the players who'd been suspended were now retired.

When it came to enforcing the league's personal conduct policy on owners, though, Roger was far more lenient. The Spygate controversy, the ordeal that had animated Pennsylvania senator Arlen Specter, uncovered how far the New England Patriots were willing to go to get an advantage against an opponent, resorting to no less than videotaping the New York Jets in an attempt at stealing the hand signals that coaches used to communicate with players from the sideline. This was the league's model franchise and, after being caught cheating, it got little more than an organizational slap on the wrist: a $250,000 team fine and the forfeiture of a draft choice.

But the team's coach, Bill Belichick, got fined $500,000, the largest fine in NFL history.

Did this represent Roger granting his buddy Kraft a favor by pinning it all on Belichick? Hard to say. Then again, I can't imagine that Kraft disapproved when Roger took the liberty of destroying the video and other evidence so the story went away.

"It was the right thing to do," Roger told Specter while testifying on Capitol Hill.

How often do you think about the fact that Jim Irsay, the Colts' owner, was arrested in 2014 for driving while under the influence with a load of pain pills and $29,000 in cash just two weeks after his mistress died of a drug overdose? Or that the Hunt family, which owns the Kansas City Chiefs, does so partly because their father, Lamar, plotted to illegally corner the world's silver market in the 1970s with two of his brothers? Or that Cowboys owner Jerry Jones has been accused multiple times of sexual misconduct in lawsuits and the press? He's denied it—but the claims more than pass the smell test.

Never?

That's how good Roger is at this. By 2012, long after the lockout ended, he and I had spoken dozens of times. It's fun to reduce Roger to a wooden and lumbering automaton, but the truth is that he's highly intelligent and clearly one of America's most skilled politicians. If the last decade or two of political turmoil has taught us nothing else, it is that the secret to political success in this country is keeping your constituency happy. Roger is better at this than anyone.

Still, the more I got to know him, the less I understood him as a person. How can such a smart guy be so stubborn, so willing to bet big on a bad hand?

Every negotiation has a deal point, that place somewhere in the middle of what I want and what you want. This is true in courtrooms, boardrooms, and the back rooms and hallways of Capitol Hill. There may be ferocious disagreements as we work toward that middle, but unless one side has a significant power advantage, deep down we're all trying to get to the same place. It may be frustrating, but it's never personal.

Or so I used to think.

Roger seemed to take every conversation, negotiation, argument personally—each one a new grudge stacked onto a growing pile. My adult life has revolved around understanding people and their motivations, all in search of potential solutions that get everyone closer to that elusive deal point. When we do, the sides shake hands, we tell our people we got the better end, and we all go home.

In those first three years, the question I couldn't shake about Roger: Why is he so dogmatic? Why does he refuse to backtrack on or even discuss an impulsive decision? Why does this man never break character, even when a negotiation ends?

■ ■ ■

**A FEW WEEKS** after the *New York Times* article, we were granted discovery materials related to what was now being called Bountygate. Among other things, the league produced its key piece of evidence, the explosive email to Saints coach Sean Payton.

Mike Ornstein had indeed put into writing what appeared to reference a bribe for any Saints player who deliberately injured Green Bay quarterback Aaron Rodgers.

**Gregg Williams put me down for $5000.00 on Rogers [*sic*]**

Williams was the Saints' defensive coordinator, and this was part of a letter Ornstein wrote from a Colorado prison camp. The long and rambling screed was mostly about his life while serving time, and the line about Rodgers was the postscript.

While Ornstein had singled out Williams, we noticed that he'd sent this to neither the defensive coordinator, Payton, nor any other member of the coaching staff—at least not directly. It had landed in the inbox of Greg Bensel, the team's public relations director, who then forwarded it to the coaches.

Another email, sent later from a halfway house, pledged the same amount for targeting Carolina's Cam Newton. Payton did receive this email directly, but so did at least a dozen other people. The head coach's email address had been among those Ornstein had cc'd. It was impossible to know if Payton had read or even opened the email.

If nothing else, these details were in conflict with the *Times*'s implication that this had been a one-on-one exchange between Ornstein and Payton. Judy Battista, the outlet's reporter on this and other articles about Bountygate, never pointed out that this correspondence had been sent to numerous recipients. If Battista or her editors at the *Times* had personally viewed these emails, none of the articles stated it.

We could only assume that the league had been the only party with access to these emails, considering its ability to summon this material as part of its investigation. Did Battista or anyone else request to view this supposed evidence? If yes, why didn't the article disclose this request and that the possessor apparently refused?

Regardless, this was not the smoking gun it had been made out to be. As disseminated, it didn't even rise to convincing evidence. But neither stopped Roger from issuing wide suspensions without pay to members of the Saints organization: linebacker Jonathan Vilma for the entire 2012 season, defensive end Anthony Hargrove for eight games, defensive end Will Smith (the same player busted for StarCaps) for four, linebacker Scott Fujita for three.

Payton also got suspended for the full season, and general manager Mickey Loomis was banned for eight games. Two Saints assistant coaches, Joe Vitt and Mike Cerullo, were summarily disciplined: Vitt was suspended for six games and Cerullo was fired. The organization was fined $500,000 and docked two second-round draft picks. Williams, who'd already left the organization, was suspended indefinitely.

It was a wide and decisive reaping, clearly meant to send a message that the league's integrity mustn't be compromised, not without harsh penalty. The villains had all been rounded up and punished, Saints owner Tom Benson claimed ignorance, and Roger could play the hero who'd restored order.

In truth, it was a heavy-handed response that Roger rushed into, bolstered by a yearning public hypnotized by a sophisticated narrative. It was smart.

But deeply, deeply flawed.

Players had recourse, at least, thanks largely to the fact that they had a union. Coaches? Not so much. Assistant coaches can belong to the American Football Coaches Association, which is a trade group that represents coaches at all levels but is not a labor organization. Even at the sport's highest level, coaching is a tight-knit fraternity in which key figures protect one another, but even the most successful and influential coaches are subject to the whims of their employer. Just to name two: Belichick, who took the fall for Spygate, and Payton, who was the public face of Bountygate.

If either wanted to continue working in the NFL, they had to accept their punishments, keep their mouths shut, and go along with the myth that Roger had done his due diligence and gotten it right. This was true before and after the lockout, when owners unilaterally threatened to drastically cut coaches' benefits and pay in the event of a work stoppage, despite the fact that coaches had absolutely no say in whether a deal did or didn't get done. A group of assistant coaches did meet around that time to discuss unionizing, spurred by the dozen or so teams that opted out of the league's pension, retirement, and 401(k) plans for coaches, but those plans ultimately dissolved.

Because players do have a union, we started outlining a defense strategy. The league responded by further deploying its PR apparatus to suggest that the NFLPA was so craven as to defend a small number of guys who had deliberately injured opponents. First off, it was debatable that any player had actually tried to hurt anyone. Second, and this may be boring legal stuff, but every labor union has a "duty of fair representation." This means that every union has an obligation to defend and advocate for its members, whether they're right or wrong, to push back against potential management overreach.

In our case, any NFL player has the right to expect or even demand the NFLPA's representation if they feel that they've been treated unfairly. In the bounty case, it wasn't so much about the accused players. It was to make certain Roger couldn't issue sweeping discipline unfairly and abuse his office's considerable powers.

In other words, whenever nobody else has your back, I do. *We* do.

The allegations did, however, create an interesting conundrum. Any union is lawfully obligated to defend its members against disciplinary action from the employer. But the archaic *code* among lawyers is that conflicts of interest must be avoided at all costs, so because the league would obviously want to interview players from the Saints and other teams, the NFLPA simultaneously represents these individuals but also must make space for outside lawyers as a way to avoid the appearance of conflict.

We reviewed the fifty thousand pages of documents, the Ornstein correspondence, and the NFL's implication that Hargrove had in fact been captured on video admitting that he was participating in the bounty program. We reviewed this footage and found that Hargrove's face was obscured, and whatever he did or didn't say was unintelligible to everyone in our office because of crowd noise and screaming coaches. Hargrove denied that he'd ever said what the league claimed.

But we had to be sure. So our office hired a voice recognition expert to analyze the Hargrove tape, and this expert concluded—beyond the shadow of a doubt—that Hargrove's voice didn't match what was on the tape. In fact, it wasn't Hargrove's voice at all, according to the analyst. It was a mash-up of two people talking at once.

The league's only evidence was Gregg Williams's "kill the head" recording, and nobody could prove whether players followed these instructions or ignored them.

Roger, though, wouldn't back off the suspensions. The "proof" he had was false. The burden lay not on players to prove their innocence but on the commissioner to prove their guilt.

Our strategy, then, was to mount an aggressive legal attack that, for the first time, put the NFL commissioner's unchecked powers in question. The league's disciplinary system goes back nearly a century, and it mirrors the power of commissioners in other sports. It's consistent with what many employers are legally allowed to do in order to protect their businesses. If you show up late to work, your boss has the right to discipline or even fire you. Roger's exclusive authority on player conduct, at least as collectively bargained, can be neither arbitrary nor based on lies. It must be consistent with previous punishments.

The NFL blew all this away, though, in its relentless PR campaign, and even when confronted with this, Roger refused to back off or rethink the suspensions or so much as discuss a compromise. I asked George Atallah and our communications department to wage a media counterattack, at least to reporters who were willing to listen, and point out that our players had the right to an appeals hearing.

The league's designated hearing officer? Roger Goodell—judge, jury, and executioner.

We ramped up the media assault. Was Roger's handling of this fair? And who the hell is this guy, whose training isn't in law but in media relations, to deploy the right legal standards and analyses? It was enough public pressure that the owners made Roger appoint a "special investigator" to take a second pass on the case. They tapped Mary Jo White, a former U.S. Attorney for the Southern District of New York, but the problem was that she wasn't exactly a neutral party. The NFL funded her investigation directly, so of course she ultimately determined that Roger had been right all along. She even held a conference call with reporters in which she repeated the lie that Hargrove had been caught on tape talking about intentionally trying to injure Favre.

If, looking back, I can point to the moment my idealism died, it was this. Because after decades of practicing law, I truly couldn't believe how many people were willing to lie, cheat, steal, or just go along with whatever the league wanted them to. They'd say, do, publish anything—all in the service of the league's predetermined narrative.

White had once supervised the Southern District of New York, perhaps the most important law office in the country, and now she was making assertions so unfounded that they suggested she was willing to abandon the truth entirely if it served her client.

I knew then that I was dealing with a different animal. This thing, this NFL *thing,* and the people who ran it were willing to get to whatever outcome they wanted, by any means necessary. There was no such thing as logic or good faith, no moral compass or, upon further review, admitting that there'd been a hasty overreaction.

Roger's train just left the station, and once it did, there was no way to reverse it. The commissioner and his underlings then set out to find—and reward—people with credibility to cover Roger's tracks or claim his initial impulses had been correct. Lawyers get paid millions to oversee investigations like the one White conducted. Cerullo, the former Saints assistant coach who'd been fired, had been the initial whistleblower to the NFL, and he was given a cushy job in the league office. Even Battista, the reporter who had written about the bounty case, left the *Times* in 2013 for a job at NFL Network, where she would work directly for the league.

The NFL doesn't just cave to common sense or public sentiment. It doesn't just move on. It has to *win.* Roger wasn't seeking justice or looking to restore integrity. He was being petty, obstinate, arbitrary—

the one thing law forbids in collective bargaining agreements. He could have backtracked to determine that Saints players had been motivated by an organizational culture that urged violence. He could have asked to interview players and get their side before handing down discipline. He could have even fined players for carrying out the instructions of coaches who *had* been directly and verifiably tied to something nefarious.

If Roger had just called me and said, "Look, I've got to hammer these guys with a huge fine," we would have taken that offer to the players. If a bounty system indeed existed in New Orleans, the collective group had as much an incentive to end it as the league.

I wanted to believe that the league could find a reasonable landing point. Paul Tagliabue had spent years keeping the peace and trying to do what was right for the league as a whole. His successor's marching orders were clearly different, and by the time 2012 started, I began to finally understand that the most important thing about Roger is that he will never cede ground.

He just can't do it. It's not who he is.

■  ■  ■

IN MY FRUSTRATION, I googled Charles Goodell, Roger's dad. There were photos of him marching arm in arm with Coretta Scott King. One website talked about how historically important Charles had been. I found out that some of his papers were at the New York Public Library, so during my next trip to Manhattan, I read through the documents from his brief but important political career.

A Republican who was pro–civil rights and anti-Vietnam? Forget his political stances. This was a level of curiosity and empathy that I would have never attached to the Roger I had gotten to know over three years. I later purchased Charles's 1973 book, *Political Prisoners in America*, and first noticed the epigraph.

To my friend, Richard Nixon—
May he do more than listen

Scribbling my thoughts on a sticky note, I affixed the first of many to the page.

**Book is written BEFORE WATERGATE. Nixon still a friend at the time.**

At the apex of Charles Goodell's career, he had followed nine years in the House of Representatives with an appointment to the U.S. Senate to represent blue New York following Robert Kennedy's assassination in 1968. He initially supported American involvement in Vietnam and campaigned with Nixon, but as the death toll skyrocketed, Charles had a crisis of conscience. Nixon told Charles that he planned to gradually withdraw troops, but this was a lie.

I dug deeper into the Goodell bloodline. More than a century earlier, Roger's great-grandfather, William, founded the American Anti-Slavery Society and even ran for president. I wondered if, in the late 1960s, Charles held similar ambitions as he chirped louder and more publicly for the White House to bring troops home. Allies told him to keep quiet, but he refused.

"Irony!" I wrote on another sticky.

Two months before Kennedy's assassination, the Reverend Martin Luther King, Jr., was gunned down in Memphis. Charles Goodell would later march on Washington with King's widow, weep after the massacre at Kent State University, and sponsor a bill known as the Vietnam Disengagement Act.

"This slaughter must cease," he demanded. But Nixon refused to throw the train in reverse, so Charles Goodell gathered his five sons at the family home in Washington. Their dad was about to do something professionally risky but fundamentally right.

Later that day, he stepped to a lectern in the Senate.

"The war drags on," he said. "It knew no real beginning, and it seems to know no end."

Nixon's secretary of state, Henry Kissinger, accused Charles of treason. Nixon ordered New York's Republican governor, Nelson Rockefeller, to cut off funding to Charles's reelection campaign and told his vice president, Spiro Agnew, to cut his "friend's" throat by calling Charles a radical liberal.

On Election Day in 1970, Roger and his brothers ran around a New York hotel as votes were cast, more against their father than for him. Charles finished third, in fact, ruined by the same machine that had created him.

"We got that son of a bitch," Agnew told Nixon.

■ ■ ■

BY OCTOBER 2012, the NFL season was well under way and Bountygate was still unresolved. Roger not only refused to back down on his player suspensions, he actually reissued them.

New Orleans vilified him, with restaurants posting signs that banned Roger from service and a house that hung a Roger effigy from its front porch. In a city that may be drunk all the time but never forgets, a Mardi Gras float later depicted a battered and bruised Roger lifting the Super Bowl trophy as he emerged from a papier-mâché vagina. I suppose fine art needn't be understood to be appreciated.

At the NFLPA, we continued our push: nasty, controversial litigation and a public callout of the NFL as liars, backing it up with facts. The league actually allowed a bounty program as recently as 1996, promoted by the legendary pass rusher Reggie White and an ambitious Philadelphia defensive back named Troy Vincent.

George educated the media in an effort to flood the zone against a league-driven narrative that some reporters were happy to parrot without pushback. We filed new lawsuits with the local federal district court that sought a court order that barred the suspensions, and as November approached and the scandal dragged on, owners finally got tired of our nuclear approach overshadowing the season and instructed Roger to recuse himself.

His response, again, was to appoint yet another supposedly independent figure to hear players' appeals. Roger's choice this time: Paul Tagliabue, the NFL's ex-commissioner and, to hear league insiders tell it, Roger's mentor.

I started to believe that owners thought Roger's public handling of this was a disaster, and they needed a solution that avoided our case going before a federal judge. And Tagliabue was the last person Roger wanted presiding over this.

Still, we didn't see this as a victory. Not yet, at least. Tagliabue is a formidable lawyer, and because the collective bargaining agreement allows the league to select an arbitrator, it was hard for us to imagine that he'd be impartial. He was still drawing a check from the NFL, still had an email address at the league, and had been aware of—if not directly behind—the idea to pay off quarterbacks in the 1980s and '90s to cross the picket line and break the union. When he was an attorney for the league, Tagliabue actually cross-examined Gene Upshaw in 1981 during a federal antitrust case in which Raiders owner Al Davis sued his own league for the right to relocate his franchise. Six years later, Tagliabue argued that NFL players should be denied free agency.

But as skilled a lawyer as he was, he wasn't much of a politician. As I researched his history, it seemed to me that he knew that, left to their own devices, owners were largely too undisciplined and selfish to collectively push the NFL forward. His job was to corral his bosses—to herd them in the safest and most lucrative direction possible. He seemed to have left a lot of the dirty work to other lawyers while Roger acted as the head of the division that drove revenue through ticket sales, apparel, and broadcast rights.

It also seemed that the most important thing Roger learned was that it wasn't Tagliabue he needed to cozy up to. It was the owners. Roger was a thirty-year-old executive when Jerry Jones bought the Dallas Cowboys, and he quickly learned how important money is to Jerry and actually advocated within the league on Jerry's behalf when the latter demanded a bigger cut of licensing revenues than other owners. When Robert Kraft bought Sullivan Stadium out of bankruptcy court in 1988 before completing a hostile takeover of the Patriots six years later, it was a baby-faced Roger who testified at a Massachusetts state commission that Kraft should get his way.

"The NFL," he was quoted as saying, "has been called the greatest social common denominator ever known to man."

Roger forged similar relationships with Carolina's Jerry Richardson, Pittsburgh's Dan Rooney, and the New York Giants' Wellington Mara. By 2006, while Gene and Tagliabue were negotiating the ill-fated collective bargaining agreement, there were whispers that owners were ready to push Tagliabue out and install a commissioner more tuned in to the desires and impulses of owners. That July, Tagliabue announced his retirement, and a month later, Roger was one of five finalists for Tagliabue's old job.

"I live and breathe the league," he told owners in a nine-page speech. "*Your* league."

Prince Valiant wasn't born, in other words. He was created, shaped by the men who'd someday elect and manipulate him, and the first time he swung his sword was to decapitate his supposed mentor.

So when it was Tagliabue who was selected to look into the bounty case, Roger may have realized that his bosses were sending him a message. And that Tagliabue, like New Orleans, doesn't forget.

His ruling, released in full to the public in December 2012, was stunning. He vacated all four player suspensions, wiping the slate for Vilma, Hargrove, Smith, and Fujita and taking his old colleague to the woodshed.

"When an effort to change a culture rests heavily on prohibitions," Tagliabue wrote, "and discipline and sanctions that are seen as selective, ad hoc, or inconsistent, then people in all industries are prone to react negatively—whether they be construction workers, police officers, or football players.

"In other words, rightly or wrongly, a sharp change in sanctions or discipline can often be seen as arbitrary and as an impediment rather than an instrument of change. This is what we see on the record here."

There's that word: *arbitrary*.

Tagliabue laid bare what we'd been arguing for months: that Roger had acted impulsively, unfairly, obstinately. He had wielded his disciplinary scythe based on nothing more than his own whims, then simply would not budge. At least to us, this felt like more than a righting of wrongs. It was a public flogging.

I can only imagine how red Roger's face got that day, when he learned of Tagliabue's decision and read his patronizing summary. The league issued a statement that said it respected Tagliabue's conclusion, but one thing I do know is that Roger didn't appear in public for a while.

When I ran into Tagliabue a few years later, I couldn't help but ask him about how Roger digested his ruling. The old pragmatist just shrugged, saying he had no idea, and the way he made it sound, Roger never got over it, refusing to speak to him ever again.

. . .

SOMETIME AFTER THE 1970 election, the Goodell family left Washington and retreated to New York. Roger was eleven years old. Humiliated and ostracized, Charles would never again run for public office.

Watergate and Nixon's downfall would prove Roger's dad right, of course, but history barely remembers Charles. He resumed his law practice and registered as a lobbyist, but news reports later suggested that Charles suffered a "mental breakdown" that required him to be hospitalized. He left Roger's mother, Jean, who died of breast cancer in 1984. Just three years later, his father was gone, too.

During and even after Bountygate, I wondered what such a thing does to a kid. How could you grow up not blaming Nixon and his cronies for not just ending Charles's political career but bringing ruin to his family? Roger's dad seemingly had it all, but the strength of his principles led him to trade it away.

A few months after Bountygate, I went to New York for a regular meeting with Roger. We usually got together before the Super Bowl to discuss a few of the things we'd be talking about during our annual news conferences. I sat in a sixth-floor waiting room with white chairs, staring at a display that holds the Super Bowl trophy. Every Super Bowl ring sits in another showcase, alongside magnifying glasses for closer inspection. This is the same room so many NFL players occupy while they await an audience with the commissioner, a chance to plead their cases in person after being accused of violating the NFL's policy on personal conduct.

Perhaps unsurprisingly, Roger rarely changes his mind on discipline, regardless of a player's explanation, argument, or contrition.

In early 2013, I waited my turn. A door opened, and I was led into the commissioner's office. Roger was running late, so I looked around his office. There's a bank of televisions on one wall, not far from a conference table and a sofa that faces Roger's desk. On the left is an old reelection poster for Charles Goodell, next to a framed copy of the *Congressional Record* from September 25, 1969—the date of his fateful speech calling for the withdrawal of troops from Vietnam.

"Mr. President," the page reads, "I ask unanimous consent that the language of the bill, which I shall introduce, be printed in the RECORD at this point."

After he spoke those words, nothing was ever the same. I was tempted to ask Roger that day about his dad and what that piece of memorabilia meant to him. But I didn't, largely because I believed I already knew. For most people, that would serve as a reminder to do the right thing, no matter its unpopularity. That there's nothing more rewarding than following your conscience.

But that's just not Roger. I believe he loves his parents very much, but I wondered if Charles's words may not have been there for inspiration. They're a warning. This, directly in Roger's line of sight, is a daily reminder of what can happen when you go against the powerful men who make you—an affirmation of the consequences that come with defying a brutal, unrelenting force.

The individuals who run the country, and indeed the National Football League, will stop at nothing to retain their power. They will not hesitate before destroying anyone or anything in their path, and the only way to stay on their good side is to make the choice most likely to please them. Then stick to it, no matter what, because the only thing worse than disappointing these men is groveling, because that is admitting that you initially got it wrong.

# 4

# THE HOMESTEAD

Every Father's Day weekend, I drive from Washington, D.C., to rural Virginia. The journey takes about five hours, though, to me, it's a trip through time. Fifteen miles north of Danville, a small city not far from the North Carolina line, is a community called Dry Fork, named centuries ago because, during the summer months, this tributary of the Banister River occasionally runs dry.

That could mean the difference between a bountiful harvest and a family that went hungry; whether my enslaved ancestors were deliberately starved or faced violence that brought them to within inches of death.

There's a small Baptist church in Dry Fork, just fifty yards off State Route 718, where we gather once a year as family. We call it Homecoming. When I was a kid, long before seatbelt laws, my dad would carry us to the car in the middle of the night, sliding us into a makeshift bed in the fold-down back seat of his Plymouth Barracuda. Around daybreak we'd pass through Charlottesville, where the smart and lucky kids studied literature and the law, before parking in the churchyard in time for my papa's sermon. Frederick Douglas Smith is why my father hoped I would become a pastor, and for much of my youth, I could think of no better path than one following in this incredible man's footsteps.

After the service, we would move to picnic tables near the gravestones of my kin, and we would feast on Aunt Bunny's potato salad, Mama Marie's biscuits, and Aunt Ruby's damson plum preserves. Then I would head downstairs to load a plate with blueberry and apple cobbler, fried fruit pie, and chocolate cake—a mighty sugar high that fueled play with my cousins and conversations with the grown-ups.

I was Smitty's son, the baby boy's baby boy, even after I became a teenager and crossed into adulthood. The ritual stayed consistent, but as I entered my twenties, I began noticing a change, not in my relatives or in Homecoming.

It was in me.

I was different from my uncles and cousins, but back then, I couldn't put my finger on why—a persistent itch always just out of reach. My personality had begun splintering, as I formed a public persona and a private one, putting further distance between them and me. My first cousins went to public schools and I attended a private Lutheran and then Baptist school. They loved me, of course, but they couldn't be sure of who I was. To tell the truth, neither could I.

When you're Black, I believe there's a certain duality that's essential to surviving in this country. You can look, talk, and engage in a certain way at home. Such comfort may not be unique to my family's traditions or even those of us born with a certain skin pigmentation. But the farther away you drift from the literal and metaphorical homestead, drawing closer to the types of individuals who once owned this land and those who think they still do, it is expected that you present yourself differently—that you will speak *their* dialect and dress in *their* customary attire.

To trade your comfort, in other words, for theirs, all the while becoming less and less like the people with your blood.

Even as a young man, I didn't realize that the stones of this path had been set long ago. If I had, maybe I would have added it up. After all, it was right in front of me, because our part of the family routine was unlike anyone else's. When the plates were empty and the stories done, my dad did something none of his brothers ever did.

Smitty loaded his car and drove away.

■    ■    ■

IN 1866, MONTHS after Virginia acknowledged the passage of the Thirteenth Amendment and freed the last of its enslaved, the Danville Railroad Company started surveying for a new line. It would connect the city with Lynchburg, seventy miles north, in what must have been a breathtaking expansion of residents' physical and psychological horizons.

Until then, the ways in and out of Dry Fork were the walking trails cut decades or even centuries earlier by the Sappony tribe. Bison and elk roamed the surrounding woodlands, and the footpaths between the trees were grass and dirt. Eventually they would be flattened and widened so that wagons could come and go, allowing traders and hunters from elsewhere to make this their home. By the mid-1600s, the new settlers noticed how easily corn and tobacco grew, so they carved their initials in the beech trees and claimed the land as theirs.

Soon after, those who had first called this home—the bison, elk, and Indigenous people—were either pushed west or had been dead for a while.

Fields expanded, plantations went up, and the first ships from Africa landed on the beaches of Point Comfort. As the crow flies, the coast is about a hundred and seventy miles east of Dry Fork. Among the passengers were those from Nigeria, and they would be stripped of their clothing and customs and identities, separated from family, and sold and transported by wagon down these recently widened trails. Upon arriving at their new homes, men were assigned to work the fields, women usually to the house.

Children were no exception. The enslavers saw them as property, not as people, so they took little care keeping records beyond those required by the state. This allowed plantation owners to shield their assets from tax collectors and census takers, one of the ways they maintained control and maximized profits. Slaves were forbidden from learning to read or write, another way to separate and oppress and manipulate even in the present day. Because of this, I am unable to know the full and complete truth of my bloodline, or even the name of the person who first carried my genes onto American soil.

I nonetheless think about how it must have felt to have been wretched away from home, stripped of everything you hold dear, and then feel the sand beneath your feet as shackles cut into your wrists and ankles. All I can do is imagine, because even during an age in which discovering forgotten ancestors is a few clicks away, the first of many liberties stolen was the chance to keep a diary or maintain family records.

And so, not unlike the stories we tell at Homecoming, there was only word of mouth: Mothers telling their daughters and sons about the things they'd seen, smelled, and felt. The ways they had made it this far. The words and customs that pleased their masters and helped the elders survive. Stories are the only part of us the slaveowners couldn't take away, so this is why we treasure and guard them so ferociously, reciting them in gatherings and putting them to music in congregations like my papa's.

One story we tell at every Homecoming is that of Mary "Grandmother" Hines. She had been "inherited" as a child, along with fifty other slaves, by a powerful Virginia family named the Fitzgeralds. Mary worked the house, and her owner, also named Mary, used her as the primary cook and caretaker of the house. Among the details that have stuck with me since childhood was that, when Mary Fitzgerald gave birth to a baby boy, she struggled to nurse the fussy infant and turned to Grandmother Hines for comfort. She was to whip up a batch of her famous cornbread, and Mary Fitzgerald told Mary Hines that she was not to burn the edges or let the center crack while it baked in the open hearth.

The crust was indeed golden, the edges crispy, but steam had caused a fissure in the middle. Mary Hines did her best to smooth the top before delivering the cornbread in a cast-iron skillet. Mary Fitzgerald noticed the crack and slammed the pan into my great-great-grandmother's forehead, opening a wide gash that would remain noticeable until her death. When my family tells this story, they do so in hushed voices, the same as their own mothers and grandmothers did, shaking their heads as they imagine what it must have felt like to live with such violence, meanness, and hopelessness.

These are stories told with empathy, of course, but it remains horrifying to me and can occasionally trigger an almost visceral anger. It is an anger that, so many generations later, I am discouraged from showing. This is another of the weapons used against my people, emotional suppression and social conformity having replaced the whip and pan.

Perhaps the most amazing thing to me is that Grandmother Hines endured this relatively recently and that, until her death in 1932, she continued living with the family that had enslaved her. The Fitzgeralds didn't even mark her grave with a headstone, though years ago, my cousin had one placed outside the church in Dry Fork.

## MARY HINES
### A NIGERIAN, SOLD AS A SLAVE AND THE ROOT
### OF THE SMITH FAMILY.

Because part of the Black existence in America is to lack certainty, I can only suspect that it's possible Grandmother Hines may have crossed paths with a woman named Amarietta Fitzgerald. They may have even worked at the same plantation. What I do know is that Amarietta, another distant relative of mine, had no choice but to take the family name of those who owned her.

Edmond Fitzgerald, a white man, had been born on a passenger ship traveling from Ireland to New York a century before. His parents had chosen to make this journey in the name of possibility and dreams, and I know this because there are records and websites devoted to describing—and probably exaggerating—the legend of a white family's arrival after braving the "high seas," as one such remembrance extols.

Edmond grew up poor, these accessible stories suggest, before acquiring a calf and trading it for a horse. Through increasingly grander exchanges, he was able to parlay his assets into a house and 500 acres of farmland near the Banister River. I can only speculate at how or by whom Amarietta became pregnant, but in 1840, she gave birth to a boy she named Moses, who would be listed in census records decades later as "mulatto."

Moses would become my great-great-grandfather, and he was twenty-five when the Thirteenth Amendment passed and he was granted freedom. From physical restraints, at least. Around this same time, a railroad company started grading the land and laying track. Nine years later, in 1874, the railroad was finished along the Dry Fork Creek.

I wonder how this development made Moses and his wife feel. On one hand, they were unencumbered now, but on the other, more outsiders had a new path in. I cannot know whether this was exciting or scary or both. Considering the scars they wore and the trauma they carried, how free were they?

I know they had nine children by 1880, and they could have taken a carriage out of town or boarded the mail train to Lynchburg. They could have left this place where their relatives were beaten and raped, coming back the way their own ancestors came, and charted their own course. Considering the things he'd seen and the stories he'd heard, I imagine the fear Moses must have felt.

Did he even *think* about leaving? How close did he come?

I have to accept that I can never be certain. All I can do is fantasize about this man watching as a locomotive roared into Danville station, hearing it screech and whine, seeing the plumes of smoke and steam as possibility surely tempted. How would it have felt to watch the white and Black passengers, still segregated and prohibited from sharing a car, board and set off into this once-unfathomable horizon?

Freedom had finally come to Danville, yes, attainable by even its Black residents. Today it seems so easy for me to think about Moses and Chaney, his wife, standing on the platform with their children. I can almost see them stepping onto the "Colored" car, Moses's stomach churning as they found their seats, the whistle sounded, and the train inched forward.

But that story lives only in my imagination, because there's no evidence that they even considered such a thing. There's one thing I know about the Black Fitzgeralds, in fact. It is that they stayed.

■   ■   ■

EVERY YEAR I was with the NFLPA, I brought these parts of myself into locker rooms and meetings with players, into bargaining sessions and discussions about crisis management, and into nights like the one when Damar Hamlin's heart stopped.

The story I told myself was that my family's struggles made me stronger and that every player had a story like mine; that they would see me as a peer or advocate and I would be welcomed in as if part of the players' extended family. This, too, was fantasy.

My greetings were rolled eyes and blank stares. Some players cursed me and the terrible collective bargaining agreement we had subjected them to in 2011, having bought into the league's highly so-phisticated messaging network. It didn't help that these meetings often occurred late in the afternoon, when players were exhausted from a day of workouts, practice, and team meetings. This was by design, of course, because owners dictated the time they'd open their facilities to us, and they wanted players to be as testy and unreceptive as possible.

The Bears, Cowboys, and Chargers went so far as to give players an unscheduled afternoon off, canceling their work responsibilities hours early so most would be gone by the time we arrived. Players on some teams suggested that we should assume our meetings were being recorded by staffers listening before compiling a report to give to the owner later.

It took me some time to realize that every player in these meetings was in his first job. The overwhelming majority was younger than twenty-seven, and many were a year or two out of college. NFL play-ers rarely worked a paper route or a summer job because, at the pinnacle of American sports and in one of the most competitive occupations in the world, football has been most of these guys' sole focus since childhood.

With this in mind, I learned to let them vent, stood there unbowed as they emoted or, in the case of Carolina Panthers wide receiver Steve Smith, stared you down and asked if you were afraid.

Sorry, Steve, but from one short brother to another, more menacing figures have tried and failed to intimidate me.

After the complaints subsided, there was an opening to educate. I reminded players that, unlike their coach or even their agent, I was maybe the only truly honest person in their football lives. Coaches say what they must to save their own skin, and every NFL agent works on commission. My salary was the same no matter how long they played or how many Super Bowls they won, and though I had trained myself for years to draw attention from a room of strangers, you need only look at me in a room of NFL players to realize I am not one of them.

"My name is DeMaurice Smith," I began, "and I do not care about the game of football. I care about the men who play it."

I told parts of the NFLPA's story, from the gnarled hands of retired players to the failed strikes, each a small step toward the pensions, benefits, and work-life boundaries today's players enjoy. I reminded them that they can repeat whatever mantra they wish, telling themselves that they're part of the supposed NFL "family," but what's the point of being in a billionaire's family if you'll never be in the will? This, I explained, is a business relationship. Nothing more. And you can give the team your body and your brain, but after you retire, the owner will still charge you full price for tickets.

When I first became executive director, my mentor, Marvin Miller, the legendary leader of the Major League Baseball Players Association, told me that players needed to constantly be reminded that they are employees. That those who employ them may *pretend* to see them as more than property, but they don't.

So I usually ended each meeting with the story of the Triangle Shirtwaist Factory. In 1911, someone dropped a discarded cigarette that ignited fabric and started a fire. The factory's owners had locked workers inside so they couldn't take breaks, going so far as to seal off the fire escapes, and 146 workers—most of them women and children—were trapped inside and died. This led to nearly three dozen rewritten laws and associated workplace reforms that included fire codes, child labor laws, and baseline measures for worker safety. Most of the victims lacked even the right to vote and, while tragic, these deaths had not been in vain. In fact, they had changed American labor forever.

"Imagine, then," I said, "if a group of the most high-profile athletes in the country came together. If they were willing to stand up to the plantation owners who run this league, what could be accomplished? What could *we* accomplish, if only we muster the will to fight?"

This was usually enough to get the guys fired up, eager to learn more, prepared to unite. A few would approach me to ask how to get more involved, and the best meetings included side sessions with committed player representatives such as Pittsburgh's Ryan Clark and Shaun Suisham, Detroit's Kyle Vanden Bosch, Tennessee's Colin Allred, and Carolina's John Kasay, maybe the only placekicker I ever met who garnered the respect of a quarterback.

I loved these meetings, because no matter how I felt upon entering, I walked away feeling like part of the team.

But then I left, headed to the next facility, to do it all over again while telling myself that *this* was the message that would stick. That players were finally buying in.

That they'd stay fired up and engaged, even after I was gone.

■ ■ ■

BY THE 1920S, the Virginia Department of Transportation began laying pavement on the old wagon lanes. Communities and towns would be connected to cities by this *auto trail*, making Richmond, Norfolk— even Washington, D.C.—accessible. This wasn't a road. It was a portal into a new world for residents who, for generations, dared not dream beyond the tobacco farm's horizon.

Moses Fitzgerald wouldn't live long enough to see it finished, but his accomplishments over seventy-six years were incredible: making it off the Fitzgerald plantation, acquiring a small plot of land in 1888, then learning that several of his relatives had purchased their own acre on the north side of Dry Fork Road. They'd paid a white family $15 for the parcel, and on it they would build Hopel Chapel Colored Baptist Church, where they'd sing and worship and bury their kin.

One of Moses's sons, John Fitzgerald, never learned to read or write. But when he married a woman named Nannie, their children grew up hearing their father's stories while obeying their mother's wishes that they become the family's first generation to experience literacy. Rather than strike marks on census papers, as their ancestors had, Moses and Nannie's children would write their names.

One of them was a daughter named Mary Lemon Fitzgerald, and her intellect and curiosity were among the things that gained the attention of a boy a few houses over. In 1917, she and Frederick Douglas Smith were married, and the young couple made their home on the Smith family's creek-lined homestead in nearby Keeling, growing corn and tobacco not far from the soon-to-be-surfaced wagon trail. On Sundays, they rode over to Dry Fork and Hopel Chapel Baptist, where Fred would become its third pastor.

From the stories I've heard and the things I had read, the family was resilient and content. The children worked the land alongside Fred, whom I'd call Papa, and like Moses when the railroad came, John Fitzgerald or Fred could have taken the roadway out of town. Whether this lacked appeal or never occurred to them, I cannot be certain, though my guess is that the only thing more terrifying than the certainty of a restrictive and bloody past was a newly opened road that represented uncertainty both coming and going.

So Pittsylvania County, home to Smiths and Fitzgeralds for generations, is where their babies were born. When they grew into teenagers, they picked the same crops on the same land as their ancestors. Fred and Mary's fourteen children attended school, albeit only when it was neither planting season nor harvesting season. This means they went only during winter, and my uncles still tell stories of getting home from school, changing clothes, and immediately heading to the drying shed to tend and rotate tobacco leaves.

By the 1940s, Fred and Mary's sons joined the military and headed off to war, staving off the German invasion while assigned to segregated units. All but one, that is. Their youngest boy, Arthur, would get his own draft notice for the Korean War. But the U.S. War Department had introduced an exemption to any last male child, in effect making it so that if all the older brothers were killed, there'd be one son left to run the family farm.

So one day Fred and Arthur rode into town, taking the newly cut State Highway 718 into Chatham. This was the nearest city, and there was a military enrollment office there. When Fred started filling out the exemption paperwork, Arthur whispered to the guy doing sign-ups for the Marine Corps.

"Please take me," the boy said. He explained that it was the only way he'd ever get off the farm. "*Please.*"

■ ■ ■

WHEN MY DAD tells this story, he says joining the Marines was the best, most important thing to ever happen to him. They made him a typist, not exactly grappling with bad guys on the front lines, but for the first time in his life, Arthur Smith didn't have to fend off his siblings at dinnertime. He could eat as much as he wanted, sleep in his own bed, wear clothes that weren't hand-me-downs.

He spent his service in Florida, and when he looks back, he says there was nowhere that felt unsafe—so long as he was in his uniform. It wasn't until he was discharged that he experienced anything that resembled overt racism. During a stopover in North Carolina while he made his way back to Virginia, Arthur boarded a bus before white passengers demanded he sit in the rear.

That was the law in 1953, two years before Rosa Parks's ground-breaking refusal in Alabama. My dad was tough. But he wasn't reckless. He owed the Corps one last assignment—make it home—and in the Jim Crow South, being defiant was enough to get a Black man killed.

Uniform or not.

He may have wanted to fight everybody on that bus, but my dad shut his mouth, did as he was told, and took a seat in the last row. Unremarkable as it may seem, this was a crossroads moment for our family. Because it's when Arthur decided to leave home for good. He returned to the homestead long enough to pack his things, talk the high school principal into letting him graduate (in his Marines uniform, no less), and tell his father that he had no desire for a life with his fingers in the dirt.

In my family, and probably lots of others, we hand down more than stories to our children. Someone's first name may be who you are, but a middle name is a reminder of who you were—one of the roads that connect now to then.

So it wasn't Arthur Smith who left Virginia and turned north, taking State Road 360 through Danville before leaving behind the Confederacy's last capital and so much else. It was Arthur *Moses* Smith, named for a man he'd never meet—but whose existence made his possible. This was a lifelong reminder of the sacrifices and agony, the fear and despair, the shackles and the forced toil on someone else's land, just for the opportunity to buy his own.

To my dad and our family, Moses was that all-important signpost not of the road ahead but of the mighty, mighty mountain we'd been climbing over the previous century.

After earning his college degree at Virginia Union University, which in Moses's day had been a theological seminary for freed slaves, Arthur continued north. He joined the millions of other Black Americans who fled the South as part of the Great Migration, leaving behind the many reminders of Robert E. Lee and so many others chanting the mantra that *the South will rise again.*

My father settled in Washington, D.C., first taking an instructor's job at the District of Columbia Teachers College, followed by an accounting position with the U.S. Department of Commerce. He had a genetic eye condition that caused his cornea to bulge, and when he needed surgery to relieve the pressure, he admitted himself to the Freedman's Hospital, which would later become Howard University Hospital, now the nation's flagship historically Black institution and the alma mater of, among many others, Pulitzer Prize winners, entertainers, scholars, and Kamala Harris, who'd be the first woman to become vice president.

One of the nurses at this hospital was named Mildred, and over time, Arthur learned her own story. Born in Georgia, Mildred had suffered burns over most of her body during a childhood house fire before her mother died of tuberculosis. Her father had abandoned the family after that, but Mildred and her younger brother boarded a train to Washington, where they had extended family. She became a nurse, took care of a dashing ex-Marine with an eye condition, and eventually fell in love with him.

This is where their stories merged, and they moved into a house off Alabama Avenue in southeast Washington. This is where I was born on February 3, 1964, exactly one week before, just a few blocks away, the U.S. House of Representatives passed the Civil Rights Act (Charles Goodell, then a thirty-seven-year-old congressman from New York's Thirty-Eighth District, was one of 136 Republicans to vote in favor of the bill).

Be it wagon, railroad, or highway, everyone has reached this moment in time following a tenuous journey down an obstacle-laden path. The one I have described isn't special. It's just mine. I have no idea what my life would have been like if my father hadn't left the farm, or if I would have even been born. It's like attempting to survey the contours of the universe, just one of those things that scrambles your brain.

My path continued down a sidewalk in Maryland, where I stepped off a bus each day from Riverdale Baptist School. Kids ridiculed me, though not for my skin color. It was because I carried a valise under my arm, a kind of bag that resembles a briefcase, and it was filled with homework I always completed. Our family went on vacations to the Poconos and Disney World, and I remember checking into the

Holiday Inn before my sister and I changed into our swimsuits and excitedly jumped into the pool.

What I don't remember is the fact that everyone else got out. This was the late 1960s, and white vacationers had no intention of swimming with Black kids. But the reason I don't remember is that our parents shielded us from this memory, distracting us so that two kids could just be kids for a little while longer.

When we went home, it was to a middle-class neighborhood that was predominantly Black, and people who looked like us could buy homes. After a white high school classmate got in my face for dating his ex-girlfriend, it didn't occur to me that he might have been angry because I'm Black and the girl was white. My parents had insulated me from that possibility, too. When our school's football team played a majority white school, I noticed, of course. Our coach made sure we did by pointing out that, win or lose, the boys on the *other* sideline would spend Saturday afternoon at their country clubs, taking breaks from swimming with their extra-thick milkshakes. We wanted to tear them apart, and we did.

To me, though, this wasn't racial disparity so much as a difference in socioeconomic class. My parents just didn't talk about race. They preferred to look ahead, not behind them, so when another classmate called me the "N-word" to my face, it wasn't fear that I felt. It was confusion, and even then, I was intelligent and confident enough to realize that it said more about him than me. When he called me that a second time? Let's just say we're both lucky I didn't crack his skull on the floor.

Other than the story about the bus in North Carolina, my dad just omitted details of his own experiences. If he and my mother were spit on, cursed at, or threatened, I never heard about it. If someone in our family tree was lynched, it's not part of the stories. I told myself that they're just not the types of people who dwell on anything bad, and as a result, my sister and I grew up aware of racism but rarely experiencing it. Racial violence and discrimination were things I read about in textbooks, not things I felt deep in my soul.

It was enough to get you fired up before a high school football game or make you stare at the sidewalk during your walk home. But that visceral fear? A white-hot anger? The idea of self-doubt or the little voice inside that suggests that, no matter your accomplishments, you don't belong or might be inferior? It's just not something I grew up feeling.

I figure that's precisely what my parents intended.

■ ■ ■

IT WAS IN high school that I noticed the first stages of my transformation. Not long before graduation, I learned that I hadn't been named to the National Honor Society. The reason? It was neither grades nor extracurriculars.

"Moral fitness," my faculty adviser said.

As it turned out, the kid whose ex I dated wasn't the only one who disliked my occasional socializing with white girls. *Whatever*. I shook it off. That's the story I told myself, at least. The reality was that I buried it, covering it not with dirt but the other key layers of my identity. I was a star athlete, a future preacher, a favorite son of my neighborhood in Prince George's County, Maryland, who carried a valise and wore emotional armor.

I got accepted to Cedarville University, a private Baptist school in western Ohio. Emotional suppression worked, I convinced myself, because the student body elected me the first Black freshman class president in the school's history. I couldn't wait for that faculty adviser at Riverdale to find out, feel ashamed, tell everyone at the school and in P.G. County how wrong he'd been.

This made me feel comfortable in Cedarville, enough that I asked out another white girl. Not long after, during a pickup football game, I planted my foot in the ground to juke a defender out of his socks. Instead, I felt an explosion in my knee, the shredding of everything connecting my kneecap to the rest of my leg. Anterior cruciate ligament, medial collateral, meniscus—all of them torn, and there, too, went that protective layer of my identity as a football player. Friends helped me to my dorm in time for my phone to ring. My girlfriend was calling to let me know she couldn't go with me to the homecoming banquet. She'd told her parents about dating a Black guy, and they flipped out and threatened to pull her out of school.

She hung up, my knee swelled, and I chased away any feelings of sadness with anger and blame. I had knee surgery and went to class in a wheelchair, and if embarrassment or vulnerability gurgled inside me, I quickly dispatched resentment and defiance to silence them.

"To hell with this place," I told myself. "And these people."

Whoever De Smith had been as a child—earnest, naïve, sensitive—couldn't cut it here. So I adopted a different persona, and this person was incapable of feeling fear, self-doubt, or intimidation. And he convinced me to stand up to anybody who wanted me gone. To make *them* feel what I didn't. So after I had initially retreated to the comforts of Maryland and family, it wasn't De who drove back to Ohio. It was this other person, and he was courageous, indignant, fearless.

There's a big rock on the Cedarville University campus, and among the school's traditions is that students paint birthday greetings or messages on it. During my senior year, I ran for student government president and painted "Vote De" on the rock. The next morning, I was walking to class when I noticed that someone had painted the N-word on it, just next to my name. Unbothered and unfeeling, I took a spray can and, in front of other students, painted over it before continuing on my way.

It worked. Again and again.

By then I was thinking of applying to law school, and in one of my prelaw classes, a political science professor assigned essays that encouraged students to take contrarian ideological stances. He assigned me Thurgood Marshall, the first Black man appointed to the United States Supreme Court. My mandate? Argue that Marshall had been unqualified and that President Lyndon B. Johnson knew Marshall lacked the educational pedigree of Oliver Wendell Holmes, Jr., and Earl Warren but had nonetheless appointed him because of his skin color.

De Smith may have felt too overwhelmed to voice his disagreement, but because this other person took the wheel, I'll never know.

"*Unqualified?*" I boomed in front of the class. "You mean the guy who argued thirty-two cases before the Supreme Court and won twenty-nine?"

The professor, an older white man, clearly disliked that I challenged him—especially in front of other students. I suppose I was meant to shut up and do as I had been told, but this felt unnatural to this changing *me*. A while later, I approached this same professor when I was applying to law schools and asked if he would write a letter of recommendation on my behalf. He refused, saying he was uncomfortable vouching for me.

Looking back, the most infuriating thing isn't that he declined. It is that the conversation was neither uncivil nor angry. He felt perfectly comfortable looking me in the eye and calmly saying that I wasn't the type of student for whom he wrote recommendations. He was right. I was wrong. There was no possible recourse, and it wouldn't be until much later that I realized the widespread nature of this subtle, glancing racism. All I had done was disagree with him, and this warranted punishment.

I don't regret standing my ground. In fact, this galvanized my thought process like nothing else had. If someone underestimates, takes advantage, or tries to humiliate you, you have to make a choice. Back down and accept it. Or engage and stand your ground in what I consider an intellectually aggressive manner.

If you look like me, there's no right answer. Submission lets them win. Fighting back provides them the validation that I'm just another angry Black man. Regardless, it was in Cedarville that I made my choice. People may not like it, but I was never comfortable just *allowing* things to sit unchallenged, especially when we both knew something was objectively true. If I'm wrong, I'll admit it. And if you're wrong, you're free to react as you desire, even if that ends by one of us storming off.

But to just refuse to discuss something? Or admit that someone's idea may lead to a resolution that may be in both of our interests? It just doesn't make sense to me.

Sure, this leads to discomfort and has the potential to get someone socially ostracized. It certainly did with me. The path nonetheless delivered me to the law school at the University of Virginia, the same campus we used to pass on our way to Homecoming.

Just a few months after I enrolled, I would meet someone who'd change my life in ways I couldn't yet imagine.

■  ■  ■

UVA WAS THE first place I had ever been that actually encouraged critical thought and radical discussion. It was crazy. Students could say the damnedest things, defy the instructors to their faces, and . . . nobody got mad.

What a concept!

Becoming a successful lawyer involves more than just good grades and learning the law. It's about gaining experience, making contacts, accumulating a diversity of thoughts, voices, and perspectives as you search for your own. Late in my first year, I lined up a job for the summer of 1987 with a successful firm in Northern Virginia, just across the Potomac River from Washington, D.C. Then, a few weeks before my start date, someone from the firm called and pulled the rug out from under me.

The guy who'd held the job previously couldn't pass the bar exam, so rather than let him drift, they gave him the job I was supposed to fill. I get it. They knew and felt loyal to him. They apologized, but suddenly I had no summer job, and it was too late in the school year to secure a different one. I was already in the later stages of the mock trial contest, a kind of competition that allows law students to practice arguments and presentation styles in a hypothetical case and in front of an actual audience. After winning a later round, one of the competition judges, Gail Starling Marshall, happened to be deputy attorney general in the Commonwealth of Virginia.

"Great job," she told me. Then she offered me a position in Richmond at the Attorney General's Office. I couldn't believe it, and I was too gobsmacked to say anything and too chicken to admit that I had no summer job.

The next day, I called Gail and told her I'd love to spend my summer in their office. The opportunity was amazing, but since it was a publicly funded job, the pay stunk. I nonetheless found a three-hundred-dollar-a-month apartment in Richmond, tried to ignore the rats and roaches—which scattered every time I flipped on the lights—and kept everything I owned in the safest place I could think of: the refrigerator.

I focused on the job, and on my first day, I checked in at a table and received a folder of materials that welcomed me to the Office of the Attorney General. The young woman who handed me the folder was a UVA business school student named Karen Padgett, and while I can't remember what I possibly said to her, she thought it was funny enough to flash a smile.

We kept talking, and I learned that this woman was utterly honest and somehow immune to what anyone else thought. Of course she was pretty, with soft features and chestnut hair, but what drew me to her was that unwillingness to place value on anything but whether you are a good person. Oh, and she liked to dance.

We were friends a full year before we started dating, and nobody at UVA gave a good, hearty damn that a Black guy was dating a white girl. Yes, I braced Karen for the potential of audible gasps she was about to encounter when I brought her to the homestead for the first time. But it would have nothing to do with her skin color. If anyone was shocked, and they were, it was because such an intelligent, lovely woman had somehow fallen in love with . . . *me*.

Or that someone whose ambition compelled my cousins to occasionally see me as a single-minded snob even had it in him to get married. Regardless, we arrived and she sat next to me during Papa's sermon, and my aunts and cousins were almost overwhelmingly effusive. My parents were thrilled.

The weirdest thing about the whole thing? It's that, for maybe the first time in my life, nobody thought it was weird.

■ ■ ■

I WOULDN'T CALL myself a romantic, exactly, but I took my first job out of law school with idealism in mind. The D.C. firm of Schwalb, Donnenfeld, Bray & Silbert was a small organization with a specialty of defending clients accused of white-collar crimes, but it wasn't the mission that drew me there. It was the idea of working alongside Earl Silbert, a former U.S. Attorney who'd been the lead prosecutor in the trials of those behind the Watergate break-in.

To me, this was the dream: to try the biggest cases, get the impossible guilty verdicts, put away the biggest and baddest people trying to skirt the rules and corrupt our society.

So, in 1991, when I was offered the chance to join the U.S. Attorney's Office to prosecute homicides and other violent crimes, I jumped at it. I'm sure deep down I felt imposter syndrome or self-doubt, but after years of shouting down those thoughts with bluster and hard work, I didn't walk into the office each day so much as I swaggered.

There was nobody in this city more dangerous than me, because I knew the law better than anyone who dared break it. There was no witness I couldn't turn, no plea deal I couldn't sell, no jury I couldn't get on my side. It wasn't De Smith who walked into the courtroom. It was this alternate side, and by now he had a name. His reputation was cold-blooded, untouchable, maybe even superhuman.

His powers, fueled by self-denial, came from outthinking everyone. Victory depended on anticipating surprises, no matter how unlikely, and having a plan in place for any possibility. While my opponents slept and my colleagues spent time with their families, I was at the office or up late, running scenarios. Victory at trial, therefore, was almost anticlimactic because I *expected* to win. I had done everything humanly possible to guarantee it.

Karen and I married in 1991, right as I became a prosecutor, and it amazed me how quickly she could fall asleep. Me? I tossed and turned, my brain identifying knots and thinking of ways to untangle them. If a witness says *this,* then I'll say *that.* If the defense attorney presents *this* piece of evidence, my response would be *that.* People asked if I wrote down questions before cross-examining a witness.

Never.

Because in my head, I had gone through every possible answer to

every possible question, devising airtight wording and the most diabolical follow-up. By the time a trial began, I had gamed these scenarios out dozens of times.

If preparing was my superpower, Armani was my costume. Public
service is fulfilling, but it doesn't pay much. I made about $60,000 a
year in the early 1990s, so it may have been off-the-rack Armani, but
nobody else knew that my suits weren't custom. My clothes came
from Raleigh Haberdasher, Garfinkel's, Britches—the finest high-end
men's stores in D.C. I turned up the volume further with big pocket
squares, trousers an inch and a half off the shoe, wing tips so clean
you could see your reflection.

Even now, I believe there are three things every American man is
entitled to by birth: shined shoes, pressed shirts, a reliable barber. It's
about pride, and, yeah, my unit's job was to put away murderers, but
the lawyers who do it? The people driven by tireless, no-nonsense
righteousness? We called those people *killers*. And if you want to be a
*killer,* you have to look like one when you cross the street. Because
people are watching. Lawyers who hope you lose, because that makes
them feel better, and judges who think you're cocky.

On the morning a trial began, my walk from the U.S. Attorney's
Office to the Superior Court of the District of Columbia, 500 Indiana
Avenue, was a procession. Riding on my shoulders were the hopes for
justice for the grieving loved ones of a murder victim, pressure from
my superiors, and my own high expectations. But that was nothing.
To me, this walk to the courtroom represented the final steps of a
family's dream—the denouement of a story that spanned two centuries.

It started when my ancestors stepped off the slave ship, continued
when Grandmother Mary nursed the wound on her forehead, turned
a corner when Moses was granted freedom from the Fitzgerald plantation.

Upon arriving at the courthouse, I disappeared into the anteroom,
the small holding area for lawyers before the doors open. I pictured
John Fitzgerald and Papa and my dad as I tucked my necktie into my
shirt and dropped to the floor. To complete my transformation, the

one set in motion and made possible by my family's enslavers and my family's survivors and my family's sacrifices, I clicked off about fifteen push-ups to get my heart racing.

This is when De Smith disappeared. Nobody on the other side of this door had come to see him, after all. The prosecutor was the star of the show, the Virginia preacher's grandson about to deliver his opening statement, and buckle up because the doors just opened.

In I marched, making eye contact with every member of the jury, opposing counsel, even the defendant. Then, the adrenaline still swirling and the story's climax arriving, the judge called on me to address the jury.

My statements always started the same way, because in my family, we're storytellers. In just fourteen words, I told one that almost defied belief.

"My name is DeMaurice *Fitzgerald* Smith," I said, "and I represent the United States of America."

■   ■   ■

ONE SPRING NOT long ago, I made my annual drive to Pittsylvania County. My BMW convertible charged down Route 29, first laid out in 1926 and completed in 1931, crossing rivers and railroads and passing tiny green signs for historic "named places."

Sites of pre–Civil War skirmishes and gathering places, churches and fields. Just west of Charlottesville is the land where Thomas Jefferson's six hundred enslaved humans toiled. A bit farther south is the community of Shockoe, where a stone wall and a row of boxwoods surround the Fitzgerald family cemetery. There's a headstone carved with "honest man and sincere Christian," a description of the white man who may have forced his way into my bloodline.

I drove past Chatham, where my father had defied his own by begging the Marine Corps to take him, then to Keeling, where the foundation of my grandfather's tobacco shed still stands. It's odd to stand and listen to the same sounds my ancestors would have heard, the insects and birds, and run my fingers along the long grass. The same sun that warmed their faces does the same to me, and when the same kinds of clouds cool the air, I walk down a trail in search of mementos of a bygone age.

My dad's older brother Willard, now ninety-eight years old, meets me there with his son. I can't help noticing how uneasy they are, the discomfort that remains from just my standing on someone else's land, and my cousin encourages me to hurry up, take my photos, and leave. When I tarry, they announce that they'll meet me back at the homestead. Their fear is something I logically know about, but it's not something I have often felt.

Finally we reconvene at the church. I'm not De Smith here, either. Nobody sees me as DeMaurice Fitzgerald Smith. I'm just Reverend Smith's grandson, Smitty's boy, the one who dresses and speaks a little differently and unabashedly confronts the exact kind of person our people have been conditioned over centuries to fear.

Not long after the 2011 lockout, I noticed a change to the Homecoming ritual. When we bowed our heads to pray, Uncle Willard made me the subject. I never asked, but I assume they read about some of the things I had said in the media about Roger, about Robert Kraft, about Jerry Jones. Maybe they were proud of me. But to cross these powerful people? To be anything but deferential to rich white men?

Standing up to those who run the plantation can get a person killed. My people in Pittsylvania County can still feel this power, and a few of them were terrified for me. Afraid because I wasn't.

"For freedom Christ has set us free," Willard said. "Stand firm therefore, and do not submit again to a yoke of slavery."

He was reciting from Galatians' fifth chapter. Then he asked God to provide me courage and strength; to protect me from the wrath of the powerful. My cousins nodded their heads. Someone usually rested a hand on my shoulder.

"Let us not become conceited or provoke," my uncle continued. "For if you bite and devour one another, watch out that you be not consumed."

CHAPTER

5

# TRIAL DOG

On the afternoon of September 9, 2014, I was on a blissfully quiet flight to the West Coast. As the plane descended into Southern California, the brown Mojave Desert gave way to mountainous greenery surrounding Big Bear Lake and the white and silver rooftops of the easternmost suburbs of Los Angeles.

When we touched down at LAX, I reached into the seatback pocket in front of me to retrieve my phone. Then I did something horrendously stupid. After nearly six hours of glorious silence, I turned the damn thing on.

Within seconds, the peaceful Zen made way for a hailstorm of text messages and voicemails. Reporters. Lawyers. George Atallah, the NFLPA's communications expert. Everyone seemed to be referring to the same person: Ray Rice, the Baltimore Ravens' star running back. I called George first and asked him to fill me in.

"It's bad," he said.

I pulled up TMZ, which George said had published a grisly video of Rice striking his fiancée in the face. Then I did a second horrendously stupid thing: I hit play.

For months, our office had been consumed by this incident and its potential for wider ramifications. Rice and Janay Palmer had spent Valentine's Day together at the Revel Casino in Atlantic City, New Jersey, before getting into a disagreement. We knew all this. So did the Ravens and the league office. An Atlantic City police report confirmed that at around 2:51 A.M. on February 15, Rice and Palmer had hit each other, refused medical attention, and been charged with simple assault before being released.

An earlier TMZ video confirmed this. Surveillance footage from a casino hallway showed Rice carrying Palmer, who appeared to be unconscious, from inside an elevator. Then she tumbled to the floor. It was hard to watch and obviously troubling, but it was consistent with what Rice and his attorney had told the Ravens and us. And as much as I would love to report that Roger Goodell acted swiftly and decisively to discipline Rice, that would be untrue.

He did nothing.

And all while the NFL was facing an intensifying crisis, both publicly and internally, involving players and domestic abuse. Paul Tagliabue, Roger's predecessor as NFL commissioner, had a mandate to grow the game's popularity and increase revenues—even if that meant covering up player arrests. Particularly heinous crimes reached the public anyway, from Minnesota quarterback Warren Moon's 1996 trial and acquittal for spousal abuse to Dallas wide receiver Michael Irvin's arrest that same year for felony cocaine possession.

The league's robust NFL Security Department assigned liaisons to each franchise, and this person's primary objective was to deal with arrests, accusations, and other unsavory incidents before the courts and media got involved. Some organizations, such as the Cowboys, hired independent contractors to be fixers and keep these matters out of the headlines.

But Roger's job was different. Owners wanted him to clean up the league's image, a desire driven in large part by a more family-friendly product that'd be more appealing to sponsors and broadcast networks. Almost immediately, Roger painted himself as the league's strongman and chief disciplinarian, introducing a wide-ranging player conduct policy that promised discipline for any number of actions that were considered detrimental to the NFL.

It sounded good, but it was deliberately vague so that the league's handpicked discipline czar could determine which actions fit which punishments. Roger, of course, was that czar—judge, jury, and executioner. Arrests the next year went up 61 percent, and the league office trumpeted its commissioner as the moral savior of a corporation going increasingly rogue. The personal conduct policy was so overwhelmingly popular that there were whispers of Roger someday running for president. In 2012, *Time* magazine featured the NFL's stone-faced leader on its cover with THE ENFORCER as the headline.

But because Roger works for the owners, he still made problems go away—for some of his bosses more than others, of course. Ravens owner Steve Bisciotti and Roger were golf buddies, so perhaps it shouldn't have been a surprise that one of Baltimore's most valuable offensive players was being allowed to skate.

A month after the incident and the release of the first video, Rice's charges were raised to aggravated assault. This changed nothing internally, and Ravens executives pointed to Rice's reputation as an antibullying advocate in Baltimore. He had met with team leaders to explain what happened that night at the casino, and coach John Harbaugh told reporters that Rice was a "heck of a guy." In May 2014, Rice and Palmer, who had recently married, appeared at a news conference at Ravens headquarters. Rice apologized to everyone but his wife, and Palmer went so far as to say that she regretted her role in the incident. The team promoted Palmer's tearful contrition on its social media channels.

That July, with a new season about to start, Roger summoned Rice to New York. The personal conduct policy grants the commissioner authority to demand that any player stop whatever he was doing and come to NFL headquarters for a one-on-one meeting. I wasn't in their meeting, so I can only assume that Rice again told his version of events to Roger, who had to do . . . *something*.

So, at long last, down came his ruling: a two-game suspension without pay.

The public crushed Roger. Women's groups and support groups vilified him. Because if a drug test showed weed or Adderall in your system, that got you suspended *four* games.

Facing this public scrutiny, and with owners surely breathing down their commissioner's neck, Roger held a news conference in which he defended his suspension. He claimed Rice "really understands the mistake he made." He wrote a letter to owners to announce harsher penalties for any league employee accused of domestic abuse. A first offense would result in a six-game suspension. A repeat offense came with a season-long ban.

"I didn't get it right," the commissioner wrote. "Simply put, we have to do better."

At least it was over.

In late August 2014, Roger called Rice to assure him that the policy's new six-game suspension wouldn't apply to him. The NFL's discipline czar had spoken, and now everyone could move on.

Then, a little over a week later, TMZ published the second video. I watched it from inside the terminal at LAX, and this new perspective is from inside the hotel elevator. Rice and Palmer are arguing before both of their arms start flailing. Then Rice's fist connects with his fiancée's jaw, instantly knocking her out cold. Then the elevator doors open, and we see Rice from behind carrying Palmer into the hallway.

The footage made me feel sick. It still does.

Because I didn't see Janay Palmer in that elevator. I pictured my own daughter, Elizabeth, getting slugged like that. My protective instincts made me want to destroy this person. And I don't mean that I wanted to fight Rice. My brain went into prosecutor mode, a kind of defense mechanism for the searing anger I felt. I started imagining a trial, me on one side, Rice on the other. There's only one way to try a case like that, and it begins with the opening statement. One popped into my mind instantaneously.

Ladies and gentlemen, Ray Rice is entitled to a fair trial. And I want you to give him that. I also want you as the jury to talk about fairness, and the "fairness" that was happening in that elevator. He's 225 pounds of honed steel. This man's job is to confront 350-pound defensive linemen at the line of scrimmage.

It's not to *meet* them there. His job is to get through them, beyond the line of scrimmage—not to give in, not to give up, not to get tackled. His job is to break the line of scrimmage. Because these collisions are a battle of wills between a group of people who, on the other side, are trained to stop him.

What happened in that elevator? Mr. Rice made a decision to turn his power against a woman who weighs 120 pounds.

Yes, I want you to give him a fair trial. In fact, I want you to give him more fairness than he gave to his fiancée.

I would expect a jury to deliver a guilty verdict in less than an hour. They'd go into the deliberation room, decide to skip lunch, and tally the votes. This fantasy was the only thing that made me feel better.

Then my phone rang again. Someone was letting me know that the Ravens were releasing Rice, and Roger announced that Rice was now suspended indefinitely. This snapped me out of my prosecutorial daydream. Ray Rice's employer was trying to take away his paycheck. His corporate office was punishing him a second time for the same thing, saying it may even prevent him from working again. There are no *indefinite* sentences in criminal law, because that's constitutionally invalid. If you hit your wife, you don't automatically lose your job.

Sitting amid the din of one of the busiest airports in the world, suddenly thrust into the center of a major controversy, I came to a confounding realization. No, I wouldn't be the one prosecuting Rice for a heinous crime we all know he committed. I would be the asshole on the other side.

Because my job, whether I liked it or not, was to defend him.

■　■　■

IN 1919, IN what has since been remembered as the Black Sox scandal, eight Chicago White Sox players were accused of accepting bribes to deliberately lose the World Series. Remember *Field of Dreams* and "Shoeless" Joe Jackson? Yep, those guys.

In the immediate aftermath, team owners approached a district court judge named Kenesaw Mountain Landis about a job that didn't yet exist. They wanted to install a single, all-powerful commissioner of Major League Baseball. The president of the National League said at the time that the most important qualification was to "rule with an iron hand."

Landis took the job and was granted broad, single-handed authority to govern the game as he saw fit. Owners therefore wrote into their league's constitution that the commissioner had the unilateral power to act "in the best interests of baseball." Though the players involved in the Black Sox matter were tried and acquitted of conspiracy to defraud, Landis nonetheless banned the players for life. That's why, in *Field of Dreams*, the spirit of "Shoeless Joe" needed a baseball diamond cut into an Iowa cornfield, because that was his only place to play and his only path to closure.

In real life, MLB's clause changed sports forever, and this got baked into the job description of the commissioner of every major sport. Even more than a century later, National Basketball Association commissioner Adam Silver's primary responsibility is "protecting the integrity of the game." The National Hockey League's commissioner, Gary Bettman, gets "full and complete power" to punish any league employee.

In 1963, the fledgling NFL faced its own crisis. Star players were found to have bet on games, and some had suspected ties to the Mafia. The league's commissioner, Pete Rozelle, had similarly sweeping power, having been granted "full, complete, and final jurisdiction and authority" to protect the league's image. Rozelle issued suspensions and fines to players implicated in the gambling scandal, but this wasn't enough.

He hired a man named Jack Danahy to form "NFL Security," a group that would act as the league's internal police force. The 1960s were perhaps the peak of American fascination with the Federal Bureau of Investigation, the protagonists in television shows and films, crusaders of justice and tireless pursuers of gangsters, Communists, and the corrupt. J. Edgar Hoover, the bureau's longtime director, was an A-list celebrity, and he strutted about in tailored suits and his signature fedora.

Hoover's right-hand man at the FBI? Jack Danahy, of course, and his new job at the NFL wasn't to keep players out of trouble. It was to keep the *league* out of trouble. Danahy's secret force spied on players, lied to them, questioned them without a lawyer present. Eventually NFL Security had someone stationed at every team headquarters, and players were instructed to alert the team if a problem arose. Get pulled over after a night out? Get caught with a dime bag? Punch your girlfriend? Call this number and some shadowy, league-employed figure would take care of it so nobody would ever hear a thing. Players just wanted to stay off the league's bad side, so they didn't question any of this.

By February 2014, when Ray Rice and Janay Palmer went to Atlantic City, NFL Security was a nationwide operation. Every team has a network of fixers, law enforcement officials, and lawyers—each with sources inside police stations, courthouses, and nightclubs. As the league's revenue and profile grew, the objective remained: Protect the league at all costs.

Get to a crime scene first. Be invisible. Make it go away.

There's nothing in the NFL's constitution about this. It's mostly coordinated and executed behind the scenes, just as owners want it. Most times an owner hires his own specialist and allows them the freedom and discretion to police the team as they see fit. Thirty-two franchises, the same number of jurisdictions and local laws.

But no matter the city, there is one thing these individuals tend to have in common. At one time or another, most worked for the FBI.

■   ■   ■

EARLY ON THE morning of February 15, 2014, the Baltimore Ravens' director of security was already hard at work. Rice did as he'd been encouraged and reported to the team that he'd been arrested. According to the NFL's report later, a man named Darren Sanders was on the phone with an Atlantic City police officer.

Sanders learned of the horrific contents of the Revel Casino security videos, including the one taken inside the elevator, from New Jersey State Police. I was later told that Sanders drove to the Jersey Shore and that it was highly likely that he had possession of at least one of the videos. Sometime later, Rice met with his coach and other key organizational figures, and those in the room relayed to me that Rice was completely forthcoming and contrite. He admitted to punching his fiancée and knocking her out. His explanation was consistent with the Revel Casino security footage.

Everyone went about their business while the commissioner decided on a discipline.

Even before I joined the NFLPA, Roger tended to come down harder on some offenses compared to others. Drunk driving? A hit-and-run? He'd drop the hammer. But there was a strange blind spot in cases of domestic assault. In 2009, an Oakland Raiders offensive lineman beat his kids' mother with a mop handle and slammed her into a wall. Roger issued no discipline. Two months later, an Atlanta Falcons player threw his wife down the staircase. Roger suspended him one game. In 2010, a Miami Dolphins defensive lineman beat up his pregnant girlfriend, and the NFL's "sheriff" did nothing.

It kept getting worse, but Roger wasn't adjusting.

In 2011, a Green Bay Packers player assaulted his girlfriend and opened a gash that required four stitches. Another one-game suspension. Then, in late 2012, the Kansas City Chiefs' Jovan Belcher shot his girlfriend dead before driving to the team facility and, in front of his coach and the Chiefs' general manager, killing himself in the parking lot.

For all of Roger's hardline stances, he mostly just let it go when it came to intimate partner violence. After all, the league's internal security network usually took care of this stuff. Prosecutors dropped charges, witnesses recanted statements, victims took the blame. Roger's personal conduct policy was just a morals clause that scared nobody straight, and, purposeful or not, this sent a message throughout the league that players could beat up their wives and girlfriends and get away with it.

Guys like Sanders are exceptionally good. Bisciotti, the Ravens' owner, rarely went anywhere without Sanders as his personal bodyguard. Trim and Black, with a close-cropped beard and shaved head, Sanders had a gift for blending in. Players loved him.

If Sanders could get an Atlantic City police officer on the phone just hours after Rice assaulted Palmer, getting a copy of the security video would have been no more difficult. In fact, we kept hearing from our sources inside the Ravens facility that that's exactly what happened. And that the team sent a copy of the video to Jeffrey Miller, the NFL's chief security officer.

One problem: In 2014, there were two Jeffrey Millers working for the league office. Security Jeff Miller was the former commissioner of the Pennsylvania State Police and a member of the federal government's homeland security council. The *other* Jeff Miller was an executive in charge of communications and the league's lobbying apparatus. In late September 2014, the Associated Press published a report that a law enforcement official had anonymously mailed the video to Jeff Miller at the league.

"I hoped it would land in the right hands," this unidentified official told the AP. Alongside the video was a note: "You have to see it. It's terrible."

Was this package sent to the wrong Jeff Miller? Was Sanders, the Ravens' security expert who died of cancer in 2021, the person who sent it or was it someone at the Revel? We can never know for sure, but because the league's job is less about the pursuit of truth and fairness than about secrecy and a rabid protection of its own interests, my guess is that Roger was so confident in NFL Security's ability to keep things out of public view that he did what he normally did: nothing.

The Ravens were supposedly handling it, the courts eventually agreed to drop the aggravated assault charge, and without the two TMZ videos, I suspect Ray Rice would have never been punished at all.

But the second video sparked such a firestorm that Roger, with his reputation of going soft on domestic violence, went overboard. It was too late. Just four days after the Rice video was published, Minnesota Vikings running back Adrian Peterson was indicted in Texas for felony child abuse. Also in 2014, a North Carolina court delivered a guilty verdict on Carolina Panthers defensive end Greg Hardy after he was charged with repeatedly assaulting a woman during a domestic dispute.

Anheuser-Busch, Pepsi, and the Campbell's soup company publicly admonished the league's handling of domestic abuse. President Barack Obama even weighed in, releasing a statement that insisted that "hitting a woman is not something a real man does."

With nowhere to turn and this becoming a four-alarm shit show for the league, Roger agreed to an interview on CBS with Norah O'Donnell. She asked him, point-blank, if he had viewed the security footage before TMZ posted it. Roger flatly said no. Nor had anyone else in the league.

"*No one* in the NFL?" O'Donnell asked.

"No one in the NFL, to, is—to my knowledge," he stammered. "Multiple occasions we asked for it, and multiple occasions we were told no."

O'Donnell rightly pressed him on this. The NFL, which at the time was a $10 billion-a-year corporation with its tendrils in every city hall in America, was just told no? By an Atlantic City casino? And the league just . . . gave up?

According to *The New Yorker*, TMZ paid more than $100,000 for the two videos. Roger, visibly cornered, tried talking through it. He insisted that current and former attorneys general could face "legal implications" from even viewing the video.

The more Roger said, the worse it got. It just wasn't credible, and we heard that the Ravens had viewed and likely possessed the security footage. The Ravens *are* the NFL. The NFL *is* the Ravens.

"Well, that's a fact," Roger told O'Donnell, "and I think it's a fact because the criminal justice system and law enforcement were following the laws. And doing what they needed to do to make sure—that

they follow the criminal activity. This is an ongoing criminal investigation, and I think they were doing what they do."

At that year's NFL draft, fans in New York booed Roger so
loudly, so mercilessly, that I almost felt bad for him. Almost.

"Freeze your face," George Atallah instructed, instead thinking
that TV cameras would catch me delighting in Roger's misery.

I was keenly aware by then, and would be reminded time and
again that summer, that Roger was concerned less about reassuring
the public of the league's steadfastness than appeasing his bosses.
Rice's case had been resolved at the judicial level, and Rice's criminal
defense attorney had a copy of the tape. It wasn't credible that the
league, which fights literally everything, just tried and failed to get it.

I could think of only one possible explanation. Maybe Roger
thought he could bury the Rice incident, let NFL Security do its thing,
and nobody would find out. For decades, this strategy had protected
the league's image. To me, this is the only scenario in which it is credible that Roger and his league office colleagues never saw the video.
It's because they never wanted to.

■  ■  ■

WHEN YOU BRING new life into the world, you remember everything
about it in vivid detail. For Karen and me, it was September 1995. I
was one of a small team of homicide prosecutors in a city with four
hundred murders a year, some of whom were the witnesses who could
help us close another case. Our group was cocky as hell, mostly young
and obsessive adrenaline junkies who worked hard and played harder,
usually at one of D.C.'s late-night taverns.

We adopted the nickname Trial Dogs and, in a paradigm that's filled
with fear, we became addicted to the idea of feeling like apex predators:
unrestrained, unburdened by emotion, invincible in the courtroom.

Then here came Elizabeth, our baby daughter, charging into the
world with the umbilical cord wrapped around her throat. I was terrified. After years of suppressing my feelings and being rewarded for

it, a wave of fear and powerlessness washed over me that felt almost paralyzing.

But then the doctor calmly uncoiled it and, let me tell you, there is no sweeter music than the relief of hearing your baby cry. Just like that, I had a *family*. A baby girl. The nurse handed Elizabeth to me, and I couldn't believe how light she was, like a helium balloon that could float away. Not if I held on tight, and I told myself in that instant that I would defend this little thing to the death, even if it meant trading my life for hers. I wanted to protect her until my final breath.

When I returned to work a few weeks later, our team at the U.S. Attorney's Office had a new colleague. Nobody knew much about him, other than that he was an ex-Marine who'd served in Vietnam before working in the administration of President Ronald Reagan.

His name was Robert Mueller, and he had just up and quit his partnership at a major firm in Boston. We were all skeptical of someone in that stage of his career becoming successful in the rough-and-tumble world of Superior Court. As it works, he also took the cases that nobody else wanted, many of them cold as ice.

Then a strange thing happened: Mueller started getting convictions. He was so thorough, so meticulous that he built watertight cases and made zero mistakes. His presentation wasn't entertaining. He just layered fact on top of fact, building airtight arguments.

Maybe it was the last of that aura of vulnerability after becoming a new dad, but one day I decided to get a look at this guy. I looked through his office door to see his eyes locked on the contents of another case file, so focused that he hadn't even removed his suit jacket. Square jaw, dark hair parted to the side, just painstakingly examining page after page in a bare office, a new level of obsession as he tirelessly searched for the weak point of the case.

■ ■ ■

ROGER'S SECOND PUNISHMENT of Rice was arbitrary. Strike one. It was also based on a series of misrepresentations and downright lies, designed to do nothing more than pacify the outcry and appease the owners. Strike two.

The league claimed the second TMZ video represented new evidence, and Roger insisted during the CBS interview that Rice had been "ambiguous" in his meeting at the league office and had deliberately misled the Ravens. Problem was, Ozzie Newsome, the Ravens' general manager, undercut this argument by telling *The Baltimore Sun* that "Ray didn't lie to me."

"What we saw on the video," the *Sun* quoted Newsome as saying, "was what Ray said."

Bisciotti, the team's owner, was *so* horrified by what he'd seen that he texted Rice after the second video to let him know that the organization still had his back. ESPN, which pays the NFL $2.7 billion a year to broadcast games and stay on the league's good side, actually published these texts in an investigative report examining the Rice situation.

> Hey Ray, just want to let you know, we loved you as a player, it was great having you here. Hopefully all these things are going to die down. I wish the best for you and Janay.

> When you're done with football, I'd like you to know you have a job waiting for you with the Ravens helping young guys getting acclimated to the league.

That second text was interesting to me. Was Bisciotti offering a quid pro quo if Rice kept his mouth shut? A carrot if Rice did right by the Ravens by forfeiting what remained on a $35 million contract he'd signed two years earlier? The team had released him, which it was entitled to do, but the public nature of the controversy made it nearly impossible for another team to sign him in 2014 or beyond. Roger's *indefinite* suspension guaranteed that Rice wouldn't be paid a prorated percentage of the $3.5 million that he was set to earn that season.

As sickened as I had been by what I saw Rice do to his fiancée, imagining my now-nineteen-year-old baby girl in a similar elevator in a similar situation, Roger's punishment violated the collective bargaining agreement, or what we call the *law of the case*. As he had done with Bountygate, the commissioner had again overstepped his authority. As written, Rice's contract granted him the right to work and receive some portion of his earnings.

There were also any number of precedents, and this wound up being strike three.

Seven years earlier, the Atlanta Falcons had tried forcing Michael Vick to repay nearly $20 million that he'd already been paid. Vick, the team's superstar quarterback, had pleaded guilty to overseeing and financing a massive dogfighting ring. It was despicable. Vick's property in rural Virginia had been the headquarters of an illegal gambling operation in which pit bulls were trained to fight before high-stakes showdowns, many of which ended in death. If the losing dog survived its injuries, it was later drowned, electrocuted, hanged, or shot anyway. When federal authorities raided the fifteen-acre property in April 2007, they discovered the remains of dozens of dogs, others neglected and tied to car axles, and a "rape stand" for forced mating. The cruelty was breathtaking.

Vick may have deserved every minute of the twenty-one-month prison sentence he'd served, a permanently stained reputation, and for the Falcons to cut him. The team was within its rights to withhold any remaining money due to Vick. But asking him to reimburse the organization for bonus money he'd already been paid? That's not how it works. The NFLPA fought on Vick's behalf, arguing that the guaranteed money that came in the form of those bonuses was, after all, guaranteed. The Falcons hadn't written a morality clause into Vick's contract, and there was absolutely nothing that stated the organization's right to recoup money if he got caught fighting dogs, convicted of a felony, or even sent to federal prison.

Vick kept his money. So did Aaron Hernandez, the New England Patriots tight end who was arrested and charged with first-degree murder in the death of an associate. Hernandez fit the clinical definition of a sociopath and may have been involved in numerous other crimes. But the Patriots, who not only have their own security experts onsite but also have access to the full might of NFL Security, signed Hernandez to a contract that guaranteed him $6 million. There was no language that voided the contract's terms in the event of his arrest, felony charge, or conviction.

The Patriots might not have liked it. Nobody has to like it. But they signed him to that deal, so they had to pay out what it said. Or we would fight. And we would sue the league so hard, make it so messy, keep it in front of the public for so long that they'd stop worrying about the money and just pay it to make us go away.

How can I sleep at night fighting for guys like that? Well, I don't sleep. I toss and turn, though not because of any ethical dilemma. But I justify it the way most lawyers do: Hernandez wasn't about Hernandez, Vick was not about Vick. Both were about the precedents that'd be set for other players and where the line is drawn on the control wielded by Roger and the billionaires he answers to.

If it were up to owners, they would find a reason to void the contract of any player who was no longer performing to his contract's implied value or his coach's expectations. What if he's at a movie theater and smacks his kid? Or gets pulled over for drunk driving? Or is seen yelling at a bar or just looking at somebody the wrong way?

Owners, given the chance to unilaterally determine the definition of abuse or even misbehavior, will do what they always do: misuse it to exert more control and satisfy their own greed. There's also a clear double standard in how the league hands down discipline. Everyone, including owners, is subject to the NFL's personal conduct policy. When seventeen executives from Jimmy Haslam's Flying J Company pleaded guilty for a fraud scheme, the NFL did not conduct an internal investigation, despite the fact that one of the executives testified that Haslam had viewed documents detailing the fraud. Same with Jerry Jones after a woman accused Jones of sexually assaulting her in 2018 after a Cowboys game. Ditto when both Carolina's Jerry Richardson and Washington's Daniel Snyder were accused of presiding over organization-wide cultures of toxicity, harassment, and abuse. Yes, the league may have compelled Richardson and Snyder to sell their teams, expelling both from their club, but they were sent off with a combined $8 billion.

So, in my mind, fighting on behalf of guys like Vick, Hernandez, and Rice was not only protecting them but also the only way to hold owners accountable, force the league to be fair, and protect players from the commissioner's whims and blind subservience to owners.

Also, maybe teams should write better contracts? Just a thought. But the NFL never even proposed changing contracts in our bargaining sessions.

We filed a grievance on Rice's behalf, and after Paul Tagliabue humiliated Roger by overturning his Bountygate suspensions, this time the league bypassed Roger and appointed Barbara S. Jones, a former United States District Court judge, to hear the appeal and arbitrate. During a two-day hearing, it was clear immediately that the league had its talking points. The NFL's lawyers claimed that Rice had told both the Ravens and Roger that Rice had *slapped* Palmer, causing Palmer to hit her head on the elevator rail and lose consciousness. The second TMZ video showed that Rice had actually *punched* his fiancée, prompting Roger to levy more severe discipline.

The judge didn't buy it. Newsome, the Ravens' general manager, testified and stuck to his position that Ray had been truthful to the Ravens and when he spoke to the commissioner. During Rice's meeting with Roger at NFL headquarters, four other league employees were in the room but curiously took sparse notes, if any.

The NFLPA had someone present at that same meeting. Heather McPhee, my longtime colleague and one of my first hires at the union, happens to be an amazing lawyer and meticulous notetaker. She had written down verbatim quotes.

Exchanged words/arguing @ elevators

Ray thinks Janay "sort of slapped @ him"

Janay moved toward him, "sort of slapped or swung"

"And then I hit her."

She fell, thinks hit head on railing

Seemed "knocked out"

Elevator opened, she wasn't conscious, pulled her out

Arrested that night. (Both)

The judge ruled in our favor, reinstating Rice immediately and allowing him to collect a portion of his 2014 salary.

"I do not doubt that viewing the video in September evoked horror in Commissioner Goodell, as it did with the public," Jones wrote in her opinion. "But this does not change the fact that Rice did not lie or mislead the NFL."

But Roger being Roger, he couldn't just accept Jones's decision and let it go. So he instructed the league to hire *another* outside investigator to look into the case—specifically whether anyone at the NFL had viewed the second elevator video.

It was mind-boggling obstinance, continuing this scandal into the season, and of course the NFL opted for an investigator with a history of employment for the FBI. I'm sure they were counting on the guy's thorough, tireless nature. But they couldn't have known one key fact about him. They just couldn't have.

Because the guy they picked? He happened to be an old friend of mine.

■    ■    ■

WHEN ROGER HIRED Robert Mueller for this latest investigation, I imagine the commissioner hoped that Mueller would perform a cursory analysis, collect his fee, and rubber-stamp a document that absolved the league of wrongdoing.

As I'd witnessed decades earlier, that's not who Mueller is. He actively interviews people, builds a case not on shock value or flash but facts, climbs deep into the weeds of a case, and barely rests until he finds the truth. I spent three years sharing space with Bob, as he eventually allowed me to call him, and long before he became a household name during his investigation into President Donald Trump and even before he was named director of the FBI, Bob was just a lawyer. Relentless. Meticulous. Thoughtful.

I used to sit in the gallery during his trials, and Atticus Finch he was not. Bob is bone-dry, but he lays out fact after fact until a jury arrives at his preferred conclusion. In other words, he does absolutely nothing in a cursory manner. He never rubber-stamps anything, and in thirty-five years of practicing law, I never met a more virtuous and incorruptible attorney.

Granted time and, I assume, encouraged by NFL owners to be as thorough as possible, Bob assembled a team that examined three million documents, emails, and text messages sent by league office employees. They interviewed more than 200 people, did forensics on 404 electronic devices, and talked to 188 women who worked at the league office not only for evidence that the video had been received but to take note of *rumors* that the video had been received. He retained a company to digitally image and then search the hard drives and phones of everyone in the league office, from Roger to the employees in the mail room.

This had to be a hint that Bob smelled that somebody—maybe multiple somebodies—had something to hide. For an organization as preoccupied with control as the NFL, it's hard for me to imagine how tense things were at the office, especially within reasonable proximity to the commissioner. I would have given anything to be a fly on the wall when Roger realized he had hired the wrong guy.

In January 2015, nearly a year after Rice hit Janay Palmer, Bob released his full, ninety-six-page report. It was damning and painted an unflattering picture of a corporate office that had made a half-assed effort to obtain evidence. Of the evidence the league *did* have, the NFL mostly buried it.

"The NFL should have done more with the information it had,"

Bob's report said. "League investigators did not contact any of the police officers who investigated the incident, the Atlantic County Prosecutor's Office, or the Revel to attempt to obtain or view the in-elevator video or to obtain other information."

In my opinion, Roger may have had no desire to see the video or learn everything about the incident. The league didn't even ask for it. As for the Associated Press report that someone sent a copy of the video to the league, maybe the NFL clearly did a good enough job covering its tracks—and sending certain individuals on unscheduled vacations—that Bob's team couldn't pin that down. According to the report:

> We can exclude the possibility that a package addressed to "Jeff Miller" was sent by any commercial delivery service, U.S. Priority Mail, or hand delivery to the League during the period from March 24 to April 9. We cannot, however, ex-clude the possibility that such a disk sent in a regular mail envelope bearing only first class postage and the name "Jeff Miller" could have been received at League headquarters and misdirected.

A little over a year later, Security Jeff Miller was gone from the NFL, moving to Southern California to start a consulting firm. Com-munications Jeff Miller is still there, and because you never go against the family, I suspect he'll never work anywhere else.

Rice never played another down in the NFL, though in December 2023 Bisciotti made good on his word to look after his former run-ning back. Nearly a decade after an incident that humiliated the NFL and further cemented Roger as one of the most unpopular figures in sports history, the Ravens honored Rice at M&T Bank Stadium as a "Legend of the Game." He walked through the tunnel in his old jer-sey, with arms draped across the shoulders of his two kids, including his own baby girl.

Rice flexed an arm, still a thick cable of honed steel, and waved. The crowd went crazy for him.

# 6

# PRESSURE

Years before the longest, stupidest, most frustrating five hundred days of my life, Tom Brady was just another guy. Okay, that's not entirely true. He was another dues-paying member of the NFLPA, yes, albeit the only one with three Super Bowl championships, a movie star face framed by an incredible head of hair, and maybe the league's most hilariously prolific potty mouth.

This is a guy whose right arm was touched by the hand of God. But that's not what impressed me. Tom's use of "fuck" compared to any other word is truly incredible. Before games, during interviews, in normal conversation, he's as careful and scripted as anyone.

But when he's animated, he becomes what I call an aggressive conversationalist. Just a real, "What the fuck?" and, "This is fucking stupid" kind of guy. It is a delight.

After a few offseasons of visiting Patriot Place, I had my routine. After the team meeting, I'd go to see Robert Kraft and try to forge an alliance with him or, failing that, a mutual understanding. Kraft is a billionaire, which makes him an oddity in the real world, plus his standing as an owner established him as an opponent, but unlike most other owners, he wasn't always this way. He grew up in a middle-class household in suburban Boston, and it's not as if his father dreamed of his boy growing up to lead a multinational packaging conglomerate. Harry Krafchinsky made dresses, believed in going to synagogue, and believed in the American Dream. He wanted his son to become a rabbi. The young man had greater ambitions, of course, and eventually he excelled in the arts of politics and the hostile takeover, going so far as to push out his own father-in-law in 1968 upon acquiring half of the Rand-Whitney container company, becoming a millionaire virtually overnight.

It's fascinating to me that, in a single lifetime, a man can go from blue-collar to billionaire, from Krafchinsky to Kraft. His life story is one the NFL relies on, and its related mythology is quintessentially American. After John D. Rockefeller became the world's first billionaire in 1916, the following decades turned extreme wealth into an aspiration. These weren't greedy capitalists or ruthless titans. Rockefeller and men like him were conquerors, self-made men who navigated a complex economic system and eventually bent it to their wills, an achievement not to be shamed but celebrated.

But this wasn't something most people thought about, at least until the 1980s, when Donald Trump emerged not so much as a billionaire, exactly, but what Americans picture a billionaire to be. With his ostentatious displays of wealth, from the construction of skyscrapers and casinos to traveling by limousine or private jet, Trump leaned into this mythology and became the first celebrity tycoon. "I play into people's fantasies," he wrote in his famous memoir, *The Art of the Deal*. "People may not always think big themselves, but they can still get very excited by those who do. That's why a little hyperbole never hurts. People want to believe that something is the biggest and the greatest and the most spectacular."

Though he and the NFL repeatedly clashed, largely over Trump's inability to join its ownership ranks, he nonetheless provided the league a blueprint of how to present its owners in public. They were aspirational, but because Trump had inherited much of his wealth, his ostentatious lifestyle and fortune may have been worthy of admiration but neither felt unachievable.

Then came along someone like Robert Kraft, the dressmaker's son, genteel and soft-spoken and kind. He had done it, becoming close friends with Trump in the process.

So, then, you or I or anyone else could do the same.

Kraft had worked hard, been smart, gotten lucky. This was the new American Dream, and it is one the league has subliminally pushed onto fans for decades. It's a big reason why so many sports fans side with ownership during a collective bargaining discussion or work stoppage. Because these owners actually *built* something. Not like the greedy players, who are somehow unhappy playing a child's game and being paid millions, willing to bite the gentle hand that feeds them, siphoning all that hard work away.

■   ■   ■

BY 2015, I had spent enough time with Kraft to believe that he retains a connection to the real world. He may not be like you and me, but unlike the other silver-spoon eccentrics who own NFL teams, he actually has a heart. He's thoughtful and truly cares about the league.

Still, I also knew that he could turn on me in a second. Drew Bledsoe had lived it and warned me as such. "He will wear you down," Bledsoe, a talented quarterback and devoted union guy, told me after I became executive director. Bledsoe had famously suffered a brutal concussion and internal bleeding during the 2001 season, making way for his backup, Tom Brady, who never ceded the job back to Bledsoe and went on to become the greatest player ever.

If not for that heads-up, it's entirely possible I would have fallen for Kraft's act. I'm certain that, during the 2011 lockout, I wouldn't have recognized him as a possible conduit to achieving a new deal, executed, of course, via Brady, Kraft's own golden boy.

Nobody believed in Kraft's inherent goodness more than Tom. Usually after I met with the team and caught up with Kraft, I'd poke my head into the Patriots' locker room. Some of the most fulfilling conversations came with Matthew Slater, one of the team's wide receivers, and center Ryan Wendell. Then Tom would walk in, appearing nine feet tall and carved out of granite, and we'd invariably get to talking, most often about his contract. My contention was that Tom accepted team-friendly deals that, over the course of his career, may have cost him $60 million.

I realize that's more money than most people could make in a thousand lifetimes and that most fans believe professional athletes make too much money anyway. I won't necessarily argue with that. But in my line of work, that's the going rate, and the truth is, I need top players like Brady and Peyton Manning and Terrell Suggs to maximize their value. Because it's those top-line salaries that set the market for everyone else. They set the curve. Imagine you're a thirty-four-year-old defensive tackle who's trying to sign one last contract and lock down a few more years of financial security. If Richard Seymour gets a huge deal, then that means you're entitled to a raise without doing a thing. Owners are capitalists, in other words, which means players must be, too.

The second part, to both me and owners, is the infamous "franchise tag." Before the 2011 collective bargaining agreement, any team could select a player to "franchise," which meant tacking on a year to his existing contract. This was originally written as a way to reward teams for drafting and developing a cornerstone player. It was as clever as it was ruthless, because that meant a player who had outperformed his existing contract was involuntarily removed from the wider marketplace and paid a bare-bones rate. Players had no recourse.

So, in 2011, we retooled the franchise tag with a compromise between the owners' desire to keep it and the players' desire to end it. Owners could still use it on one player per year, delaying having to sign a multiyear deal. But rather than the player getting paid the same as the year before, he was now due the average salary of the top five players at his position. Those contracts were fully guaranteed, a first in NFL history. In my mind, this arrangement made sense and was a decent compromise for both sides. Averaging the salaries of the highest-paid guys meant that ownership had to think twice before exercising the franchise tag, and this at least introduced the possibility of fully guaranteed contracts, which every other major sport already had. The calculated salary also set the floor for the players' eventual move to free agency and made it difficult for owners to collude.

In 2012, Washington drafted two quarterbacks: Robert Griffin III in the first round and Kirk Cousins in the fourth. Cousins eventually outplayed the injured Griffin, became the starter, and became the textbook reason why we changed the franchise tag. But during our team meeting in Washington, it was Cousins who declared the new franchise designation a "problem."

While I understood his feelings and the insecurity of being stuck in a contract that paid him less than an injured teammate, it was important to point out that the NFLPA doesn't select players. Owners do, and the collective bargaining agreement designates contract lengths to *protect* players who may not live up to a team's expectations. Our change to the franchise tag had actually made it so that owners now had to think twice about assigning it to guys like Cousins. They had to choose between letting those players enter the free market or fully guaranteeing their salary at the high-dollar average.

Sure enough, Washington applied the franchise tag to Cousins. *Twice.* So because of the work of his union, Kirk Cousins wound up getting paid the average salaries of Eli Manning, Ben Roethlisberger, and Matt Ryan. Unlike those guys, Cousins wasn't a first-ballot Hall of Famer, but for two seasons, he'd be paid like one, to the tune of $19.9 million—a 3,000 percent raise from his previous salary. When I visited Washington the following year, just before the team was about to franchise him again and guarantee him $23.9 million, Cousins was far less naïve.

Now, the reason Cousins got paid so much, and the reason why Washington's then owner, Daniel Snyder, couldn't just pocket the difference, is because Manning, Roethlisberger, and Ryan had signed contracts worth their market value. Their *maximum* market value.

This is something Tom Brady never did.

Contract after contract, Tom agreed to deals that made him the biggest bargain in sports. No one knew why. Endorsements and off-field earnings? The fact that his wife, Gisele Bündchen, was a wealthy supermodel? Tom's money is his business, but my job is to make sure that all players understand how the NFL market works. That includes the fact that taking undervalued contracts actually devalues the entire market for players in the same position. I had no interest in what guys did with the cash. But not taking it? All that accomplished was doing the team owner a favor while allowing general managers to use one's experience as a bargaining chip to pay other players less.

Tom never told me why he accepted less money, but I suspected it was rooted in his relationship with Kraft. The two were genuinely close, and Kraft had convinced Tom that he was like another son. He had also promised to pay Tom the difference on the back end of his career. The Patriots went on to convince the public that Tom's altruism made it so the team could spread the savings by paying other players, thereby keeping Tom surrounded by talent and in Super Bowl contention every season. The public ate it up, and local and national reporters never questioned it.

Neither did Tom.

The collective bargaining agreement required teams to spend at least 89 percent of the salary cap on a rolling three-year basis. Any unspent money could be carried forward year after year. The NFLPA tracks league revenue and expenditures to the penny. The Patriots never came close to exceeding the salary cap. Not *close*. In fact, they routinely hit that 89 percent on the nose. So for all the Super Bowls the Patriots won, how many more did they *not* win if they had just spent as much as they could have?

This was the brilliance and ruthlessness of Kraft. It was a flat-out lie, and Kraft knew his trusting quarterback would fall for it. So, feeling feisty one day, I told Tom about a blowup Kraft and I had after the lockout. When owners opted out of the 2006 collective bargaining agreement, it triggered a number of fail-safes that had been put in place to compel the sides to hammer out a new deal. The incentive on players' side was that no insurance, retirement, or continuing education benefit payments would be made in 2010. For the owners, the provision was that the 2010 season would have no salary cap.

Everyone speculated that this would send owners on a spending spree, resulting in chaos and the end of competitive balance. Snyder, Jerry Jones, and others could just go wild and buy themselves a Super Bowl contender.

Sure enough, player benefits got canceled and there was no salary cap. A few players got signed to big contracts but nothing crazy. A few months after we ratified the new collective bargaining agreement, Jeff Pash, the league's general counsel, contacted our legal department. The NFL wanted to dock four teams' cap space as a punishment for spending too much money in 2010.

*What?*

In an uncapped year, with no agreed-on limit, how was it possible for teams to spend too much? How can you surpass a ceiling that doesn't exist?

Because the salary cap is collectively bargained, the league needed the NFLPA to approve the cap reduction to the four teams, which we immediately knew wasn't trying to punish those owners so much as it was taking money away from those teams' players. We refused. Pash countered that if we didn't agree, they would spike our previously agreed-on deal for a salary cap shortage plan. Hundreds of veteran players would get cut. In either scenario, they were using the union and me as their scapegoat.

I was livid. We had a deal. The league was trying to cheat, but it was somehow more sinister than that. The owners had clearly agreed to a secret salary cap in which no individual franchise would dramatically overspend. But Jerry and Snyder had done just that, and now the other owners wanted to penalize Dallas $10 million and Washington $36 million. This wasn't just foul. It constituted collusion, which is a clear violation of the very antitrust laws that had been written to prevent business owners from suppressing wages and stifling the market for workers.

I was as angry as I had ever been. As taxing as the lockout had been, Kraft had helped save the 2012 season.

"You lied to us," I hissed at Kraft over the phone.

"We have to keep order," he said. "We have to keep owners in line. I'm thinking about the league, and . . ."

"I don't care," I said. "Fine Jerry Jones, fine Dan Snyder, I don't care. But you know you're punishing players and shivving me."

Kraft didn't care for my tone, but I didn't care and ended the call. He later emailed me to explain.

"I understand your concern," he wrote, "but believe me we did the right thing for the integrity of the game long term."

Below this text was a chart that actually outlined the illegal salary cap in 2010. Owners had agreed to a $123 million ceiling, and Dallas, Washington, Oakland, and New Orleans had ignored it. Washington had blown past the threshold by $102.8 million, and Dallas had over-spent by $52.9 million. The Raiders and Saints had surpassed it by nearly $42 million and $36 million, respectively.

"[T]hese teams got an unfair competitive advantage," Kraft wrote, "which is not good for the game or in my opinion the union long term."

I couldn't believe my eyes. The NFL's most powerful owner had sent me proof, in writing, that the league not only had broken their own collective bargaining agreement but it had committed a crime, and Kraft delivered the smoking gun. It also provided a perfect di-lemma. As executive director, I never stopped being a lawyer for my twenty-five hundred clients who played in the NFL. This email from Kraft meant I had to use it to get relief for my clients. But burning Kraft as the source would cut off my ability to communicate and negotiate with the most important owner, effectively ending any chance of reach-ing across the aisle to discuss better deals and other options for players.

So I had to let Tom make his own decision—I didn't have to agree with it—because I believed that Tom actually thought the Patriots would cut or trade him, and I came to realize that this was just life inside the Bill Belichick paranoia bubble. In the name of keeping ev-eryone humble and in line, you condition them to question their self-worth and remind them, day after day, that they are replaceable assets that can be discarded at any moment.

A year later, I returned to Foxborough with paperwork. Before 2011, teams engaged in a practice called "not likely to be earned incentives." For instance, a savvy general manager could sign the punter to a contract that promised a $20 million bonus if, say, he led the team in tackles. That was obviously never going to happen, the punter didn't care, and this tied up $20 million that would count against the salary cap and was therefore unavailable to players demanding more money. As we did with the franchise tag, we redefined the cap system to become a *cash* system. That money must be spent, not just earmarked, and this represented a minimum amount each team was required to pay out to players.

The documents showed that, in 2013 and 2014, New England spent less than 83 percent of the cap. They were just spending as little as they were required. Tom absorbed the information and, to me, did not look happy.

Star tight end Rob Gronkowski, the only other player in the room, got up and left the locker room and, I assume, marched right up to Kraft's office. I don't know what happened but I do know that when he exited the Patriots' locker room, Gronkowski's salary was $630,000. After a later negotiation, his pay had ballooned to $3.75 million.

■   ■   ■

EARLY ON A Monday in January 2015, my phone lit up with a familiar number.

"What the fuck *is* this?" Tom said.

And a hearty good morning to you, too, sir. The previous evening, he and the Patriots had carved up the Indianapolis Colts in the AFC championship game. He threw for three touchdowns in a 45–7 victory to reach yet another Super Bowl. Nothing about that was unusual, and I hadn't watched the game. Not long after it ended, a respected Indianapolis reporter named Bob Kravitz posted something odd on Twitter.

Breaking: A league source tells me the NFL is investigating the possibility the Patriots deflated footballs Sunday night. More to come.

Shortly thereafter, Chris Mortensen, the legendary ESPN reporter and my friend, had a source high up in the league office who'd told him that eleven of the twelve footballs used in the first half had been deflated by more than two pounds per square inch.

*Who cares?* I wanted to ask Tom. But I didn't, instead asking him to explain what it was I was missing about this. He told me that the league was launching an investigation into the possibility that the Patriots had broken rules by purposely letting air out of the balls, which may have improved Tom's grip on the ball and therefore provided an unfair advantage against the Colts.

Even now, a decade later, it's hard for me to believe this wasn't some bizarre and confusing dream.

But it wasn't, and I assured Tom that I would look into it. My next call was to Don Davis, my right-hand man at the NFLPA and a retired player who'd once suited up for the Patriots. I told him what I knew, which wasn't much, and that George Atallah would brief me on the specifics when I got to the office.

"I just don't get it," I told Don. "If it's an advantage for one team, isn't it just as much of an advantage for the other?"

Don didn't immediately respond. He is much too kind to call me an idiot.

"They, uh, don't play with the same balls," he finally said.

I had no idea. I have never concealed the fact that I don't watch much football, bolstered by my belief that no rabid fan of the game could effectively lead the league's players union. Still, all of this struck me as arcane and weird. Don explained that, in every NFL game, each team must provide a dozen footballs. Each must be inflated to a league-mandated air pressure of between 12.5 and 13.5 pounds per square inch. Don said officials even check the balls before games prior to handing them back to the team, where some are made available to the kicker and punter, others to the quarterbacks. Each can push on and massage the ball to their liking before selecting the balls they intend to use.

Maybe I should've known this wasn't like baseball, whose umpires just provide fifty or so balls to both sides. But, no, this is the National Football League, whose rulebook underscores the league's military precision on matters from jersey length, to helmet size, and the visibility of players' socks. Players who violate the uniform code can be fined.

When I got to the office, George helped me piece together some of what hadn't yet been made public. With the Patriots leading the Colts 17–7 the night before, representatives from the league office had confiscated the balls on New England's sideline before whisking them inside Gillette Stadium. Then those balls had been replaced by twelve different balls.

"So what'd they do with the other ones?" I asked.

The league had removed them for further testing, George explained, but nobody seemed to know who would examine them or how they'd be tested. The night of the AFC championship game, Foxborough was an unseasonably warm fifty-two degrees, which compelled some people to wonder if ambient air temperature can significantly affect a football's internal air pressure.

I called Tom back to relay the information I had, but the truth was, we had more questions than answers. Among them: Was this a routine examination? Or was it a kind of sting operation? No one seemed to know.

What we did know is that, even with the reissued balls, the Patriots had torched the Colts in the second half. In fact, Tom was a sharper and more efficient passer than he'd been before halftime, regardless of any supposed grip advantage.

We nonetheless started hearing that the NFL would be gearing up for an investigation into the Patriots and Tom. My call to Roger was perfunctory, though I do recall his being dismissive about what was happening. Like with Bountygate three years earlier, I couldn't help but think that this meant owners were readying their weapons. Most of us suspected that, like with Bounty and the secret salary cap, one or more other teams must have raised concerns and tipped off the league about something untoward going on in New England. Owners are nothing if not tattletales.

Before Kravitz had received his tip, a different news report suggested that Indianapolis linebacker D'Qwell Jackson had been the first to notice how flat the balls had felt. He'd intercepted a pass in the first half, squeezed the ball, and wondered aloud if something was off. Then he handed it over to coaches for safekeeping.

But now Jackson was publicly denying that he'd noticed anything unusual about the feel of the ball, or that he had brought the ball to his sideline because it was crucial evidence. He'd done so because he had picked off the great Tom Brady and wanted the ball as a keepsake.

I didn't have much of an update for Tom when I called him yet again, but I figured that the league would go through some performative "testing" of the footballs and, at worst, issue a fine. The Super Bowl was less than two weeks away, and by then, I told him, nobody would remember or care about the Indianapolis game.

"You have to let it go for now," I told him. "I'll call you when I hear something."

For the second time that day, I had been careless with my words. Tom doesn't let anything go. Literally every interaction, debate, or conversation is a competition—a contest with a winner and a loser. I should've realized that he'd never allow the possibility of being the loser, even against the mighty NFL, with its half-baked investigation into whatever this was.

And Tom was right to have his hackles up. By the following Friday, my calendar remained packed with calls with Roger and Robert Kraft, followed by long meetings with our legal and communications teams. Then, after each of those conversations, I made a call to brief Tom.

Even in the earliest possible stages of a controversy we'd come to know as Deflategate, Tom could see the entire field. He never forgot, even for a moment, that the NFL values nothing more than the public's perception of accountability and fairness, this rigid system that is supposedly the backbone of competitive balance. Their business is built on the belief that, on any given Sunday, any team has a chance to win.

This, like so much else associated with the NFL, is part of its mythology. Anyone who works at a law firm, corporation, or any other regulated business knows that most companies are subject to audits and compliance checks. Every office has material information that may not be made public, but breaking rules or stacking the deck will undoubtedly be discovered, either internally or externally. This leads to consequences, in some cases a conviction for fraud.

Senior executives are bound to this not only by morals and an unspoken code, but by signing documents that, under the penalty of perjury, hold them accountable. Coaches never have to certify that they have abided by league rules, and general managers and owners are under no legal obligation to keep things aboveboard, on the field or off. For more than a century, the NFL has been allowed to self-regulate, meaning that they are accountable only to one another. They owe no disclosures to the public and allow no oversight by the federal government.

In other words, each of these multibillion-dollar corporations with their player and coach workforce, a group of win-or-die alphas, are on the honor system.

The league office didn't hire a director of compliance, or someone to actually enforce the rules, until 2019. Then again, even the job description of that position is curious: "NFL Compliance supports all League offices, including international, and provides guidance to NFL teams."

Guidance. Not investigation, audits, or supervision.

As a result, I believe that every team pushes boundaries when it comes to following rules, either to improve their chances of winning or to exert more control over players. There's a saying in sports, in fact: "If you ain't cheating, you ain't trying." Baseball players cork their bats, jam their bloodstreams with steroids, and steal opposing teams' signals. Racehorses and cyclists get loaded up with performance-enhancing drugs. Basketball players and officials have been accused of deliberately altering game results because they had been compromised by illegal gambling operations, and boxing has been hollowed out by its history of bribed fighters and corrupt judges.

That's just what happens when thousands of people exist within a system in which everyone is clawing for trophies, glory, and their piece of a multibillion-dollar pie. But damaged as boxing's reputation may be, it has an independent commission that oversees, supervises, and regulates its integrity. Neither the NCAA, which oversees college athletics in America, or any of the major professional sports leagues can say the same. They police themselves, and everyone pretends that the people in charge will just do the right thing.

That's why Kraft's public persona is so brilliant. In college football and basketball, fans never see school presidents and rarely see athletic directors. There's no trust in what happens above the head coach's office, therefore, which partly explains why many fans just accept that cheating, illegal recruiting, and other nefarious behavior is an inevitable part of the game. This is something the NFL does not abide. If a player breaks a rule, he is punished by the coach, who has oversight by the front office, which is monitored by ownership. If you see and hear the owner and that person is thoughtful and steady, with a slow speech pattern that gives the impression that the speaker is being hyper-careful with his words, then you are receiving a subliminal message the league carefully manages. These owners wear the finest suits, are well groomed, and are dutifully articulate.

Then they are returned to the shadows before they say or do anything that threatens that perception. Unless the conditions are perfect, owners are kept mostly out of public view. If something happens that could make the owner or organization look bad, then Roger gets involved. He is the rodeo clown there to distract the bull before it charges the cowboy.

When Spygate happened in 2007, nobody from the NFL announced that this malfeasance was discovered by a random audit or search of the press box. To my knowledge, nobody in the league ever has their playbooks or cellphones searched to check for evidence of tampering or gambling as a part of random audits. NFL Security possesses the technology, of course, but this department reports to the commissioner, whose powers are ceded to him by the owners. Translation: The owners decide how or if something should be handled, and Roger executes their orders. So when the league got word of Spygate, Kraft was embarrassed by what his coaching staff had done and was effectively hauled in front of a tribunal of his fellow owners and forced to issue an emotional apology. Then the group, which included Kraft, signed off on punishment.

By 2015, though, Kraft's embarrassment had hardened into contempt. Other owners whispered that the Patriots had cheated their way to all those Super Bowls, and with their quarterback deflating footballs for another illegal advantage, they were now doing it again. When Kraft and I spoke, he was livid. He was furious that owners were suggesting that Tom was a cheater, but I also sensed that he felt this ordeal had been ginned up by his rivals as a form of payback.

I do not know if any other owners objected to the punishments to Dallas and Washington for defying the agreement for the secret salary cap in 2010, but my guess is that Robert was not on that list. Jerry Jones and Daniel Snyder had been humiliated, not just for cheating the secret cap but for cheating *and* losing. Both teams had gone 6–10 in 2010, with neither reaching the playoffs.

Now, with Kraft's team advancing to yet another Super Bowl, the story of that week wasn't Seattle's quest to win two championships in a row or Tom and Belichick attempting to win their fourth title. Deflategate was swallowing those storylines whole. The chatter was that New England had cut corners, with its superstar quarterback finally unmasked as a cheat. Most curious was that the league was letting this sideshow overshadow the game itself, essentially forcing Kraft and his organization to publicly defend themselves, day after day. The NFL does nothing by accident, certainly not when it comes to public relations, so it was clear that this was a coordinated message being sent by other owners.

Kraft met with reporters and tried to conceal his rage, insinuating that the league would eventually come to its senses about the absurdity of Deflategate. To twist the knife, the league released the results of its ongoing investigation: forty interviews, the analysis of outside experts, a cache of forensic data. The report went on to state, in no uncertain terms, that the game balls against Indianapolis had been tested before kickoff and found to be of satisfactory inflation. The investigation "thus far supports the conclusion that footballs that were under-inflated were used by the Patriots in the first half."

That's when Kraft had enough.

"I believe, unconditionally, that the New England Patriots have done nothing inappropriate," he told reporters. "Tom, Bill, and I have been together for fifteen years. They are my guys. They are part of my family. And Bill, Tom, and I have had many difficult discussions over the years, and I have never known them to lie to me."

The Patriots went on to win the Super Bowl, but even weeks later, the league was doing nothing to put out the PR fire. Tom was growing increasingly irritable, and my earlier advice that he let it go was dying a painful death. When, a month after the Super Bowl, the prevailing story at the NFL's scouting combine was deflated footballs and air pressure, it was clear that the league office had decided on its position and would never walk it back.

I knew that a fight was coming, and I suspected Tom did, too. The only question: Was he ready?

■   ■   ■

BY MARCH, A full two months after the AFC championship game, Deflategate remained front and center. Karen and I were at dinner one night when she handed me her phone.

"You need to read this," she said, pointing to a news alert.

Not long after we got Ray Rice's indefinite suspension lifted, which was another public humiliation for the league, Roger announced his plan to hire someone to enforce player discipline and investigate potential misconduct. Roger had previously filled both roles, which we had challenged again and again, and during the Rice debacle, I tried a new strategy. Rather than waging public battles, I spoke directly with owners, attempting to maneuver from the inside.

"How is this good for our business?" I asked. "Outsiders keep coming in to clean up a mess the league office has made. Wouldn't a neutral party that we both paid for be better for everyone?"

It was pure advocacy, and I had practiced my pitch down to the syllable, not unlike a closing argument. The owners had steadfastly resisted hiring an arbitrator, but after years of losing both in the courtroom and in public opinion, they were open to something new. The league's narrative was that it would hire a conduct czar, and this person would investigate and recommend punishments to the commissioner. Roger would retain final say, but for the first time, his powers would be neither unilateral nor autocratic.

The news story on Karen's phone was about the person they hired, B. Todd Jones, set to begin his new position a week later. I was impressed. Jones's considerable résumé included four years leading the Bureau of Alcohol, Tobacco, Firearms, and Explosives—one of the most influential positions within the Department of Justice. He'd been a longtime U.S. Attorney in Minnesota, a partner at a big firm, and an ex-Marine.

Oh, and one more thing: Todd was also my best friend.

I found it impossible to believe that this didn't come up in his job interview. Jeff Pash, the NFL's general counsel, is perhaps the best lawyer I have ever known and is definitely the most unscrupulous. In a corporation filled with ruthless people, Pash has everyone else beat. To continue the feudal metaphor I like so much, with Roger as Prince Valiant, Pash is Merlin: the sorcerer the kings all turn to when they need a spell cast onto an enemy.

To call Todd's hiring a coincidence feels disrespectful to Pash's cunning, but at the time, all I felt was betrayal. Todd hadn't so much as called to give me a heads-up. This is someone who had been my mentor at the Justice Department, my drinking buddy every time I went to Minnesota to visit the Vikings, the guy who stayed with Karen and me when Todd and his wife came to Washington. This was a kick to the gut, and I knew my friendship with Todd would be damaged.

Hurt as I was, I did what I've always done: suppressed my emotions, ignored most of what I was feeling, and channeled it all into work. I believed Todd could be fair and that he respected due process. But could he be the disciplinary hearing officer for NFL players? Nope. Because his appointment—*anyone's* appointment—to this position was a violation of the collective bargaining agreement. In 2011, owners had insisted that Roger, and Roger alone, must preside over all matters of discipline and misconduct. We didn't like it, but we agreed to it because there were more pressing issues that players have always prioritized, like reconfiguring an economic system that inherently favored ownership.

The league had been so protective of Roger's position as discipline czar that, from a legal standpoint, we had to make the NFL die on that hill. With an asymmetrical strategy, it was important that the media and players know that hiring a czar would not satisfy our desire to change the collective bargaining agreement to give players better due process protections. As we headed into the Brady hearing, a memo the league sent us correctly pointed out that Roger wasn't an attorney. So we amplified the fact that this was the NFL *admitting* that Roger was unqualified to preside over discipline. We also kept reminding everyone that this was Kraft and the Patriots the league was going after, the wider kingdom training its sights on the most powerful king.

This was our play, and the flurry of activity made me almost forget that the NFL was playing dirtier than ever. The league's body shot had connected, but I refused to spit blood. I never called Todd to congratulate him on his new job, and he didn't call me.

I reminded myself that it's common for lawyers, even friendly ones, to be on opposite sides. It's not personal. Hardball is just part of the job, I told myself, and Todd and I would figure out our feelings later.

. . .

THROUGHOUT THE SPRING of 2015, we began structuring a potential defense case for Tom, who I was talking to daily. At this stage, I couldn't do much more than explain the process and remind him that the league's investigation was ongoing.

"Do we have to be part of that?" he asked me.

"No, but . . ." I replied.

"Well, why the fuck not?"

Any employer is entitled to do their own investigation.

I knew Tom wasn't actually interested in the arcane tenets of labor law or whatever procedural challenges we might face. He just wanted to vent, stew, and plan his attack. I had seen this scene play out on the sideline, with Tom grinding his teeth as he waited for his team's defense to get a stop so he could jog back out and cut the opponent's throat.

But what seemed to drive Tom craziest wasn't just that he was powerless while the process played out. It was the cartoonish nature of it all. A question about deflated footballs, of all things, had become a sideshow. Neither Bountygate nor Ray Rice had overshadowed the Super Bowl, and flawed as those cases were, both were at least rooted in the pursuit of righting a wrong.

This had been half-assed from the start.

So I started asking questions. Why had the NFL sprung its trap during the AFC championship game? How did the league even know to check the air pressure in the balls? Considering the magnitude of what was about to happen, did anyone alert Kraft? And most interesting to me: Who was it that confiscated the footballs?

Prosecutors and police officers live by many codes, among them the "chain of custody." That's a strict accounting of who was physically present at the scene of an incident, which person made certain decisions, and which piece or pieces of evidence were collected, examined, and by whom. This chain must be an unbroken factual link between what is being alleged and what can be proved, and all evidence is subject to inspection by opposing counsel before it can be admitted into evidence.

The NFL abides by a similar code, albeit only selectively. In anticipation of Peyton Manning breaking Brett Favre's record for career passing yards, the Pro Football Hall of Fame sent senior adviser Joe

Horrigan to the game in Denver to immediately retrieve the ball. Flanked by security, Horrigan was whisked off the field, the ball taken by him to the press box; it is likely sealed in a bag, marked by his initials, and then certified as accurate when it arrives in Canton, Ohio.

That's just one example of the league's process for a ball they intended to display at its museum. But the confiscation of Tom Brady's footballs? There was no sophisticated undertaking, certainly not one executed under the direction of Roger Goodell or Jeff Pash. So who was high enough on the league office's flowchart that they'd be granted access to Gillette Stadium and had the authority to remove game balls from the field, while *also* doing all this in the most ham-fisted way possible?

Certainly no one from either team. We learned that two individuals from the league had been on the sideline before storming the field to collect the balls.

"You're in big fucking trouble!" one of them screamed at Patriots officials.

The mastermind would have had C-suite authority, and the more we heard about the execution of this caper, the same name kept coming up. This was a person with a history of ruthless ambition occasionally blunting his judgment, with name recognition and the authority to leak details to ESPN's Chris Mortensen.

When the NFL released the findings of its investigation, I saw the name and started chuckling. Of course this had been the person who had put his entire organization in a pinch. The highest-ranking league official on the sideline that night?

None other than Troy Vincent.

■　■　■

WHEN REPORTERS ASKED Roger about testing the footballs and insight into the collection of them, the commissioner talked in circles. He deflected, time and again, and assured the public that a full report was forthcoming. The league nonetheless denied us any opportunity to

conduct our own investigation or even examine evidence and interview witnesses.

As the topic overshadowed the combine and continued to be an
everyday source of sports media chatter, it was becoming clear that
Troy, not Roger, was emerging as the unofficial spokesman of Deflategate.

Mike Florio, who founded the popular NFL blog *Pro Football
Talk,* would later accuse Troy of initiating the entire controversy by
leaking potentially false information to ESPN reporter Mortensen.
"It's unclear," Florio wrote, "whether Vincent deliberately lied to
Mortensen. Things were muddled and hazy and confusing in the early
days of the scandal."

What *was* clear as the months dragged on is that, once again, the
train had left the station, and Roger couldn't throw it in reverse.
Roger may have wanted this one to go away, but this time, sliding it
under the rug would ignite a political firestorm. Kraft and Roger are
exceptionally close, and the other owners are keenly aware of that.
Kraft and Dan Rooney, the late owner of the Pittsburgh Steelers, had
been Roger's two biggest champions during his 2006 elevation to
commissioner. During the 2011 lockout, I knew that Roger leaned on
Kraft for guidance, which is why I first contacted (and often lobbied)
Kraft when I needed Roger to adjust his thinking on something.

More problematic for Roger, though, was that his other bosses
still had the lingering taste of Spygate on their lips. Owners weren't
shy about their whispers that Roger had protected Kraft, making a
problem go away despite being a considerable threat to the league's
competitive balance and integrity. This was perhaps the first time I
realized how difficult Roger's job is. It's not just managing the egos,
moods, and compulsions of Jerry Jones and Kraft. There are twenty-
nine other owners who think they are no less important and are
equally deserving of the commissioner's attention and advocacy.

On paper, this is undeniably true. But in reality, several of the
owners are either not particularly smart, completely uninterested in
the league's wider aspirations and health, or a combination of the

two. This is not to suggest that I felt sorry for Roger. He is paid enormously well, has a private jet at his disposal, and knew what this job was when he took it. Still, fans hate the guy with a passion and boo him relentlessly every year at the draft, and I have witnessed owners berate and emasculate Roger, knowing full well that he works for them and cannot defend himself.

Roger therefore couldn't show favoritism for Kraft. But I could. Behind the scenes, it was critical that Kraft be on Tom's side by standing firm against his own league. Even following our usual playbook—airing grievances, filing lawsuits in federal court, waging a public battle—the NFLPA had little to no ability to win representing Tom alone. But forging an alliance with Tom and Kraft? That gave us a shot. So I called Kraft several times a week, allowing him to vent but also to keep him angry: angry at his fellow owners for being so petty, angry at Roger for letting this play out for so long, angry at the league as a whole because it had now turned its mighty guns on its most powerful and successful owner. These conversations gained me access to Kraft's outside lawyer, who was considering the Patriots' legal case against the NFL, which allowed me and us to form a potentially multifaceted attack in a case pretty much everyone wished would go away.

I was well aware that Kraft was also communicating with Roger, and possibly others, on their own way to end this with a settlement we could all live with. Kraft wanted to handle it peacefully. Just in case he couldn't, there I was, the devil on his shoulder, ready to declare war. For once, none of these options were bad, and if it came down to playing two sides—Kraft and Tom—against the middle, I liked our chances.

Tom and I spoke sometimes multiple times a day. I have gone through the checklist hundreds of times with clients: Enforce a complete and total press embargo, say nothing to anyone about the case, stay aggressive but positive, and do not destroy any relevant material. "We may not win, and you have to consider that possibility," I said, "but I will fight like a junkyard dog."

Just as I knew Kraft was speaking with Roger, I also knew Tom was speaking with RKK. That's how Tom and I both referred to Robert Kenneth Kraft, and just as I had to assume that everything I said to Tom would make it back to Kraft, this also represented an opportunity. I had no juice in the league office, so any settlement proposal would have to be generated not by the NFLPA but by RKK. Tom was to be the angel on Kraft's shoulder.

Shortly after the initial reports by Bob Kravitz and Chris Mortensen, the league announced that it had appointed Ted Wells to lead the investigation. I knew and respected Ted, a fantastic litigator and criminal trial lawyer. He was one of the small circle of trusted white-collar Washington, D.C., lawyers who, like I did, sometimes referred cases to one another. Like it or not, our business runs on referrals, and this means it can be chummy but more often a product of mutual respect. Ted is meticulous, reasonable, and fair.

This also wasn't his first association with the NFL. In 2014, the league commissioned him to investigate the conduct of Richie Incognito, a Miami Dolphins offensive lineman who had been accused of being the ringleader of a locker-room bullying scandal that targeted a teammate named Jonathan Martin. The young man had been harassed to such a degree that he'd quit the team. It became another situation of the NFLPA representing both the alleged abuser and the victim. Mark Schamel, a smart young lawyer, would represent Richie, and the union would cover his costs because of our organization's duty to members.

When Ted began his investigation into that case, he requested that we hand over Richie's phone so that Ted's team could search its contents. We refused the wholesale delivery of Richie's phone, but we were willing to agree to run any search terms offered by the league and hand over any resulting material. Ted, myself, and the other lawyers are all officers of the court, we trusted one another to handle these things honestly. Even if the search turned up something damaging, we had a responsibility to submit it to the league.

And, we would learn later, Richie's phone included references to a rifle scope that was "[p]erfect for shooting black people" and a photo of Richie holding his penis next to the ear of a sleeping teammate. He had made graphic sexual remarks about Martin's sister, used homophobic slurs about Martin and other teammates, and tormented an Asian American assistant trainer with racist language and abusive behavior.

When Ted's 148-page report came out, it concluded that Richie and two other players had engaged in "a pattern of harassment" against Martin and others while outlining a toxic culture in which "the statements in question were an accepted part of the everyday camaraderie of the Dolphins tight-knit offensive line."

Richie had already been suspended, and this marked a turning point for hazing in professional sports. More important to me, though, was that Ted's report repeatedly mentioned that the NFLPA had been fully cooperative during the investigation. There had been no limitations or constraints. This was an important message that we wanted to be made public, not only because it underscored our commitment to fairness and the protection of our players, but also that we knew how to ensure the integrity of an investigation.

As Ted's investigation into deflated footballs intensified, the sides agreed on an interview at Gillette Stadium. Two of our lawyers traveled to Foxborough for the meeting, but they were denied entry into the interview room. Tom and his agent, Don Yee, were inside but without support from the NFLPA.

Heather McPhee, the union lawyer who had been the difference maker in the Ray Rice case, was left outside the door alongside another NFLPA attorney while the interview took place.

Every player is allowed to choose who they want in the room with them, and I am admittedly biased when I generally prefer someone from the union to be included.

As he had done with Richie Incognito, Ted Wells asked for Tom's phone. Yee is a terrific agent and a skilled lawyer, but there's a difference between someone who handles investigations on a daily basis and someone who does not. Yee falls in the latter category. And while he surely knew about how we had handled the Incognito matter, Yee and Tom refused to turn over the phone or any of its contents.

On May 6, 2015, fourteen weeks after the Patriots beat the Colts, Ted's team released its findings. This report was 243 pages, far longer than the Incognito document, and it determined that it was "more probable than not" that the Patriots had deliberately broken rules. It singled out two team employees, locker-room attendant Jim McNally and equipment assistant John Jastremski, for releasing air from footballs after officials had examined and approved them. Video evidence had shown McNally taking two bags of footballs into a bathroom, where he spent less than two minutes before emerging with the bags.

The Colts had notified Troy and the other league official after D'Qwell Jackson's interception, but by then Troy had already decided to collect the balls.

Yee publicly attacked Ted's integrity, which I saw as another strategic error. The first rule of a good defense is that you never attack the lawyer. On our side, we instead decided to target the purported scientific findings in the report and the source of those findings. The team had retained an engineering and science consulting firm called Exponent, which I had used myself as a lawyer in private practice and found to be reliable. But the firm hadn't actually tested the footballs, rather extrapolating on the supposed findings of others.

What bothered me most about the report was its passage about Tom's phone. As written, it bolstered the argument that Tom was hiding something, suggesting that Ted's team had "offered to allow Brady's counsel to screen and control the production so that it would be limited strictly to responsive materials."

Yee and Tom had simply refused. The NFL would surely seize on this and use it as public relations sleight of hand, manipulating a doubting public and convincing it that the case was no longer about deflated footballs but about whatever may have been on Tom's phone. Nearly a decade later, I'm still haunted by a single thought: Our lawyers were just a few feet away.

The league wasted no time, suspending Tom four games to begin the season. We appealed the decision and made Roger the focus of our appeal. In addition to going after the testing procedures and the entire goofy process, we made technical jurisdictional and procedural arguments that were meant to prove that Roger was incapable of rendering a decision that complied with due process.

Moreover, it was telling and legally significant that it had been

Troy, of all people, who had recommended that Tom be suspended four games without pay. And that Roger had done precisely that. The Patriots were fined $1 million and stripped of first- and fourth-round draft choices, the most severe team punishment in league history. The whole thing was absurd, but to no one's surprise, the league justified its punishment by combining the infractions of breaking rules and a "failure to cooperate in the subsequent investigation."

The phone. That damned, infernal phone.

This is like every defense attorney's recurring nightmare: an allegation that your client obstructed justice, because regardless of whether it's true or false, the very claim provides the opposite side with an avalanche of leverage. It almost always leads to a worse punishment than whatever the client originally faced, and judges and juries use any proof of obstruction as an indicator that the defendant was trying to cover up his or her guilt. It just changes the atmosphere of a trial, considering it's easier to prove obstruction than the underlying offense.

Reading the league's letter informing Tom of his suspension, I could not shake the notion that, yet again, the NFL had issued punishment for something they hadn't set out to investigate. The supposed refusal to cooperate allowed Troy and Roger to escalate the punishment beyond that of an on-field infraction and declare it conduct detrimental to the NFL's integrity. The four-game suspension was more than what Ray Rice had initially received and was the same that Pittsburgh quarterback Ben Roethlisberger had gotten after being accused of sexual assault.

I still believed that this was less a search for truth than a legal consistency. It was an end-around way to pacify bitter owners who wanted to humiliate Kraft and punish Tom. The NFL was *going* to find a way, and rather than be honest about it and fix a small problem, the league office found it more politically useful to leverage it into a much larger problem, just a bucket of chum to distract the sharks encircling Roger.

■ ■ ■

TOM WAS PREDICTABLY furious, and we informed the league the following day that we intended to appeal. We demanded that the league appoint a neutral arbitrator in part because we were assembling a powerful list of witnesses. Roger and Troy were at the top of the list.

We would also learn that while the NFL had publicly presented Ted Wells as independent and impartial, his report no less than the gospel, the league's general counsel, Jeff Pash, had edited the document before its distribution. So we added Pash to the witness list, too. What information had been deleted or altered? Which characterizations, facts, and conclusions, if any, had been manipulated?

Neither of those guys would be our star witness, though. That designation belonged to RKK. He had pledged his full support to Tom, so I wanted to see what this entailed. Like he had been in 2011, Kraft could be our principled hero, the man powerful and righteous enough to end this.

And, just like in 2011, one of us was better positioned to make the ask.

The NFL's bylaws forbid owners from suing the league, but Kraft *is* the league: his relationship with Roger, his role in negotiating broadcasting rights deals, his ability to whip up a coalition of supportive owners and bend them toward his will. Besides, breaking the bylaws had been done before. Al Davis sued the NFL twice because it tried to prevent him from moving the Raiders to (and later from) Los Angeles.

"We need this," I told Kraft.

If he wasn't willing to go weapons-hot with a lawsuit, Kraft's lawyer and I discussed the possibility of a tolling agreement from the NFL, preserving Kraft's ability to sue if he didn't like the outcome of our case to protect Tom. Kraft was livid about how far this thing had gone. But to me, he sounded more hurt than angry.

I told him I understood. The league represented Kraft's corporate interests, but the team—and Tom in particular—was family. A lawsuit from an owner, even if it never resulted in a hearing, would work collateral magic in this kangaroo process. The NFL may fight the NFLPA until the end of time, but it wouldn't do that against an owner. Certainly not one as plugged in as Kraft. We just needed to ratchet up so much pressure on Roger that, amid the chaos, he would have no choice but to hand down an amicable resolution.

And that's where I come in. My name is DeMaurice Fitzgerald Smith, and I settle chaos. I must admit to laying it on thick. I reminded Kraft that the other owners either hate or envy him, and in some cases both. Tom? Wonderful, innocent, handsome Tom? He of the trophies and confetti and glory?

"You owe him this," I kept telling Kraft. "He's like a son to you."

I went on to explain that the system had always been rigged, and now Kraft was witnessing it for himself. If Roger heard our grievance, we would of course lose. The firm that employed Ted Wells was on the league's payroll, so any investigation by that firm wasn't exactly independent, especially given Pash's edits. Roger denied our request to view those edits or Wells's original draft, underscoring that nothing about this process had been impartial.

Everyone from NFL players to NFL fans likes to accuse me of taking every case to court, with some going so far as to say I prefer to litigate than negotiate. And on some level, I get it. The management rights clause spells out employer power to discipline, but the law requires that punishment or arbitration systems comply with "industrial due process." Translation: Management can neither cheat nor sidestep the system, and punishments must be consistent and based on facts. It would be great if the league did everything by the book and, on the odd occasion that it runs afoul of industrial due process, we merely informed them of this oversight before it was swiftly corrected.

That's not how the NFL plays. They bend or outright break the rules, you call them on it, and they deny it. You present evidence, they act flabbergasted that you'd take it this far, then refuse to correct their original act of malfeasance. It's not until you haul them to court and *force* them to do the right thing that they even consider it. And throughout the litigation process, they keep hiding cards up their sleeves and dealing from the bottom.

Example: We demanded that Roger recuse himself from hearing our grievance on behalf of Tom. Immediately before the hearing, Pash informed us that, because Roger isn't a lawyer, he would indeed be assisted by an outside attorney named Gregg Levy. Levy works for

Covington & Burling, which is the NFL's longtime firm, and whose partners include former commissioner Paul Tagliabue. Roger, of course, succeeded Tagliabue in 2006. The runner-up? Gregg Levy.

Conflict of interests? You tell me.

I kept milking the absurdity of all this to Kraft and Tom, the latter of whom was breaking bad. He became laser-focused on whatever needed to happen to win; to cut his opponent's throat before it could cut his. This was exactly what I needed from him. I assured Tom that this was never going to be a situation in which Roger and I would just work something out. Some players suspect there's a magic handshake or safe word for when we need to get something done, but while I had some success appealing to Roger on business issues, nothing worked when it came to discipline. The owners depended on him being a dictator, and I think Roger also loved the power to determine a player's destiny.

Tom may know the football field as his workplace, but as the interview with Ted Wells proved, neither he nor his agent was experienced in the labyrinthine nature of courtrooms, judges, and the glacially slow process that is the American judicial system. There are twists and turns designed to frustrate, surprise, and bankrupt you as you feel yourself being slowly choked out.

He learned this one afternoon in May 2015, not long after I arrived at his home in Boston. Kraft lived nearby. When I walked in, suit with no tie, a woman greeted me before suggesting I leave my shoes at the door. There was a large bin filled with Ugg slippers, one of Tom's many brand ambassadors, and I was free to help myself.

No thanks, considering Uggs don't exactly go with Armani, but when I removed my shoes, I saw my big toe sticking through a hole in my sock. I pulled the toe through, cinched the mangled sock, and tried to turn my foot into a fist to hold it there.

"Thomas," the woman said, was in the basement with the other gentlemen. I walked down, extended my hand to Tom and Jeffrey Kessler, one of our outside attorneys, and a small army of lawyers. I was the only person not wearing Uggs. We were about to sit down for a prep meeting in advance of the upcoming hearing when the massive television in Tom's basement, tuned to NFL Network, announced breaking news. Kraft was about to make a statement.

My stomach sank. I knew what was about to happen. Tom didn't.

So he watched as RKK approached a lectern and told reporters at an owners meeting that, after all this, he had chosen his side.

"At no time should the agenda of one team," he said, "outweigh the collective good of the full thirty-two."

In that slow, deliberate tone, Kraft said aloud what I suspected to be true. The team may be his family, Tom his de facto son, but there's no allegiance like that of a billionaire to his partners. As much as I wanted to believe the dressmaker's son still saw the world as we did, that was another lie I told myself.

"I don't want to continue the rhetoric that's gone on for the last four months," he continued. "We won't appeal."

Watching Tom take all this in, I expected him to scream "Fuck!" so loud that it'd rattle the basement walls. Instead, and perhaps more jarring, he sat there and said nothing. He just nodded, as if to finally accept that he could never win enough trophies or accumulate enough fame to be seen as one of them.

■ ■ ■

I YEARNED TO make Tom feel better; to assure him that this wasn't the end. But that's not my job, and as a competitor as cold-blooded as Tom, I doubted he *wanted* to feel better. So I left Tom to it, with his pit bull mix, Lua, to comfort him. I called Kraft and his lawyers later that night for a final Hail Mary, but it was hopeless.

Kraft made it clear he still loved and supported Tom, and his public support of Roger and the league had been professional posturing. He remained angry at the other owners, indicating that while he wouldn't change his mind about suing the league, we had his full blessing to fight this thing to the death. Maybe he was just trying to make *me* feel better.

Regardless, a month later, Tom and I met at NFL headquarters. Roger refused to withdraw as hearing officer, so our audience was with him and Levy, the commissioner and his trusty sidekick. Tom made it clear that he was willing to pay a reasonable fine or even play games for free, but I didn't love the precedent that would set. It's not as if his pay for those games would go to hungry kids or unhoused Bostonians, or even be dropped from a helicopter into the Gillette Stadium crowd. It'd go right back to the owners.

Another possibility was that Kraft pay the supposed fine by donating it to charity and therefore allow Tom to play. I suspected that this would put pressure on the NFL if this were offered at the hearing.

The only problem was that Kraft skipped it, disappearing to Israel but sending a sworn affidavit that supported Tom and torched the league. Tom and the lawyers sat before Roger for ten hours, with Tom treating the appeal with the same intensity as the Super Bowl: patient, respectful, prepared. I deliberately avoid sitting in on hearings, largely because my presence seems to put Roger on the defensive, threatening the possibility of a settlement. I kept hoping Kraft had cut a deal with Roger in advance, if only to end the drama, considering that now the news media was flooded with stories about air pressure and the ideal gas law.

Five days after the hearing, the league announced that there'd be no reduction or modification in Tom's punishment. I made the call to Tom. This was horrendously bad for the NFL's business and image, from the sloppy investigation to doubling down on the supposed win. Like Bountygate, it appeared that the league had predetermined its own ending and rigged the process to reach it. The league was counting on the fact that fans will come to the games, buy merchandise, spend their Sundays in front of a screen that pipes a zillion Bud Light, Visa, and AT&T ads directly into their brains. Owners and the commissioner believe in control and that no player can ever be bigger than the NFL shield. The NBA sells superstars, but the NFL's product is its system. John Mackey, Freeman McNeil, Michael Vick, and Ray Rice had all learned this.

Now it was Tom's turn.

A year before all this, Domonique Foxworth completed his single term as NFLPA president. He had been a terrific successor to Kevin

Mawae, deploying a mix of youthful exuberance with beyond-his-years wisdom and intelligence. Fox's playing career ended after the 2011 season, meaning the union's constitution forced him to step aside after the closing of the 2013 league year. I don't imagine he missed the owners' ruthlessness while trying to engage players to face off against management. Eric Winston, a veteran offensive lineman with a reputation for being fearlessly outspoken, was elected to succeed Fox.

I knew of Eric as a member of the board of player representatives, where he was a vocal ally for players during the lockout and a conduit between the union and agents, many of whom were suspicious of me. It wasn't until Eric's ascension, though, that I would learn his most valuable quality: a willingness to admit that he doesn't know something. "I don't understand that," he'd say. "Explain it to me."

There was a lot to explain, considering he became president in March 2014, during the heart of the Rice domestic assault matter and just months before Deflategate. I briefed Eric every step of the way as Tom's case gained more attention, generated more scrutiny, and traveled through the various processes. Once Roger dug in his heels after Tom's hearing, I told Eric it was go time: We were about to sue the league, taking the fight to federal court. And it was our last move.

Once Eric understood something, his true gift was getting critical players off my back. It's easy for someone to suggest a commonsense solution, unaware that this idea wasn't new, and grow a coalition that believed I just wasn't trying. Or that Roger and I were somehow in cahoots. Eric, a three-hundred-pound west Texan, could defuse this in a way I never could.

"Wait," he'd say, leaning forward and flashing a wide grin. "You think we haven't figured out the magic words?"

Then he'd chuckle, disarming the poor soul, and explain the reality of the situation. I never realized how much additional weight I had been carrying until Eric's easygoing way lifted it from my shoulders.

By late summer 2015, Eric and I were on a call with Tom to discuss next steps. We had recently learned that the league had preemptively sued to certify Roger's ruling in federal court, a savvy move considering that Roger, Pash, and the owners assumed I'd be pushing to sue. They beat me to it, filing in New York four years after the 2011 collective bargaining agreement ended the oversight by David Doty, the Minnesota judge who'd decided disputes between our sides for two decades. New York's Second Circuit also has a reputation for being friendlier to a business itself than its employees, and while I wanted to challenge this and get the forum moved to, say, Boston, I felt it would inevitably land in New York.

I had almost forgotten the thrill of being back in a courtroom, in this case on the legal team of one of the most famous men in the world. Tom was eager to take the spotlight as plaintiff in a battle against the NFL. To the outsider, a federal proceeding looks like any other hearing or trial. But to seasoned trial attorneys, it is more complex. Federal judges are appointed for life and often take their power to render judgments as an opportunity to push both sides toward a settlement. The technical legal issue before the court was whether Roger failed to provide due process to Tom, but Judge Richard Berman would pressure us to reach a conclusion by holding conversations with the parties in his chambers.

I have always insisted that my client, who has the final say on whether to settle, always be present in the courtroom. Tom was there front and center, I was in attendance on behalf of the NFLPA and prepared to make arguments, if necessary, and Jeffrey Kessler would act as lead counsel.

During our first meeting with Judge Berman, he asked who had settlement authority for the NFLPA, meaning which of us could sign off on a resolution. I raised my hand. Berman turned to Levy, who was lead counsel for the league.

Levy hemmed and hawed before saying that the league's governing body had to approve any settlement.

"Well, who is the head of that?" Berman asked.

"John Mara," Levy said. Mara was the co-owner of the New York Giants and a former lawyer.

"And is he here?" the judge said.

He was not. But the next day, he was. Tom seemed to delight in how irritated Mara looked, grimacing as if working through the final throes of an encounter with bad sushi.

. . .

NOW IT WAS August. Football season. Five weeks before the Patriots would open the season against Pittsburgh. Tom coped by sending me articles about the ongoing saga, including a Yahoo! Sports column that called it "truly one of the dumbest scandals in sports history."

"I still can't believe we have gotten to this point," he told me. "This is truly unreal."

His anger at Roger was explosive, and his feelings toward Kraft went from shock to disappointment. I couldn't help thinking about Troy's role in this saga, speculating about how his zany gambit had unfolded: no hard evidence, no video proof, no consideration of the impacts of cold versus warm air. How had a guy as meticulous as Jeff Pash been a party to such drama, with more unforced errors and clumsiness than a middle school play? I couldn't square it, which led me to believe that no lawyer was aware of this.

Had Troy, with aspirations bigger than his intellect, fired a silver bullet in some misguided attempt at currying favor with certain owners? Was this a shrewd political move to position himself to someday become commissioner? It wouldn't be a terrible idea in concept, considering how poorly Jerry Jones and others think of Kraft. But this level of unsophistication could bury even the most intriguing concept, to say nothing about what Roger must have thought when he learned of it.

A day after our appeal in New York, the NFL announced the hiring of a new executive. Tod Leiweke had worked for professional football and hockey teams, and Roger named him chief operating officer, effectively the no. 2 position in the league office. Troy wasn't demoted outright, but Leiweke leapfrogged him on the organizational chart. Mike Kensil, the other NFL employee alongside Troy at Gillette Stadium the night their trap was sprung, would be reassigned later before leaving to start a consulting business.

With the season approaching, we asked Judge Berman to render his decision before September 4, less than a week before the Steelers–Patriots game. I occasionally wondered if I was talking more to Tom than my own family, though deep down I knew I absolutely was. He would call or text me before sunrise, and we'd connect a few times throughout the day, sometimes to talk strategy and other times just to shoot the breeze. We'd FaceTime some days as he reviewed game film, and almost every evening we included a summary call. Then we'd part ways for a few hours, one of us in a hyperbaric chamber designed to extend life and the other slamming premium spirits to numb it.

"I'm sure people are getting tired of this," he told me during one of the exchanges.

It was indeed hard to believe it was real. The hysteria surrounding a federal court case was unlike anything I had seen, and outside the courthouse each day was a herd of reporters and quasi-reporters, including a braying ignoramus named Dave Portnoy, who'd shout smart-assed questions and the occasional obscenity. Inside wasn't much better. The court sketch artist was so mesmerized by Tom that she wound up drawing a misshapen head that appeared to be melting, then scurried over afterward to have Tom autograph it.

Tom and I passed the time by making fun of the sideshow nature of the case and most people on the league side, and reliving our first meeting a half-dozen years earlier at Patriot Place. He was so naïve back then, so much of that wide-eyed innocence and belief in meritocracy-above-all having been beaten out of him.

"You like our chances?" he asked me one day.

"Like a Hail Mary in the dark," I said.

Berman ordered us into his Lower Manhattan court in late August, uncertain that a decision could be reached by our requested deadline. Anything later would mean that Tom would serve at least one game of his suspension, which was a bad sign for how Berman was leaning. The judge kept urging us to settle with the NFL, but all the league office would accept was Tom's full confession that he was a cheater who'd been lying this whole time.

Tom had no intention of saying any such thing or indicating that the league's investigation and process had been sound. He also stead-fastly refused to blame any Patriots employee. I was proud of him, and of the fact that I could say I was briefly one of his teammates. We relayed to Berman that we had tried reaching a settlement by all rea-sonable measures, including that Tom was now offering to play *four* games for free. The NFLPA would discard any further challenge to the league's findings so long as the league did the same, and the sides could issue a joint statement announcing an agreement to the sordid affair.

But because it's the league and Roger, they effectively told us to go screw ourselves.

This motivated Tom even more, and he shook off the considerable risk that we could lose. Perhaps not surprisingly, he wasn't thinking that way.

"We will win," he told me as September arrived.

We both sensed that Berman was growing frustrated with the league's obstinance, seeing as how judges at his level deal with major corporations all the time. In virtually all of those disputes, the sides want things to end as quickly and cleanly as possible. Not the league. Roger and Mara sat there, day after day, imperious to the verge of petulance.

On the first Friday of the month, I was at my desk at NFLPA headquarters when my phone rang. It was Tom. He had heard that a decision had been made and that internet chatter was suggesting the same. I hadn't heard or read anything, but then someone entered my office with a printout of Berman's forty-page opinion. I put Tom on speakerphone and started reading.

"What does it say?" he asked.

A kid on Christmas morning, I flipped to the last page and saw the words. But I'm a lawyer, so I said nothing and, refusing to make a mistake, read the whole thing carefully. I could almost hear Tom grinding his teeth as I mumbled the sentences aloud. I couldn't reach the end fast enough. Then I reached the key passage: Berman wrote that we had been improperly denied the opportunity to question Pash, that Roger had refused us equal opportunity to examine evidence, that there was a conflict on the so-called independent investigation.

"*De,*" Tom said again, "what does it say?"

"For the reasons stated herein," I read to him, "the Management Council's motion to confirm the arbitration award is denied and the Players Association's motion to vacate the arbitration award is granted. Brady's four-game suspension is vacated, effective immediately."

There was a pause.

"It says we win," I said.

"Holy fucking shit!" he said.

"Holy fucking shit," I replied.

There aren't many moments like this in a lawyer's career. We both sat there and soaked it in, regardless of what we probably both knew was coming next. Tom Brady had won championships by conquering the St. Louis Rams, Carolina Panthers, Philadelphia Eagles, and Seattle Seahawks. Now he had beaten the National Football League itself.

"Man, *fuck* them," he said.

I couldn't have agreed more.

■　■　■

I NEVER WATCHED football, damn sure didn't support a specific team, and cannot ethically root for a particular player. Unless . . . well, the 2015 and 2016 seasons were different.

As much as I would love to report that Judge Berman's ruling was the final dagger, there is no zombie like the NFL and its commissioner, especially when he's determined to send a particular message to the owners. That message, in this case, was that a player cannot be allowed to win.

Ever.

The league immediately announced that it would appeal Berman's decision, which swayed public opinion back in Tom's favor. Even the most devout NFL fans demonized Roger as out of touch and driven not by principle but by hubris. It had to win. *He* had to win. Or die trying.

The federal appeals court announced in November 2015 that it would hear the league's side the following March. By then, Tom had begun what felt like a revenge tour. I took the entire legal team to Foxborough for the Steelers game, and we stood on the field while every Patriots fan I met vowed that I'd never buy a beer in Boston ever again. Dave Portnoy's *Barstool Sports* handed out thousands of T-shirts featuring Roger's face with a clown nose, and I must admit that I found this so delightful that I took a photo with one.

The Patriots started 10–0 and were the Super Bowl favorite. With the circus having chugged back into town, and with the team having to loan out its star quarterback to the judicial system, New England lost four of its last six games and saw its season end following a defeat to Peyton Manning's Denver Broncos in the AFC championship game.

"Any update or a fight till the death?" Tom asked me as the season drew to a close.

"At this point, death," I said.

The Patriots' on-field woes sent Kraft into a frenzy. Then the league won on appeal, reinstating Tom's four-game suspension, now to take effect to start the 2016 season, and Kraft finally agreed to join the legal fray in support of Tom and us. The Patriots filed an amicus brief that accused the league of being interested in "less a search for the truth than pursuit of a pre-determined result."

It wasn't a lawsuit against his own league, and it led to no leverage or avenue toward a settlement. But it was something. I noticed something familiar in Tom that, until then, I had been unable to put my finger on. The guy was a *killer,* and it was the league itself that had completed his transformation. He wanted to take it out on everyone, all the world an enemy—Tom hell-bent on cutting every throat in his path.

Tom wanted to hit the league office where it hurt. He would go on to spearhead union efforts within his team and beyond, showing solidarity by telling rookies that players must take charge. He pressured teammates to do nothing without compensation, especially if it benefited the league. No voluntary practices, no autographs the league could sell, no interviews on NFL Network.

Tom had apparently made the decision to become more involved in union business. While most players agree to give away their time to the league and its vast apparatus of media and marketing entities, Tom seemed to understand that this gave the NFL power—which could be shifted if players just stopped supplying these things for free.

Later, when longtime Patriots spokesman Stacey James told Tom that he was obligated to make these appearances, I contacted the club and corrected this error, having learned that the league relies on nickel-and-diming players.

It was similar to when Seattle running back Marshawn Lynch refused to answer reporters' questions after games, which drove owners crazy. I will never forget being on a call with Pash, Marshawn, and his agent, Doug Hendrickson, the day before the Super Bowl's media day. The league had threatened Marshawn with a $500,000 fine if he failed to participate, though I jumped in to remind Marshawn that his contract only obligated him to be available. Nothing more.

The next day, Marshawn emerged from behind a curtain as a row of microphones and tape recorders waited.

"Hey, so when do my time start?" he said. Then came the questions. He answered every one the same way. "I'm just here so I don't get fined."

A middle finger to the league, yes, but also a player exerting his power. It was a correction from five years earlier, when union reps for the Steelers and Green Bay Packers agreed to talk only about the impending lockout. As the Steelers' Charlie Batch and Ryan Clark waited, Packers quarterback Aaron Rodgers went up and ruined it all by talking about everything *but* the lockout. If only the Steelers had gone first. Alas, always a few feet away.

Tom's motor, fueled by vengeance, kept humming.

"Imagine the draft without any draftees," he'd suggest later. "They need to feel some fuckin' pain."

So, in 2017, Texas A&M edge rusher Myles Garrett was widely expected to be the top overall pick in the NFL draft. It's a huge night for the league, and for Roger, because he makes himself the star of the event every year. It has become a tradition, albeit one that makes my eyes roll, that top draft choices wrap the commissioner in a hug while cameras click and the league's broadcast partners issue a league-friendly image to the world.

Before the draft, we spoke to Myles and learned that he didn't care to attend. We arranged for him to stay home and collect a $5,000 check for the trouble of allowing us to send a film crew. We threw in a surprise guest: Bruce Smith, Myles's idol and the Hall of Fame pass rusher, to hand the young man his first jersey. The league begged to tap into our YouTube broadcast, and we said no.

Not for free. Not anymore.

In April 2016, the appeals court reinstated Tom's suspension. We appealed again, but the Second U.S. Circuit Court denied our request. The next stop, after more than five hundred days, was the U.S. Supreme Court. I told Tom I was game if he was.

But he was ready to move on. He was done fighting, at least in the courtroom. He served his four-game suspension, sunbathing in Italy, and finally put an end to Deflategate. Most people were so angry at Roger and gobsmacked by the league's crusade that nobody seemed to care if Tom had ever deflated footballs. Owners had shown the world how petty and ridiculous they could be, and how vengeful they were. Remember the three names on the lawsuit the NFLPA filed when we took on the league during the lockout? Tom (Deflategate), Drew Brees (Bountygate), and Peyton, who was the subject of a failed seven-month league investigation into whether he'd had human growth hormone sent to his home. All three guys got drilled, I'm sure, by total coincidence.

I watched almost every Patriots game during the 2016 season. Correction: I watched Tom on an absolute warpath. New England stomped Pittsburgh in the AFC championship game, the two-year anniversary of Deflategate, and I saw Tom later at the Super Bowl media day.

"When you win this thing," I told him, "you're a bitch-ass if you don't snatch the trophy out of Roger's hand and say, 'Fuck you.'"

He flashed that Hollywood smile, and we had a good laugh. That Sunday, I watched the first half from the NFLPA's box at NRG Stadium in Houston. This was the infamous 28–3 game, when Atlanta built a massive lead and was primed to win the franchise's first championship. It would never be that easy, though.

The union's chief of security, Tim Christine, joined me on the sideline for a better view. Tom passed for 466 yards as the Patriots scored thirty-one points in the final seventeen minutes, and I was close enough to see Tom drenched in sweat and emotion. After New England's astonishing comeback, Roger grabbed the microphone and prepared to hand over the Vince Lombardi Trophy before being greeted with a thunderstorm of boos.

Roger then handed the trophy to Kraft, who gave him a dead-fish handshake, and Roger quickly left the stage. "This is unequivocally the sweetest," Kraft said without thanking or even mentioning the commissioner.

When Tom walked up and raised the trophy under falling confetti, he conducted a brief interview with NFL legend Terry Bradshaw. He was the consummate gentleman. But I knew what he was thinking, because I was thinking the same.

"Fuck 'em."

# 7

# "RACE HUSTLERS"

It was chilly when the mob gathered, worsened by a breeze drifting off the Arkansas River. The white kids drew in close. The seniors of North Little Rock High were to have six new classmates, and to greet them that morning, many students lined a walkway.

One of the more enterprising boys, not quite fifteen, wore a striped shirt as he slipped between the taller students. The Wildcats' football coach had told players to stay away, but the young man couldn't help himself. He had to see.

Six days earlier and three miles south, nine Black students had been similarly welcomed to Central High by order of the U.S. Supreme Court. Six years had passed since a Kansas welder named Oliver Brown sued Topeka's school board because his daughter had to travel past the closest elementary school. But Linda was Black, and Sumner Elementary allowed only whites. Her school was supposedly separate but equal, but neither the academic environment nor weathered facilities were at all equal. The Court ruled that public schools in America should be desegregated, ushering in a period of opposition, violence, and trauma.

Many Black families adapted by being obedient, quiet, and humble. They learned that displays of deference and gratitude to their white classmates and educators, just appearing thankful for being allowed to merely exist alongside society's supposed royals, could be traded for leniency.

On the morning of September 9, 1957, previously segregated schools in Arkansas were declared legally open to Black students. At Central, 116 kids had been preliminarily selected to enroll based on a variety of factors: grades, good behavior, and—maybe most important—a history of keeping their mouths shut. Nine actually made it to class.

"Don't give anyone the slightest opportunity to accuse you of being out of line," Melba Pattillo Beals, one of those nine, later wrote in her memoir, *Warriors Don't Cry*. "Don't be late, don't talk back."

At North Little Rock High, the boy in the striped shirt wormed his way up the stairs near the school's front door. Other students sang "Dixie" as Black students arrived, and just two years after fourteen-year-old Emmett Till was tortured and lynched, a Black effigy hung from a nearby lamppost—a reminder of what happens if you step out of line.

The kid craned his neck for a better view. He was a sophomore, with a crew cut and blue eyes, and he watched as other students jeered four Black classmates, screaming and shouting and sneering as they blocked the entrance. At the precise moment a photographer for the Associated Press snapped a picture, the boy in the striped shirt had a curious smirk on his face.

Seven decades later, most American sports fans know that smirk. The boy is an old man now, Jerral Wayne Jones, though few people know him by that name.

He tells everyone to call him Jerry.

■　■　■

WITH DEFLATEGATE SETTLED, the 2016 NFL season was looking to be the first in seven years to start without some off-field controversy or legal battle. It was an odd feeling, the momentary calm you feel during the eye of a hurricane.

Then, just as when the air pressure changes and the breeze stiff-ens, my phone rang and the storm's wall arrived. It was George Atal-lah calling. Our communications expert wanted to let me know about something unusual that had happened before a preseason game be-tween the Houston Texans and San Francisco 49ers. A reporter had noticed a 49ers quarterback, Colin Kaepernick, sitting on the bench during the pregame performance of the national anthem. The reporter later called George to ask if Colin was sending a message by defying the tradition of players standing at attention.

The short answer? We didn't know.

Colin had undergone shoulder surgery the previous offseason and was still recovering when training camp and the preseason began. He wasn't in uniform for that Texans game, so it was possible that he was on the bench because he was injured. George and I ended the call, and I just forgot about it.

I knew of Colin, but not well enough to say we had a relationship. He came across as a different kind of person who, based on our most memorable interaction, could sometimes fall between obstinate and difficult. When I visited teams before each season, it wasn't just to give them a rah-rah speech about what the union was doing, or could do, for players. It was also a chance to do some legal housekeeping. At every facility, our staff makes sure that each player has signed a group licensing agreement, which is a card that grants permission to the union's corporate partners to use any player's name, image, and likeness: on trading cards, for example, or video games. Every fan jersey comes with an NFL seal of authenticity and the NFLPA logo, and at the time this was generating nearly $300 million for the union every year. After operating costs, salaries, and litigation and over-head, every NFL player receives a royalty check for about $30,000. We are the only labor union in the country not funded by member dues.

During our visit to the 49ers, one of our directors told me that Colin was refusing to sign his card.

"What's the problem?" I asked.

The director shrugged.

I sighed, grabbed a card and pen, and marched into the locker room. This process is tedious enough as it is, but it's a formality most guys just accept. On rare occasions, however, there are misunderstandings or conflicts. It was up to me to find out what was bothering Colin, lest one player start a domino effect that leads to trouble down the road. In the 1990s, the NFL "Quarterback Club" was a separate entity with its own video game franchise, and after that was disbanded, the NFLPA's stance was that no player or position group is more important than the full collective.

I didn't see Colin in the locker room, but when he came in, he saw me waiting at his stall.

"Hey brother," I said, "is there some issue?"

He ignored me. I kept at him while he changed clothes. He finally told me he wouldn't sign because his arm tattoos hadn't been included in the previous year's edition of Madden NFL, the highly popular EA Sports video game. It was a fair dispute, and even I had no idea why the tattoos weren't in the game. A quick call to EA Sports generated an answer: Tattoos are art, and Colin didn't own the rights to the artwork on his arms.

When I returned to the locker room, I relayed the issue. "Who owns the artwork?" I asked. He just looked at me.

His body art, his prerogative. But I told him I wouldn't be leaving the facility without his signed card. He sighed, took the card, and signed it, and I told him to call me if he bought the rights to the tattoos and that I would make sure EA Sports updated his avatar. He later had the tattoo artist sign a waiver, allowing Colin's full likeness to appear in the 2015 edition of Madden.

Two weeks after that 2016 preseason game, an NFL Network reporter again noticed that Colin, now in uniform against Green Bay, was sitting on the bench during "The Star-Spangled Banner." The reporter posted about it on social media, George called me again that evening, and, yes, this was officially a thing. In the months prior, Colin's own social media posts had grown increasingly political, most of them taking aim at repeated acts of police violence and brutality against Black people. In 2014, five St. Louis Rams players raised their hands on the field as a show of solidarity with protesters in nearby Ferguson, Missouri, the St. Louis suburb where a police officer fatally shot an unarmed teenager named Michael Brown. The following year, Walter Scott died in Charleston, South Carolina, after being shot in the back five times by a police officer who'd stopped him because of a broken taillight. Eight days after that, Freddie Gray died in the custody of Baltimore police after being transported to jail.

The summer of 2016 had been especially bloody. Alton Sterling died in Baton Rouge, Louisiana, after police shot him, and a Minnesota man named Philando Castile was shot dead by an officer while his girlfriend and four-year-old daughter watched. The girlfriend live streamed the grisly aftermath, showing Castile covered in blood and slumped over. It was a horrifying scene that kick-started a national conversation about police overreach, their mental health and trauma responses, and the methods in which officers were trained.

In all but the Charleston case, police officers were never convicted of a crime. Most weren't even charged. They were allowed to carry on, in some cases placed on leave, before the matter just went away.

To be Black in America is to accept things like this as irrefutable truths, a by-product of living in a country where we should be grateful we're allowed to exist. It's not leniency many of us are afforded. It's survival. At seemingly any moment, regardless of your education or character or job, you could be the next Alton Sterling or Walter Scott, and this is a feeling of powerlessness that is almost impossible to explain to someone with a lighter skin pigmentation.

It's something I thought about almost constantly. My son, Alex, was about to start his senior year of high school. At six feet and 180 pounds, he played lacrosse and basketball and walked with a certain invincible swagger that's common among teenage athletes. But because he's a Black male, his extracurricular activities included training sessions with me on how to avoid getting shot by police during a traffic stop. I would stand behind his car, playing the role of a trigger-happy officer, and run through scenarios. If he reached into his glove box too abruptly as he grabbed the car's registration . . . *bang-bang.*

Sorry, kid, you're dead.

Next time, stick your hands out the window so they're visible, de-escalate the situation, and come home alive. Then we'd run the drill again the next day.

After the 49ers' preseason game against the Packers, reporters encircled Colin in the locker room. Steve Wyche, a reporter for NFL Network, asked him why he sat during the anthem.

"I am not going to stand up to show pride in a flag for a country that oppresses Black people and people of color," Colin said. "To me, this is bigger than football, and it would be selfish on my part to look the other way. There are bodies in the street, and people getting paid leave and getting away with murder."

It made me think about what my dad and his siblings endured—the hardship and bloodshed that, for centuries, was assumed to be a fair trade for freedom. Colin's protest was important and sophisticated, but like my uncle Willard, who prays for me every year at Homecoming, I feared it came with unimaginable risk. The pro football ecosystem rarely makes time for nuance, and the league culture runs on militaristic compliance and a hyper-specificity to detail. Eric Winston, our union's president, had to remind me of this often.

"You've got to stop saying fifty percent," he'd say, "when it's actually forty-eight-point-nine. Football players don't realize you're speaking in generalities."

George booked me to do an interview with Dave Zirin, a reporter whose work and intentions I respect, so the NFLPA could begin establishing a narrative that was supportive to Colin. No matter the issue, the union needs players to be united. Or at least *appear* united. In the early stages of what our office correctly predicted would become a national tempest, we couldn't afford to wait for players to conduct interviews in which they might voice a counternarrative and potentially fracture our coalition. My words to Dave, about murdered Americans of color, were directed less toward the public and more toward our players. I also wanted to send a message to the league to leave this one alone.

"I know the NFL likes to call themselves the family. The union is the only family our players have outside of their own families," I told Dave. "We are dealing in conflicted times, and the only beauty that we can elicit from this is to embrace the things that have kept our country surviving—things like freedom of speech, freedom of expression. Those are things that don't necessarily come without cost, but things that we have tried to ensure and instill for generations to come.

"There is never going to be a day where this union is going to sit back idly and allow anybody to trample our players' rights. . . . My hope is that it doesn't get to that point in this case or any other case. We never pick a fight with anybody, but we certainly don't shy away from one if the league brings one to our door."

For the moment, it didn't seem as if a fight would be coming. It may seem hard to believe now, but grievance and political crossover were rare in professional sports and almost unheard of in the NFL. In 2016, my only direct experience in this arena had been in 2009, not long after I became executive director, when Rush Limbaugh announced a plan to buy the Rams. Limbaugh was a right-wing zealot with a radio megaphone, so in my process-oriented mind, it wasn't that Limbaugh was a racist, misogynist, and sexist. It was strategic: that we simply cannot have an owner like him, with a daily audience in the tens of millions, telling fans what to think—especially as we were approaching a lockout.

My second thought was that Limbaugh was a racist, misogynist, and sexist, someone who had no business owning an NFL team. I was new to the job, still working without a salary or contract, and feeling my way through the protocol of what I could or should say, or not, without checking with the executive committee. Limbaugh's ownership hopes seemed to be gathering momentum, and after calling Roger to express my thoughts, I decided a leader doesn't need to ask anyone's permission. George and I walked through a statement lambasting Limbaugh as a potential owner, and I sent it to the executive committee just moments before its release to the public.

I have asked our players to embrace their roles not only in the game of football but also as players and partners in the business of the NFL. They risk everything to play this game, they understand that risk, and they live with that risk and its consequences for the rest of their life. We also know that there is an ugly part of history, and we will not risk going backwards, giving up, giving in, or lying down to it.

Rams players later spoke out against Limbaugh buying the team, and a week later, the league informed Limbaugh that he would not be welcome to join the owners' fraternity. He went nuclear, of course, using his show to unload on me, the Reverend Jesse Jackson, and the Reverend Al Sharpton, all of whom criticized Limbaugh as the potential owner of an NFL franchise. He called us "race hustlers" and went on to suggest that Barack Obama had personally ordered the league to end his ownership bid.

"The owners are not going to admit that. They don't want to," Limbaugh said during his rant. "That is one of the things that I do know is going on behind the scenes."

An army of his listeners flooded the NFLPA offices with calls, overwhelming our entire communication system—effectively a DNS attack on our servers.

Seven years later, therefore, Colin's understated act of protest and thoughtful statement would barely register as a potential crisis. I doubted that it would get any attention, let alone set off a transcendent, generational movement. When Roger and I spoke shortly after Colin's first remarks, the commissioner seemed unbothered. This was one player, a backup quarterback for a bad 49ers team. The league had stopped short of disciplining the Rams players who had demonstrated amid the unrest in Ferguson, even after the St. Louis police union urged the NFL to send a message. Yes, a union attempted to influence a corporation to punish members of its workforce.

Roger and I barely spoke about Colin's point, and my position was that as long as fans were still coming to games and spending money, no one from the league should care. To my surprise, Roger agreed. After all, life was good in Billionaire Land.

"Just let it play out," he told me.

. . .

JERRY JONES'S GRANDPARENTS had been sharecroppers, working the loamy Missouri soil. His dad, Pat, worked alongside poor people, many of them minorities, on a chicken farm. He watched as chickens were slaughtered and workers pulled meat off the carcasses to prepare it for market.

Pat Jones decided this wasn't the life he wanted, so when he married, the couple moved to Little Rock and opened a small store in the predominantly Black and low-income neighborhood of Rose Hill. They called it Pat's Super Market.

Long before Pat's son initiated a stadium arms race, outgunned his own league on branding and apparel revenue, and became a vigorous champion of the potential of TV money, the grocery owner dressed in an elaborate cowboy costume and carried a six-shooter. A local radio host entertained shoppers, and there was a bandstand in the center of the store. Young Jerry was part of the experience, wearing a suit and bow tie as the market's greeter. If someone dared question whether a melon was ripe, Jerry would cut a chunk out of it and extol its juiciness.

The kid suited up for the football teams at North Little Rock High and the University of Arkansas, where he played alongside Jimmy Johnson and Barry Switzer. He figured out that a good football coach could command attention and captivate a group like a revivalist preacher, and before he graduated from Arkansas, he wrote a master's thesis and called it "The Role of Oral Communication in Modern-Day Football."

It was essentially a deep dive into marketing, just another way to get customers in the door, and he interviewed legendary Alabama coach Paul "Bear" Bryant and Louisiana State's Paul Dietzel. Jerry tried to buy the San Diego Chargers when he was twenty-three, submitting an offer of $5.8 million, which he didn't have. Investors wanted nothing to do with him. So he returned to Middle America, borrowed $1 million, and started a string of pizza parlors in Missouri. That venture failed, too, but this wasn't the first time bad luck hit the family.

Pat's Super Market burned down in 1958, when Jerry was a teenager, and his dad went into the insurance business and worked at a drive-through zoo. After college, Jerry joined his dad in the insurance trade and became vice president of Modern Security Life. The company sold in 1970, and twenty-seven-year-old Jerry took the $500,000 he received from the sale and started an oil and gas prospecting company. Any dark clouds hanging over the family were gone. Jerry struck gushers on twelve of the first thirteen wells he commissioned, and he and an associate came to an exclusive deal for him to drill on the associate's 40,000 acres of land.

When he again struck oil, Jerry had such a bounty that he could sell his product above or below the market rate, depending on the customer. There are winners and losers in this world, Jerry seemed to learn, the sellers who keep the money and the shoppers who fork it over. This naturally earned Jerry some enemies and attracted suspicion, but by the time he'd sold $43 million worth of oil, he had convinced himself this wasn't luck at all. Wealth was about hard work and determination alone, he believed, just the fruits that'd been watered by the sweat of his brow.

In 1986, Jerry's oil and gas company drew up a contract that forced a utility company in Arkansas to buy his land for $175 million. Jerry and other prospectors were finding so much oil that, in 1986, retail gasoline prices dropped 30 percent. The utility company couldn't sell the product Jerry had sold it, which kicked off an investigation into possible self-dealing from the state's public service commission. That investigation went away, and with gas prices as low as eighty-six cents a gallon (the equivalent of about $2.41 in 2024), another ambitious Arkansan set his sights on the White House. Bill Clinton cruised to reelection in the state's 1990 governor's race, a year before *Newsweek* called him the most effective governor in America.

In the late eighties, the Federal Deposit Insurance Corporation had acquired 12 percent of the Dallas Cowboys after three of its minority owners defaulted on their loans. Because the federal government owned a chunk of the franchise, it truly was America's Team, and fresh off another $49 million windfall, Jerry ignored his financial advisers and bought the team for $140 million.

Intoxicated by his power, Jerry cleaned house. Out went stuffy coaches and boring executives. In came people like Jerry: charismatic and cutthroat men, virtually all of them white, who didn't just put on a weekly football game but understood a *show*. Jimmy Johnson, the flamboyant coach of the Miami Hurricanes and Jerry's old teammate at Arkansas, became the head coach of the Cowboys. Jerry named himself the team's de facto general manager, drafting UCLA quarterback Troy Aikman with the first overall selection.

Jerry immediately ruffled feathers as he challenged the NFL's status quo. He told reporters that he'd sell beer at Cowboys games, and he confessed to one reporter that he occasionally leered at the team's cheerleaders through a two-way mirror former general manager Tex Schramm had installed.

"It is obvious that a Beverly Hillbilly is stationed at the Cowboy helm," Dallas's *D Magazine* wrote in a 1989 profile. "The question is, which one? Jethro or Jed?"

He ran the business side of the Cowboys like his father's grocery, but the player roster was run more like the old chicken farm. Pat Jones had seen co-workers' fingers become gnarled and useless as they separated meat from bone, compressing nerves and inflaming joints. These days, Jerry speaks proudly about what his daddy saw, because there's always a solution when a worker can't perform his duties. You replace them with someone younger and healthier, because that's not just the NFL's business model. It's show business, and long after Jerry put away his bow tie, he still knew how to get customers in the door.

■   ■   ■

A MONTH AFTER Colin's initial refusal to stand for the anthem, one man's protest was sweeping the nation. Players throughout the league were demonstrating, whether kneeling or raising a fist in the style of John Carlos and Tommie Smith during the 1968 Olympics.

And I won't lie: I was proud.

In my mind, these acts of quiet protest were an acknowledgment that not all paths are equal. Even those that lead us forward, such as the one my ancestors took, are fraught. The leaders of college and professional sports bodies would prefer that athletes avoid cultural and political issues, and for much of the previous century, even star athletes obliged. Michael Jordan, the rare athlete to have gone from player to owner, made that leap by putting capitalism above conscience. In 1990, Jordan infamously refused to endorse Harvey Gantt, a Black North Carolina Democrat, in Gantt's bid to unseat Senator Jesse Helms, the incumbent and an unapologetic racist.

"Republicans buy sneakers, too," Jordan said.

Many fans assume that many young players are just in it for the money, and while sports is their profession and a job is rooted in trading services for compensation, that assumption isn't so much wrong as it is incomplete and intellectually lazy. In my experience, the overwhelming majority of professional athletes care about their wider world and have creative thoughts and ideas about how to improve society. But there are few incentives to vocalizing them.

It's also unfair, in my view, to think of NFL players as a monolithic bloc. It's true that these are some of the biggest, strongest, sweatiest human beings on the planet. But these are individuals, each with intense competition and delicate job security, and most of the athletes I have come to know well have a visible delineation between their on- and off-field personalities. In 2010, during the "One Team" salute the season before the lockout, Peyton Manning was among the most steadfast participants and one of the players most responsible for whipping up continued enthusiasm about showing unity. But he's the same person who, the Monday morning after his team's first pregame display, called me to express dismay that fans had . . . *booed* him.

This was the same quarterback who, as a rookie in 1998, set an NFL record with twenty-eight interceptions while the Indianapolis Colts went 3–13. These guys have faced intense criticism their whole lives, and the job description of every football coach is to scrutinize and correct, often without mercy. These boos weren't about a missed tackle or dropped pass or boneheaded interception.

What was difficult for Peyton and others was that they weren't being jeered as athletes but as men—as human beings with the very complex thoughts and emotions that aren't often seen. The "One Team" gesture represented an interruption to fans' in-game experience and the league's most addictive product, which isn't a sporting event so much as it is a loud and violent distraction. To add an unannounced wrinkle was disruptive to the experience, and fans let players know it. Peyton urged me and the union to do a better job of relaying to fans what players were doing, and because I didn't have the heart to tell him that no amount of messaging would change a century of sports and entertainment dynamics, I assured him we'd do our best.

What also struck me was the game-day transformation that turns man into gladiator. It begins not when a player arrives at the stadium but when the shoulder pads go on. The pregame routine can last three hours, from warm-ups to final prep meeting to gathering on the sideline. Even then, there's a hint of normalcy with the guys. You can have a conversation with them—talk about relationships or travel or the previous night's college game. The transformation, in other words, isn't complete.

It is often the playing of the national anthem that acts as that final mental trigger, when jets and other military aircraft thunder overhead, the crowd roars, and a prayer or a couple of deep breaths later, it's time to rock and roll.

Which, to me, is partly why choosing that moment to protest in 2016 was so moving. Guys were interrupting their personal routines and making themselves vulnerable not as players but as individuals. As men. As three-dimensional human beings who shed their real and imagined armor to push forward a great rethinking. And not because someone told them they had to. Quite the opposite. Boos and vulgarities were raining down on these guys like never before, and it wasn't because players were breaking their own pregame ritual. They were daring to snap some fans' primal trance.

Early in that season, I scheduled a second visit to each team. I needed to check on guys, remind them of the NFLPA's resources, and remind them that their union was behind every single player, whether they chose to demonstrate or not. I also wanted to lay the groundwork of Colin's case, what I thought the NFL might do, and explain why it was an important stand. Also, given the very real possibility of dissension, a union leader is never more worried about leading a group than when it feels impossible to discern the difference between a quiet that is okay and a quiet that is not.

"Everything good?" I had asked in previous years. This was my way of inviting them to vent or share any thoughts about the collective bargaining agreement, Roger, or problems in the workplace.

"Man, De, we're good," players would often say in some way. "We're chilling."

But the responses now felt different.

"How's everything going?" I asked.

"We're really fine," they told me.

"So how's everything *really* going?" I'd say again.

By the time that season started, Donald Trump had ridden a wave of hate, distrust, and grievance to win the Republican nomination for president. When Colin started his protest, Trump publicly invited Colin to leave the United States and move to another country. Trump later said that political displays at NFL stadiums showed "a lack of respect for our country."

The league itself has draped itself in conservative politics for decades, largely because its owners and fan base have a tendency to vote for the same party. In 2007, one of Roger's first acts as commissioner was to hire Jeff Miller—PR Jeff Miller, that is—as an in-house lobbyist. The next year, the league formed its own political action committee, called the Gridiron PAC, which owners and the league office pumped millions into. This was in addition to what individual owners were contributing, and it was among the reasons we cited when we suggested to player leadership that the NFLPA create its own PAC.

In 2010, not long after the New Orleans Saints won their first Super Bowl, owner Tom Benson used his political connections to somehow get legislation introduced in the Louisiana statehouse that would strip workers' compensation benefits from Saints players. This was on top of salary cap deductions each team received for the cost of their workers' comp insurance, but these savings of course weren't enough. I couldn't understand Benson's strategy, especially given the poor optics, but two of the union's in-house attorneys, Tom DePaso and Richard Burleson, figured it out immediately. If a state somehow passed a law that decreed that no player can receive workers' comp, owners wouldn't have to pay for the insurance *and* could keep the salary cap credit.

The initial straw poll suggested that the Louisiana Senate would vote to pass it, suggesting that players being on the hook for their own injury care would save taxpayers because this financial burden wouldn't come out of state or local funds. When I heard about this, I flew to Baton Rouge, the Louisiana capital, with the lobbyists we had recently hired. Despite lawmakers assuring us that the measure would never pass the state's House of Representatives, we learned upon returning to Washington that those politicians had lied to our faces. They would be voting the next morning, and it was expected to pass.

So I called Drew Brees, the Saints' quarterback, and shared the bad news. We had been outfoxed, and members refused to delay the vote.

"What should we do?" Drew asked me.

I told him to encourage players to do interviews and attempt to create enough public pressure to get the vote delayed. It was our only hope. But Drew had a better idea. After practice the next day, Drew and forty teammates traveled to Baton Rouge by bus and paraded into the statehouse while one union-friendly lawmaker played "When the Saints Go Marching In." Elected officials stopped what they were doing to get autographs from and snap selfies with the very players they were trying to screw over. Then Drew walked to the lectern and addressed the chamber.

"It's about showing how important protecting our workers' comp rights as Louisiana workers is," Drew said, "and we're here to make sure those rights are protected."

Drew was a killer.

Lawmakers tabled the bill, effectively killing it on the statehouse floor, and this became the best example of my tried-and-true rallying cry at the NFLPA: The most dangerous weapon against imbalances in pro sports is a well-informed player who is willing to act. Even with a lobbying arm, we could never spend what the league does. But by being strategic with our lobbyists and empowered players, we had footholds both on Capitol Hill and in state legislatures, which, if nothing else, was an impediment to the NFL getting everything it wanted.

The league's political influence is obvious even during games, when fans claim to want separation between entertainment and the so-called real world. Every pregame flyover by a military aircraft, any time a service member returns home to surprise their loved ones on the field, the pageantry of every "Salute to Service" campaign—these are all rooted less in patriotism than in greed and entertainment. In 2015, it was revealed that the U.S. Department of Defense had paid the league $5.4 million in taxpayer funds to stage those events. Senators Jeff Flake and John McCain, both Republicans, issued a joint oversight report that concluded that the Pentagon had funded this "paid patriotism," as they called it. They demanded that the contracts with sports leagues be voided.

To NFL owners, this had never been about the Stars and Stripes. It was just another revenue stream, and a direct result of this deal had been that, starting in 2009, teams started requiring players to be on the field for the national anthem.

So Colin wasn't even protesting some decades-old tradition. Players could do whatever they wanted during the anthem just eight years earlier. But just weeks before the 2016 election, Trump was using this demonstration to animate his supporters and transform a nuanced issue into a simple one that wrongly accused spoiled NFL players of disrespecting veterans, the military, and the flag. His supporters gobbled it up.

I called Kraft, who had introduced me to Trump years earlier at the funeral for his wife, Myra. The two had been friends for decades, so I tried appealing to Kraft's business acumen by suggesting that nothing about Trump's comments was good for the league or our shared brand. Could Kraft tell his buddy to stay out of our business?

"Oh, De," Kraft said, "he doesn't believe half the things he says."

The implication was that neither of us should care about what Trump said, so long as he might not actually believe it. But I cared that the Republican nominee for president was sowing division and making our jobs harder, and maybe putting players in harm's way off the field. If it had been anyone besides Trump, I believe the NFL would have rebuffed this person with extreme prejudice. This is a league that waged a battle to prevent a neurologist from publishing a paper about CTE and made a habit of co-opting journalists to do its bidding. Kraft and others had made huge donations to Trump's campaign and inaugural committees, which somehow gave him license to say and do whatever he wanted. (It was around this same time that Tom Brady kept a "Make America Great Again" hat in his locker, and while I assumed Tom had met Trump through Kraft, I never asked if he actually supported Trump's politics, in part because I was afraid of the answer.)

As Election Day approached, I scheduled a meeting with Roger to try generating a cooperative strategy. Up to that point, we had been on the same page about the growing tension and how none of it was good for the league or players. Now I heard hesitation in his voice. He admitted that Trump's attacks weren't good for the NFL, but for the first time, he indicated a desire for the union to quietly pressure players to stop kneeling.

That wasn't going to happen.

So he took it a step further, indicating that a few of the league's big-ticket sponsors had expressed concern that protests were dividing people rather than bringing them together. This is another key part of the league's business model: that the NFL is a great unifier, even during periods of considerable polarization. This was, of course, ignoring the fact that the NFL was the last league to integrate, with the Washington Redskins refusing to add a Black player until 1962, when Bobby Mitchell signed with the team amid public pressure from the federal government.

I was getting nowhere. Kraft was Trump's friend, and Roger was likely hearing from furious owners and, at the very least, was trying to avoid jumping into the fray. Neither of those guys could help me. I needed to talk to someone who thinks like Trump—a circus ring-master like Trump, who got rich in as dubious ways as he did and has made himself rich and famous by saying and doing outrageous things.

Late one night, I was tossing and turning, trying to figure out my next move. Then it hit me. I emailed my assistant, asking him to book a flight for Don Davis and me. We needed to get to Dallas.

■ ■ ■

NOT LONG AFTER Jerry's Cowboys won the Super Bowl in 1993, the team was invited to the White House. Bill Clinton walked across car-peting in the East Room meant to look like a football field, straight up to Jerry, and wrapped him in a hug.

"I watched this team win the way I think Americans win best," the president said. "They hung in there. They were strong, they were dedicated, they started a lot of games slow, and they always finished fast. And that's what we have to do as a country."

Then the world's most powerful man made way for one of its wealthiest.

"The Cowboys were something very special: not down-and-out and on their back," a fifty-year-old Jerry said, "but just needed a little lifting hand to get up off that knee and become great again."

It had been Jerry, of course, who had bankrolled the revival of the franchise and this symbol of Americana.

Then, just two years later, Jerry decided he wasn't rich enough. He sued the NFL for $750 million, alleging that a league he called "an unlawful cartel" had illegally restrained trade by pocketing a large percentage of team-licensed merchandise. The sides settled, and the Cowboys were the only franchise allowed to keep its own marketing and licensing contracts separate from the league itself. This sent a clear message: There is Jerry, followed by everyone else.

He has manipulated league business ever since, often becoming its richest beneficiary. These days, the Cowboys put $200 million worth of wholesale product in the retail chain, some years doubling or even tripling up. A franchise he bought for $140 million is now worth $10 billion, the world's most valuable professional sports organization.

And it's still not enough.

I sometimes think about fourteen-year-old Jerry and the choice he faced upon descending the steps that day at North Little Rock High. He could have absorbed what he'd just witnessed and vowed to stand up to the country's traditional power dynamic. Or he could manipulate it to enrich himself. We all know which path Jerry chose, but the thing that bothers me is that Jerry actually grew up playing with Black kids. He considered them friends, though he never actually attended school with them. The intimidation and protests worked, after all, and North Little Rock denied entry to the six Black students. The school wouldn't desegregate until 1970, long after Jerry was gone.

Black families had also been the "largest clientele" at Pat's Super Market, Jerry would tell the University of Arkansas as part of an oral history in 2010, but there was a clear dividing line between the shoppers and the sellers. Jerry spent summers in his grandfather's cotton fields, learning to communicate across race and class. Then again, when one of the Black kids got "a little sassy," he'd say in that same oral history, Jerry dumped a bucket of ice water on the boy's head and ran off.

"I can remember back then," he said. "I could take just so much of that BS."

There was always a limit, in other words, to Jerry's views on equality. He could tolerate them as long as they stayed in their lanes, kept quiet, and showed gratitude for being allowed to exist alongside him. Anything less would be seen as an affront, with players replaced and coaches fired and league commissioners bullied. Rather than stand up to Jerry, the NFL has *become* Jerry.

And he is the personification of greed. His lust for *more* can never be satisfied, and it has blunted any sense of right and wrong he may have once had.

In four decades of team ownership, Jerry has never hired a Black man to be the Cowboys' head coach. Only twice has Dallas had a Black coordinator, and though a Black man, Will McClay, leads the team's scouting department, he's not the general manager. Jerry is one of two people to face discipline for violating the Rooney Rule, which is the league's requirement that teams must interview a candidate of color before hiring a head coach. In 2003, Jerry had already decided to hire legendary New York Giants coach Bill Parcells before conducting a sham interview with Dennis Green, a Black man who had coached the Minnesota Vikings. The NFL handed down no actual penalty on Jerry, though, making it clear that Jerry is above the rules of his own league.

And that, when it comes to Jerry himself, Black people can play for him, drive him around in his luxury bus, and clean the stadium and team facility. But lead with him? Shape the league with him? Attend owners' meetings and affect policy and stand up to systemic failures with him? Those are lines he will not cross.

When Don Davis and I got to Dallas in 2016, Jerry took us on a side trip to nearby Frisco. Construction was under way on The Star, a $1.5 billion team headquarters and mixed-use complex north of the Dallas–Fort Worth metroplex. It was impressive and over the top, the result of more than a decade of Jerry having collected 1,200 acres of undeveloped farmland in rural Collin and Denton Counties. The Star itself took up 91 of those acres.

But rather than savor his latest accomplishment, Jerry was angry. The league was poking around allegations that Ezekiel Elliott, the Cowboys' most talented running back since Emmitt Smith anchored three Super Bowl championships in four years, had beaten up his girlfriend. The woman posted pictures of bruises on her body to social media, and the league had opened the most high-profile domestic assault investigation since Ray Rice. It was to become a public litmus test for the NFL's revamped personal conduct policy.

Jerry was furious, suggesting that one or more owners had put the league up to this. I didn't know much about the alleged assault other than what had been made public. One of our lawyers was working with Elliott and his outside counsel as we awaited the league's report, which would be coming from Lisa Friel, the NFL's new special counsel for investigations. Jerry complained about the power Roger had, ripped the commissioner for being overpaid, and kept talking about how this stage of his life was supposed to be a victory lap.

We took our tour of The Star, and Jerry confessed that he had donated $1 million to Trump. I didn't get the sense that he cared as much for the man as it may have seemed, but Jerry liked that Trump was a wildcatter like himself—a carnival barker whose persona is tied to extreme wealth and who will do whatever it takes to make his point. I detected a hint of admiration in Jerry's voice.

"But what if he ups the ante on this protest thing?" I asked. "How is any of this good for our business?"

We both knew Roger wanted it to go away. The commissioner wanted some sort of agreement that appeased not only Trump but his core supporters. He was looking for a way to pacify owners and, I have to assume, get them off his back. Jerry acknowledged this, but he wasn't keen on making life easier on Roger.

"We've got to figure a way out of this," he told us. I took this to mean he wanted the NFLPA to order players to stop protesting.

I reminded Jerry that the demonstrations weren't occurring during the game. The national anthem is no more part of the contest than an Olympic medal ceremony is part of the bobsled competition—part of the event, yes, but not the game. No player had knelt during a time-out or even during a touchdown celebration.

Jerry seemed to agree that Trump's tone was too harsh. Then he went on about how, for the first time in thirty years, the ol' Arkansas boy might have a direct line to the Oval Office.

Jerry was again faced with a choice. What was he going to do with it this time?

Climbing back into the SUVs that would take us back to the Cowboys' aging Valley Ranch facility, where all those Super Bowl teams had been assembled, Jerry said he'd call Trump. Maybe, he said, he could get him to lower the temperature.

■   ■   ■

ON NOVEMBER 8, 2016, Karen went to bed early. I stayed up late, watching the election returns. Ohio and its eighteen electoral votes went for Trump.

"Geez fla is close," I texted my friend Eric Holder, who had stepped down as Barack Obama's attorney general fourteen months earlier.

He tried to reassure me but admitted it was unsettling that Democratic nominee Hillary Clinton wasn't exactly crushing Trump and issuing a full-throated repudiation of his inflammatory rhetoric. Someone else sent me a "firewall map" of supposed blue states whose electoral votes would be safe: Virginia, Pennsylvania, Michigan, Wisconsin. A narrow Clinton victory was the worst-case scenario, this person insisted.

Hours passed. I drank wine before switching to Johnnie Walker Blue around the time newscasters called Florida for Trump. Clinton took Virginia, Trump claimed Iowa and Utah, leaving it to the supposed firewall. Then, at 1:35 A.M., Pennsylvania went for Trump.

"OMG," I texted Eric.

An hour later, Wisconsin went red. Michigan would follow, and Clinton called Trump to concede. I stumbled to bed and told Karen that our country had just elected Donald J. Trump as president. It would be okay, I told Karen and myself, the voice of Kraft echoing in my mind that Trump didn't believe the things he'd said. It had all been an act; a revolutionary, if vulgar, way to energize normally inattentive voters.

The next morning, I woke into a landscape that felt alien. On an intellectual level, I understood the implications of Trump's election. But emotionally? I distracted myself from my feelings of dread and fear, a skill I had honed since I was an undergraduate at Cedarville, with my dark skin and blown-up knee. I would go on to perfect the art of denial, shedding my self-doubt as easily as a snake leaves behind its skin. De Smith needn't be afraid, because at the snap of my fingers or the clicking off of a few push-ups, here came DeMaurice Fitzgerald Smith to save the day.

If anyone insisted that I face my fears or process unpleasant thoughts, it had always been easy enough to muffle those voices with alcohol or work. The chronic discomfort in my belly or the tension in my chest wasn't anxiety; it was adrenaline. Because this is what suc-

TURF WARS

cess feels like. It is simply what it takes, and if it were easy or comfortable, everybody would be successful.

Adrenaline, I could live with. Anger, I could manage.

Fear? Doubt?

No room in my mental inn, or in the world I had created, where I was always at the top of my game. If I failed or even struggled, it was my fault. Half-hearted effort—on the track, in law school, in a courtroom. I'd work harder tomorrow, push myself a little more, rack my brain until the right strategy struck. Often it was during the wee hours that inspiration struck, tomorrow's solution to today's mistake. Rest could always wait.

Back in college, I'd run the quarter-mile relay twenty times in my head before lacing my shoes. In the courtroom, I had already considered every possible question, answer, and surprise. In either setting, all that was left was the performance. I became addicted to preparation and game strategy—the thrill of the hunt—and I'd invent new problems to solve to feel as if I had done enough.

This went on for decades.

Then I got the NFLPA job, trying to apply logic and common sense to an ecosystem composed of young adults, the agents and financial advisers who cared less about morals than their commissions, and owners whose interests consisted of dollar signs and control. When I got elected, I honestly believed I could approach and engage owners like businesspeople. An outcome may not be a win-win, but businesspeople always factor in the cost of the fight. I had represented Halliburton and Bear Stearns and Ford Motor Company.

I wasn't some Nat Turner of K Street. I had gone to their law schools and worked in their firms. I was one of them, I told myself. Or at least I could speak their language.

It's amazing now how quickly the NFL beat this notion out of me. Owners refused to negotiate fairly or in good faith, and the Dallas Cowboys team doctor sued me personally when the NFLPA took a stand against prescription painkillers. These are men who, when challenged, are flabbergasted that you dare challenge them—then, once you corner them, they say: "We owe players money, yes, but you'll have to sue us to get it."

Players elected me because I vowed to stand up to a cadre of bullies. Because I truly believed that, if you stand up to a bully, they will back down. That the bad guys, with their corruption and racism and misogyny, will always lose.

Now one of the owners' guys had been elected president. Kraft was his apologist and friend, Miami Dolphins owner Stephen Ross would host a fundraiser for Trump, and New York Jets owner Woody Johnson would become Trump's ambassador to the United Kingdom. Eight NFL owners donated a combined $7.25 million to Trump's campaign and inaugural fund, each of them groveling to a man who'd been denied entry to their private club. Just two years earlier, Trump had attempted to purchase the Buffalo Bills. But he had challenged the league in 1983, founding the United States Football League's New Jersey Generals and suing the NFL for antitrust violations. But rather than discuss a merger or let Trump into their club, owners blackballed him, ignoring his 2014 attempt to bypass the league's bidding process for the Bills by offering $1 billion in cash.

After Trump was elected, my mind kept calling out for the New York State Department of Financial Services to get into the game. We would no doubt be dragged into a prefabricated culture war in which images, disinformation, and social media were Trump's preferred tools. When I visited locker rooms, I sensed anger but not contempt. Some guys felt strongly about standing during the anthem, but nearly everyone respected their fellow player's choice to kneel and understood that the union had to protect the rights of everyone. We owed it to everyone to make sure their voices were heard, and nobody was trying to force teammates to kneel or stand. Every union member is entitled to what labor law refers to as a "duty to defend," which means a legal obligation by the NFLPA to defend its members.

This is a legal obligation, but I believed it was also a moral obligation. And as the weeks and months passed, I felt overmatched at my inability to find a solution. I drank more, slept less, gamed out dozens of scenarios about messaging—especially when it came to Colin.

In 2014, he'd signed a six-year contract with the 49ers that would pay him a reported $115 million. The team could cut him before the 2017 season but would nonetheless owe him $14 million in guaranteed salary. In that scenario, Colin would be free to sign with another team, and if no team signed him, we had an easy collusion claim.

What wasn't easy was the repeated unforced errors on Colin's part. He was photographed at practice wearing socks with cartoon pigs dressed as police officers and later wore a T-shirt in Miami with a photo of Malcolm X meeting with Fidel Castro, the Cuban dictator. "Like minds think alike," the shirt read. Colin publicly defended Castro's education policies, drawing controversy in a city with more than a million residents of Cuban heritage.

I had no choice but to defend Colin's rights, but in private I couldn't help questioning his messaging discipline. Most times when we reached out to Colin or his team, we never heard back. What was he trying to achieve from this? What was his endgame? We had no idea.

Then, on March 1, 2017, Colin presented a scenario that my restless mind had never imagined. He voluntarily opted out of his 49ers contract to become a free agent. We learned that along with everyone else, from ESPN. This decision not only absolved the team from paying him the $14 million he was guaranteed, but it also severely undercut a best-case scenario for a grievance against the team. He was not cut. The free agency period came and went without Colin signing with a team, so he hired Mark Geragos, a celebrity lawyer based in Los Angeles whose clients included Michael Jackson, Bill Clinton's brother, and the lead singer of the Village People.

It's not uncommon for players to hire outside lawyers, but I believe it's in everyone's interests if all the attorneys are coordinated. I called a meeting in Washington and invited Colin and the various legal teams so that we could talk strategy. How might we manage a possible collusion case over the absence of offers for a quarterback who, in 2013, had started for San Francisco in the Super Bowl? What are the next moves? How should he engage with teams that do reach out to him?

On the morning of the meeting, the NFLPA legal team waited in a conference room. The start time came and went, and Colin wasn't there. Eventually a colleague poked his head in. Colin wasn't coming, the colleague said, but his representative was in the lobby. His manager? An adviser? Geragos?

No, it was Colin's publicist, wearing an all-white jumpsuit.

■ ■ ■

DURING THE SPRING and summer of 2017, Roger and I were talking more frequently than ever. There were days when I honestly believed he understood the purpose and power of player activism as a necessary stimulant to an overdue national reckoning.

There were other days when he seemed desperate to silence them. "How do we fix this?" he asked me during one of those latter days.

Fix . . . *what*? Police brutality? Racism? Or merely force an end to demonstrations?

"We just need to resolve it," he said.

But I would be skeptical of any league-endorsed resolution, because this was an organic movement by players. We didn't control it, and I wasn't going to try. My politics aside, these were grown men using their voices before the game actually started, and it was during one of my conversations with Roger that I let it be known that we would go to war if the league tried to silence them. An NFL rule change would have to be collectively bargained, and a unilateral decision to restrict a player's speech before a game would immediately result in a federal lawsuit. Besides, what constitutes the acceptability of one political display but not another? Players and groups of players kneel in prayer all the time, be it after a teammate is injured or after scoring a touchdown. The league has no problem with that, but it now wishes to regulate the same display but for different motivations? And who is the arbiter of those motivations?

Roger? The owners? Please. We would never agree to such a thing, especially given the league's history of overreaction and Roger's own tendency to be zero-sum. Any recommendation by the NFLPA would result in political Whac-A-Mole: snuff out one act only to watch another crop up in its place. This simply wasn't a straight-line issue, as I told the commissioner, so there could be no simple resolution. Roger made it clear that he needed *something* he could take back to owners. They were breathing down his neck and demanding he fix this, led by one particularly ornery owner in Dallas.

But I reiterated to Roger that I wasn't going to change my position. Beyond the philosophical impediments, American history has made a few things clear: Protest has always been a necessary catalyst to change, and oppressors always want to rid protest from their lines of sight. My ancestors got the whip or the cast-iron pan, my parents' generation had dogs and firehoses turned on them, and if Colin's experience was any clue into how owners were thinking about this, players were at risk of having their employment opportunities suppressed.

Roger was usually huffy by the time our calls ended. Then he'd call me again the next day, and though I was never excited to see his name pop up on my phone's display, he was at least trying to talk through an amicable solution rather than escalating this into another stupid war.

NFL training camps opened that July, and Colin still wasn't on a roster. It was undeniable what was happening. The league's PR machine had successfully disseminated a narrative that Colin's play had dipped the previous season, decreasing his chances of being a team's starter, and this—and this alone—explained why he didn't have a job.

It was ludicrous. Colin's best season wasn't 2016, but he nonetheless appeared in twelve games and passed for sixteen touchdowns to four interceptions. He wasn't a liability to his team, and it stretches credulity to suggest Colin was so bad that he didn't warrant an invitation to a training camp, where nearly one hundred players were competing for roster spots. With the utmost respect to some of the other quarterbacks in the NFL during that time, it was just impossible to believe that Brett Hundley (who accumulated a quarterback rating of zero in 2016), Bryce Petty (seven interceptions to three touchdowns), and Cody Kessler (twenty-one sacks in nine games) were good enough for roster spots but Colin was not. He was unemployed because of his refusal to back down. This was, pure and simple, a way for the league to show force against one rebel to the industrial fiefdom, lest the other serfs get any ideas.

Roger and I kept talking, but without the NFL making a move, we were at a stalemate. We would file a grievance on Colin's behalf, but in my mind, I knew that Colin's decision to opt out of his contract had made things more difficult.

Then a bomb dropped.

Two weeks after the regular season began, on a Friday night in Alabama, President Trump appeared at a rally in support of Luther Strange's run for Senate. Trump was bouncing from topic to topic when he landed on the NFL and player protests.

"Wouldn't you love to see one of these NFL owners, when somebody disrespects our flag, to say: 'Get that son of a bitch off the field right now,' " he told the crowd. " 'He is fired. He's *fired*!' "

News reports later would suggest that White House staff had no idea Trump would go there, but on Air Force One hours after the rally, Trump was watching television and noticed that this had been the line that drew the loudest, most enthusiastic response. Ever the opportunist, Trump realized he had struck political gold.

My phone went crazy. Player reps were calling from around the NFL, reporting that their teammates were furious. I'm not sure Trump realized the message he was sending to players, but I did. He had effectively called their mothers a "bitch," and especially for guys who welcome an opportunity to unleash their aggression, players were ready for a battle royale. Some Black players were discussing a mass protest by refusing to play that weekend. While that sounded good, it's not that simple for the lawyer running the NFLPA.

A mass action refusing to work qualifies as a strike, and our collective bargaining agreement includes a clause that forbids strikes by players and lockouts by owners. Initiating a work stoppage, or what we call a "wildcat strike," would nullify our collective bargaining agreement, granting the league an opening to sue players for damages. Such action would also shift the messaging away from the cause and allow owners to take the position that they had no choice but to sue players for breach of contract. The financial damage would be catastrophic.

My responsibility was to advise players of the risk, and ultimately they decided to play the games. By Saturday morning, most players had calmed down. I stayed in touch with staff whose job was to speak, and listen, to players. I had no information that caused concern. In fact, I heard nothing. That made me nervous. So I called Roger. I still wanted the league to publicly stand up for our players. My experience told me that this president would just drop an issue if it didn't take hold—then move on to another one.

"Now you have a much bigger problem," I told Roger. I could hear in his voice that he knew. None of the supposed friendly calls to the president, whether from Jerry or anyone else, had done any good.

The Sunday before Trump's remarks in Alabama, six Black players took a knee during the national anthem. The weekend after, two *dozen* guys knelt during a single game, before the Jacksonville Jaguars and Baltimore Ravens played in London.

"We're a unified front," Ravens linebacker Terrell Suggs told reporters. "There ain't no dividing us. I guess we're all son-of-a-bitches."

■  ■  ■

ON SEPTEMBER 20, 2017, a massive hurricane tore across Puerto Rico—already ravaged following a different storm that made landfall two weeks prior—killing nearly three thousand people and causing $90 billion in damage to the U.S. territory.

Trump spent his time not organizing aid or assessing the damage but rage-tweeting about the NFL. He posted nearly a dozen times about anthem protests and rescinded a previous invitation for the NBA champion Golden State Warriors to visit the White House.

"If a player wants the privilege of making millions of dollars in the NFL, or other leagues, he or she should not be allowed to disrespect our Great American Flag (or Country) and should stand for the National Anthem," Trump wrote on September 23. "If not, YOU'RE FIRED. Find something else to do!"

This sent the league into full-blown panic mode. This had all been avoidable, but because of the NFL's inaction and Roger's insistence on coddling owners, the train had gained steam and speed. Roger issued a statement that appeared to back players, saying that Trump's comments were "a failure to understand the overwhelming force for good our clubs and players represent in our communities."

I distributed a statement of my own, pointing out that "NFL Players are part of a legacy of athletes in all sports who, throughout history, chose to be informed about the issues that impact them and their communities. They chose—and still choose today—to do something about those issues rather than comfortably living in the bubble of sports."

That Sunday before every game, in every NFL city, players were kneeling. They had no intention of backing down, and nearly a decade later, I look back and think that this was my proudest day on the job. Hands had been forced, lines drawn. Before a nationally televised Monday night game, the Cowboys facing the Cardinals in Arizona, I traveled to Phoenix. The NFLPA director whose responsibilities included the Cowboys reported that he had heard that players were discussing a moment of unity. The entire traveling party was planning to kneel. Because the game was to be broadcast on ESPN, millions of eyeballs would be trained on whatever happened.

What would Jerry do? I had to see for myself.

So I walked through a tunnel at University of Phoenix Stadium and stood on the boundary as a long line formed. The display was to take place before the anthem, not during it. I saw Jerry, at the end of the line, dressed in a powder blue blazer and black pants. His eyes were following the TV cameras, whose operators were swarming toward the line's center. So there went Jerry, bolting down the sideline, jamming his way between punter Chris Jones and receiver Dez Bryant. Right near the middle. I had to chuckle at Jerry being Jerry, forever the grocer's son, as he locked arms with the players at his side.

Then, in a sight I could barely believe, everyone dropped to a knee. I didn't care that there were audible boos in the crowd, in part because it proved that people were just pissed that players dare protest. It wasn't about the anthem or the military. They just wanted our guys to shut up and dance for them. I also didn't give a damn that Jerry had made himself the center of attention, winding up in every major photograph and highlight montage from the event.

Because this was one of the coolest, most moving things I had ever witnessed. For once, the league and its players were united. The sides had come together, if only for a moment, to issue a collective middle finger—knowing full well it was being beamed directly into the Oval Office.

■  ■  ■

A COUPLE OF weeks later, all hell broke loose. Attempting to capitalize on the Monday night moment, Roger and I arranged for a group of owners and players to meet in Washington, D.C. It would be a safe space where perspectives could be exchanged without judgment or penalty.

I should've known this plan was doomed when owners dug in their heels on the meeting place: a conference room inside the private terminal at Dulles International Airport. We had offered our downtown office, but apparently the thirty-minute drive into Washington was more than they could bear.

Roger made sure Kraft, Pittsburgh's Art Rooney II, and the New York Giants' John Mara were in attendance. Don Davis and I brought Washington players Kirk Cousins and Josh Norman, the Ravens' Benjamin Watson, Saints linebacker Demario Davis, and recently retired wide receiver Anquan Boldin. Josh and I hadn't seen eye to eye on certain issues, namely that he had suggested I was "in cahoots" with owners during an interview with *ESPN: The Magazine,* but I had nothing but respect for him attending the meeting, because he was nursing a set of bruised ribs from a recent game.

Demario explained the work that he, Josh, and Philadelphia safety Malcolm Jenkins were doing with what was being called the Players Coalition, a new group of mostly Black current and former players who were interested in possible overhauls to the criminal justice system. Anquan told the heartbreaking story of his cousin, Corey Jones, a musician whose SUV had broken down in Florida two years earlier. Jones was on the phone with roadside assistance when an undercover police officer pulled up and asked Jones if he was okay. Then the officer fired six bullets, three of which struck and killed Jones. This, Anquan explained, was why so many Black men fear law enforcement.

Another player explained that a former teammate with the Houston Texans had been tased by police during a routine traffic stop. Mostly just listening, I wondered if owners had ever thought about how closely police brutality hit home for players—and for everyday Americans of color.

This, Anquan continued, was why players were protesting: a way to get the nation's attention and inspire change. The owners seemed to be absorbing Anquan's words when, unprompted, Kirk Cousins chimed in.

"I just think we all need to understand," he said, "that kneeling may be hurting the game and having an effect on revenue."

My eyes widened.

I always liked Kirk, even when we had our disagreement about his understanding of the franchise tag, but I wasn't the only one flabbergasted that the only white player at the table was making this point. There's also a code that NFLPA business is family business; you never attack one another in mixed company. Now Kirk was doing just that, effectively discounting what Anquan and Demario had just passionately explained.

"Are there other ways?" he continued. "I'm just saying we should consider those."

I leaned forward, ready to interject. Before I could, Don beat me to it. By then he had become my consigliere, someone I trusted with my life and a man who could put into twenty-five words what I sometimes needed a thousand to do. No one loved players more than Don, in large part because he used to be a player, having gone from undrafted linebacker at the University of Kansas to eleven-year NFL veteran.

"Kirk," he said, "do you know what the Black players hear when you say that? That the n—rs need to shut up."

The room went silent, Roger's jaw dropped, and I reached under the table and squeezed Don's knee. *Eeeeaaassssy, big fella.* Sometimes a scalpel is more useful than a machete, at least conversationally speaking. But Don was right, and his point got the other players involved in the discussion again. We may not be fully united, as the owners just witnessed, but we weren't about to let them think we were desperate to find a solution.

It also allowed us to address the lost-revenue argument, which owners had been leaking to friendly reporters for weeks. The league's audit and finance team is highly sophisticated, with the ability to generate a spreadsheet that details the number of beers sold in a particular stadium during a time-out in the third quarter. Despite our requests, the league had produced no documentation to back up their claims that protests were hurting business. I had no doubt that owners loved the fact that Kirk had bought the lie and was now trying to advance it, largely because quarterbacks aspire to be owners and have the most in common with them.

The other thing was: Who gives a damn if the owners lose revenue? Some things, believe it or not, are more important than money. Should Rosa Parks have shuffled to the back of the bus because sitting up front was bad for Montgomery City Lines? Should the four Black teenagers in Greensboro, North Carolina, have ended their sit-in because it was bad for the bottom line at Woolworth's?

Kirk's remark had been simultaneously pandering to owners and intellectually lazy, and Don's rebuke of it wasn't so much a way to redirect the conversation as to reflect our collective exhaustion as we tried to teach a group of players that there is no success without sacrifice—that the key part of my old rallying cry wasn't just about well-informed players.

It was about those willing to act.

Josh, Anquan, and Demario were there to prove that willingness and that they would accept whatever consequences came their way. They were there to look owners in the eye and prove that this moment was heartfelt and genuine.

The rest of the conversation was cordial, but two of the owners across from us clasped their hands and leaned back. I had noticed a change in Kraft after Trump's diatribe in Alabama. His friend had come off as unhinged, and Kraft made it clear in our meeting that he was appreciative of the players' perspectives and that he hated the president's attempts to divide Americans based on race and class. He explained that he had experienced racism, too, when owners of radio stations decades earlier had refused to sell to Kraft because he's Jewish.

This comparison wasn't the best, especially on the heels of Anquan's story about his murdered cousin, but Kraft was trying. That's more than I could say for Rooney and Mara. It was also Kraft at his best, because he was negotiating with his fellow owners without taking them on directly. His story wasn't even directed at our side of the table. It was meant to convey to Rooney and Mara that this was all personal and that he hadn't once brought up the league's business interests. Once again, it had been Kraft who exuded both gravitas and morality.

"I hear what everybody is saying," Rooney said quietly. Then he leaned forward for emphasis. "But I'm in Pittsburgh, and let me tell you one thing: No one in Pittsburgh is *ever* going to kneel there."

His statement had nothing to do with his or any player's act so much as it was a rebuke to any notion that the owners had softened their stance. Rooney and his father, Dan, had always been nice to me. But this showed the steely side of the ruthless negotiator I had dealt with during collective bargaining agreement negotiations in 2011. He didn't raise his voice. A trained lawyer, Rooney is careful with his words but can speak in a condescending tone, especially when he gets impatient.

The following Sunday, Trump dispatched Vice President Mike Pence to Indianapolis. In what clearly was a staged event, Pence dramatically left the Colts game before tweeting that neither he nor the president would attend an event that "disrespects our soldiers, our Flag, or our National Anthem."

Trump continued on his social media soapbox, suggesting that NFL games were boring and that television ratings had plummeted. Roger, he suggested, was presiding over a league that was increasingly soft and losing its way.

Not long after that, Roger called me. When Roger is stressed, he skips all small talk. There was desperation in his tone. I wouldn't learn until later that Jerry had spoken with Trump, as he had promised Don and me. But it hadn't resulted in the president laying off the league and protesting players.

Something had gotten Jerry so animated that he was threatening to go nuclear, and by the sound of Roger's voice, Jerry had his sights trained on the embattled NFL commissioner.

. . .

**AS I HAD** learned, time and again, the controversies I dealt with and those the public learned about were usually rooted in secret wars among the owners. Jerry's Cowboys ruled the 1990s, but the next decade belonged to the Patriots and Kraft.

This was a time of considerable jealousy, which led to shots being fired.

I can't definitively say who was behind Spygate, but I have a theory. Next came Kraft insisting that Jerry and Washington's Daniel Snyder be penalized for overspending the secret salary cap during the 2010 season. Deflategate followed, dragging on for years, with Kraft's golden boy sullied, and applying an asterisk to those three New England championships.

In August 2017, my old friend Todd Jones, the league's discipline czar, found "substantial and persuasive evidence" that Cowboys running back Zeke Elliott had been physically violent with his ex-girlfriend. Video had emerged from a separate incident in which Elliott was seen pulling down a woman's shirt at a Saint Patrick's Day festival, exposing the woman's breast. The actual investigator on the case, Kia Roberts, interviewed complaining witnesses and others before recommending that there be no suspension because of credibility issues surrounding those witnesses.

We learned that her conclusions never made it into the final NFL report, which resulted in a six-game suspension for Elliott. That's tantamount to a federal prosecutor pushing through a case despite a lead

detective or FBI agent dropping by our office and insisting the defendant was innocent. Things work differently behind the NFL shield,
but I couldn't help wondering if this was just the latest battle between
a pair of silver-haired generals.

The NFLPA nonetheless sued the league, and front and center
was Lisa Friel, a former Manhattan district attorney who had been
appointed by the NFL as special counsel for investigations. Friel had
failed to include her own direct report's recommendation in the Elliott
case, and we later learned that this wasn't the first time Friel had been
accused of withholding credible information that someone may not
be guilty. In 2011, she was accused of failing to turn over exculpatory
evidence, which falls under material that lawyers are required to disclose, and Friel stepped down from her job after allegations of misconduct surfaced. According to Yahoo! Sports, multiple sources
claimed that Friel had been asked to resign.

This is the individual the league office turned to when it came to
investigating and potentially prosecuting players.

Our suit alleged that the disciplinary process in the Elliott case
had been an unfair sham, just another example of the league deciding
on an outcome before an investigation even began. We won the first
round, and a judge issued an injunction so that Elliott could play. The
NFL appealed, of course, and we refiled our suit with a higher court.
Back and forth we went, again, until Elliott dropped his appeal that
October.

Jerry, who I believe would trade years off his life for just one more
Super Bowl victory, would see his Cowboys trudge to a 9–7 finish. He
was absolutely livid, blaming Roger, his highest-paid employee, all
the while. But I was actually impressed by Roger's political prowess.
In just a few years, he had drawn the ire of the league's most powerful
owners, Jerry and Kraft, and survived. It was truly a marvel. Roger
had long eschewed having a second-in-command, throwing Troy Vincent to the wolves after Deflategate and, in 2018, accepting the resignation of Tod Leiweke, the league's chief operating officer.

Roger wasn't just playing key owners against each other, surely
knowing that Jerry and Kraft would be unable to bury their differ-

ences long enough to fire the commissioner. But just in case, Roger had summarily eliminated the most credible threats to his job.

Now Jerry was throwing a public fit, questioning Roger's tenure and his salary. Roger of course emerged stronger than ever, with a pay raise and a private jet as part of his compensation package. I couldn't help wondering if Kraft helped nudge through Roger's new contract as a way to stick it to his frenemy from Texas.

With the commissioner safe, Jerry turned his anger toward his own players. He threatened to suspend any member of the Cowboys who knelt or otherwise demonstrated during the anthem. It would be nearly impossible to enforce such a suspension, even by the great and powerful Jerry Jones, especially if more than a few players called his bluff. I knew that no player would test him, but more than that, I knew Jerry didn't actually care about the anthem *that* much. The words were more important to him than the potential actions, and that is precisely what drives other owners crazy.

At every owners' meeting, Jerry will stand up, say something wild, and then the league has to deal with it. I truly believe that if he declared that the moon were made of cheese and that the NFL should dispatch a rocket to get some of that cheese money, Roger would find a way to commission a rocket.

People outside football may think that's just Jerry being Jerry, but everyone on the inside knows he isn't just saying something crazy. As he did on the oil fields and in his first years as an owner, Jerry is talking something into existence in a way nobody else would. Now he'll try to find a way to back it up. Crazy talk is not idle talk, not with Jerry.

A few days after Jerry's threat, quarterback Dak Prescott said during a news conference that patriotic displays weren't "the time or the venue" for protests. I respect Dak, but when a Dallas artist painted a mural featuring Dak confined to the "sunken place" from the film *Get Out,* I had to chuckle.

Jerry wasn't in a joking mood. He was becoming more defiant and unhinged, prompting some owners to call me to vent. During an owners' meeting, Jerry had stood up and declared himself the "senior ranking owner," which is not an actual designation, and demanded to be added to the league's compensation committee. The NFL has about a dozen small committees—usually made up of owners, executives, and coaches—that oversee various league matters, including stadium issues, on-field competition, and guidelines for health and safety. Owners compete against one another for what they deem the most prestigious committees and chairmanships, the pinnacle of which is the league's management council executive committee, consisting of the handful of owners who negotiate with me and the NFLPA during collective bargaining meetings.

The compensation committee isn't particularly prestigious or interesting. It has five members, all owners, and their only responsibility is determining the pay of top executives in the league office. Jerry has been part of fifteen committees since he bought the Cowboys, but this was the first time he had expressed interest in joining the compensation committee, ostensibly because it was a surefire way to manipulate Roger's salary or hold it hostage.

"He talks more, and he makes less sense," one owner told me. "The whole room is kind of sick of listening to him."

Another pointed out that Dan Rooney, the Steelers' longtime owner and Art's father, grew into a statesman as he aged. Not Jerry. I was certain Jerry couldn't care less about how other owners viewed him, considering his contempt for most of them, but it was clear that Jerry was channeling his frustration into being increasingly offensive, disrespectful, and vengeful. And proud of it.

Roger, for his part, avoided fits of emotion. He was stoic and measured around owners, several of whom wondered aloud if Roger's refusal to placate Jerry had further incensed the Cowboys owner. Some were vocal in their delight that Roger had punished Elliott despite Jerry's hostility.

But with me, whether over a drink or in our now-frequent phone conversations, Roger wasn't measured. He sounded exhausted and stressed. The commissioner's drink was chardonnay, mine scotch, and no sooner had the glasses arrived before Roger was insisting that the league had to do something about the protests. He claimed it was about pacifying sponsors, but I knew it was really about silencing Trump.

Roger was the same old commissioner, but over the previous year, it didn't feel as if I were dealing with the same person. He had traditionally presented himself as all-powerful and omnipotent, the guy who bends television networks and streamers to the NFL's will and has never shied away from declaring war on anyone, including his league's biggest stars. At all times, Roger was the apex predator, impervious to any threat.

Trump's onslaught had gotten to him, though. The guy came across as something that jarred even me: powerless.

"What do you think is going to happen?" I asked him.

"It's just that a number of sponsors . . ." Roger stammered.

"Which sponsors?" I asked.

"You know, they're expressing concern."

"*Who* is concerned?" I asked.

Papa John's, the pizza chain whose owner, John Schnatter, was a Trump donor, was blaming the NFL for his company's sluggish sales and pressuring the league to end protests. Schnatter, whose face frequently appeared in Papa John's commercials, would be forced out as chief executive officer in December 2017 after making controversial remarks about NFL protests during a call with investors. He quit the company outright months later after using the N-word during a media training session.

"Is our business so fragile that we need to worry about a pizza sponsorship?" I asked.

Roger didn't respond.

I knew it wasn't Papa John's he was worried about. It was Uncle Jerry and the other narcissists who pay him. Roger was used to dancing for them, and now he was working overtime to indulge both their political preferences and their entitlement. At least to me, this seemed like the first time Roger acknowledged that he was in the employ of madmen, along for the ride with Jerry and others at the wheel. The commissioner had tried to take the keys, disable the vehicle, call a taxi. But they would never let him drive, so all he could do was ride, cross his fingers, and attempt to navigate.

Roger, in other words, had lost control.

■  ■  ■

WHEN I RESUMED my visits to team facilities, my assistant, Mark Cobb, called when I was in the Steelers' locker room. This was highly unorthodox, so I stepped aside and answered. "Call George immediately," Mark said in his crisp, big voice.

I did, and George told me that he'd been contacted by *The Wall Street Journal* about a story regarding Roger's "secret defender" on social media. It was his wife, Jane Skinner Goodell, who had been posting supportive messages from a handle by the name of "Jones Smith," usually directed at media outlets who'd been critical of her husband. The same account had taken shots at me, including suggesting that "D Smith sounds like D Trump with the inaccurate fire-bombs" following my comments in an ESPN story.

George told me that Kraft had attempted to get Rupert Murdoch, the media tycoon who owns the *Journal,* to kill the article. Murdoch had refused. George then said Roger was planning to call me and apologize, but all these years later, I'm still waiting on that call.

The guy clearly had his hands full, and I heard that Jerry was gathering a group of anti-Roger owners. I have had clients who Jerry reminded me of, and time and again, I was relieved when they fired me or I parted ways with them. Roger couldn't fire the owners, but he could stand up to them and tell them to knock it off or get on with firing him.

He could tell them that indulging Trump was stupid and dangerous. Paul Tagliabue had reached his own breaking point as commissioner a dozen years earlier, learning that, left to their own devices, owners were irrational and self-defeating. Tagliabue had spent years protecting them from their worst impulses.

Roger had always let the billionaires be billionaires: ruthless, petty, petulant. He was never going to wrestle the keys from Jerry or Kraft, even if it meant doing the right thing.

■  ■  ■

IN OCTOBER 2017, I joined several protesting players and a few members of the NFLPA executive committee for a meeting at NFL headquarters. I watched Roger the whole time. I couldn't decide if his deference to owners was admirable or pathetic, even when they put him in an impossible position.

It had recently become public that Bob McNair, who owned the Houston Texans, had said during an owners' meeting that the league couldn't have "inmates running the prison." McNair attended our meeting, too, knowing Roger would clean up any mess.

When Philadelphia Eagles owner Jeffrey Lurie tried to relate to the players' cause, clumsily saying that it had been *his* generation that ended the Vietnam War by protesting, Roger just squirmed. Nobody understood that era or the fallout better than Roger, considering that his father's bold stance killed Charles Goodell's career and possibly shortened his life.

The worst part was that Lurie never arrived at a point to his statement. If players were waiting for him to suggest that he understood the power of protest, their reward was silence. Lurie, whose family fortune came from a chain of movie theaters his grandfather started, just wanted to take credit for something else he hadn't done.

The meeting accomplished nothing except allowing owners to claim they'd sat down with players. Roger kept the trains moving, and three months later, he signed a new five-year contract extension that would pay him at least $200 million. Jerry had hired a lawyer and threatened to sue his fellow owners, which got him booted from the compensation committee he'd forced his way onto, another of his oddball gambits.

I spoke with Jerry the following spring, and he winked at me and claimed that he'd just been tuggin' on the ol' commissioner's tail, just playin' politics and generatin' competition.

"I'm a showman, but you gotta have some reasonableness in you," he told me. "If I hadn't had concussions, I might've been president of the United States. But I had to settle for just runnin' the Cowboys."

Owners are so uniformly mean and nasty that, by virtue of being folksy and amusing, Jerry strikes me as different. I got along with him, helped by the fact that we both prefer our Johnnie Walker Blue, and despite our obvious contrasts, our family stories aren't all that dissimilar. Both of our fathers left home, took a chance, and never looked back as they tried to cut a better path for their sons. Jerry and I both learned to speak to and get along with people who have a different skin tone, to see the world and talk about it in a new way, which in some ways alienated us from the places that made us.

But that's where the similarities ended.

Because when our paths brought each of us to life's biggest crossroads, whether to sell our soul or keep it, Jerry made his choice and I made mine. Jerry, who came of age during the Civil Rights Movement, chose greed. I elected to fight corruption, greed, and men like him. That doesn't mean we can't share a drink and a laugh. It does mean that we'll never be on the same side.

When we finally reached the end of the 2017 season, it felt as if it had lasted four years. I went on vacation to Italy, attempting to escape the realities of home, and I had already decided that we would file a grievance in the event of unilateral action by the NFL. Owners were busy trying to trick our guys, including calling a secret meeting at the league office without alerting me or Eric Winston, our union's president. This was the NFL attempting to bypass collective bargaining, hold an informal conversation, and issue some sweeping ruling before claiming that they had gotten approval from players.

As soon as we heard about the meeting, Eric and I started calling guys and telling them the meeting was a farce. When I reached Zak DeOssie, the New York Giants' long snapper and a member of our executive committee, he told me that John Mara, the team's co-owner and the chairman of the league's management council, had personally invited Zak to the meeting.

"I understand if you need to go," I told Zak. That's a lot of pressure, especially for a long snapper, for his team's owner to ask him to attend.

"Fuck it," he said. "I'm not going."

In May 2018, owners met in Atlanta to welcome David Tepper, a hedge fund billionaire with a short fuse, into their fraternity of coolest nerds in America. They also unilaterally voted on a new anthem policy. Every vote was in favor of requiring players to "stand at attention" during the performance, and individual clubs could set their own policy. Any offense would result in the league issuing a fine to the *team,* which it could then pass along to the player.

Clever as it may have seemed, it still violated our collective bargaining agreement. George called me as soon as the news broke, and because I had already downed a bottle and a half of wine, I ended that call and initiated another. Kraft picked up, and I let him have it: about the rule, about him not even giving me the courtesy of a heads-up, about the general audacity of the owners. He encouraged me to call Roger, and I told Kraft that wouldn't be necessary because my next call would be to instruct our lawyers to file a federal antitrust lawsuit: Our players' rights were being violated.

I remember saying something about a bloodbath, and that I planned to suggest to every player in the league that he kneel during the sixteen commercial time-outs during every game, during every end zone celebration, before the anthem, after the anthem, and during the coin toss. Before I could conjure more nonsense, Kraft conferenced in Roger.

"The one year we can kick off a season with no pending case," I said, "and damned if you bunch of freaking Einsteins didn't decide to kick another round of shit toward us again."

I repeated to Roger my plans to have players kneel every chance they got. He hemmed and hawed, again spouting talking points about sponsors, because he knew. Nobody was losing money. Fans were still coming to games and tuning in. No sponsor was dropping out. This was solely about the owners' need to control. He knew that I knew that, because Roger and I had already had this conversation.

"But hey," I continued, "now I get to make it an issue again, because America needs to keep talking about it."

As soon as I was back in the office, we filed a noninjury grievance and began preparing the most aggressively wonderful First Amendment complaint. The league itself had said players were allowed to use their platform to elevate issues important to them. Why was *this* a problem? What made them change their minds? What delicious morsels existed in the cellphones of people like Jerry, McNair, and others from certain high-ranking government officials like, say, the president?

This is Christmas morning for a trial lawyer, and we didn't even have to win. The lawsuit would extend the conversation in a way that not even the on-field protests could.

"De," Kraft told me during another call, "we are not in the straight-line business."

Yeah, no shit, because owners were making a simple trip between point A and point B routed through Connecticut, then Kansas City, with a side trip to North Dakota, around their asses to touch their elbows, before an overnight train to Atlanta. And because it's owners at the wheel, the league still careens off a cliff before exploding on impact.

Absolutely none of this was sophisticated or professional, and this extended to our side. The Players Coalition was imploding, dealing with internal issues that revolved around poor communication. We offered them support and organizational resources, and it was important for us to make it clear that we were there to help. But the union couldn't create a reason for them to exist, nor could we define their endgame. At first the objective seemed to be getting Colin onto an NFL roster, with some players pledging to continue protesting until he was signed. But did he even *want* to get signed?

Colin and Eric Reid, a former San Francisco teammate who had knelt alongside Colin, filed their own collusion grievance against the league in October 2017. Had they done so in order to compel the league to help Colin get a job? Who knew? Because neither of those guys communicated with us. Ever. Malcolm Jenkins, an intelligent and thoughtful person on top of being a Pro Bowl safety, took up the mantle of leading the movement after Colin and Eric ghosted. Then, late in 2017, the NFL made a deal with the Players Coalition in which the league pledged to spend nearly $90 million over seven years on social justice causes and grants targeted at predominantly Black communities. The day before the deal was announced, several players left the Players Coalition over disagreements with the founders, and protests essentially ended.

Looking back, I cannot imagine that Colin was prepared for how big his protest would become or what would be required of him to sustain it. It was clearly the right time and right issue for such a demonstration, but the messenger was a disorganized exemplar of the message. This was no time for naivety, considering the stakes, and Colin began his protest out of nowhere, without the weeks of groundwork, messaging, and goal setting that can protect both messenger and message. Why he declined our help, I can only speculate. I assume he wanted to carry it to the finish line himself. The grievance the union filed on his behalf was working its way through the process.

Compare this to Bill Radovich's suit against the league in 1946, after teams blacklisted him when he left the Detroit Lions because he wanted to be closer to his dying father in California. When no team signed him, Radovich took a job as a Hollywood stunt man and funded his own ten-year legal battle against the NFL, taking it all the way to the Supreme Court. The Court ruled unanimously in Radovich's favor, and while he was no longer physically able to play football, he won on principle. His tenacity also subjected the league to antitrust laws, which, forty years later, allowed players to sue the NFL in their own cases to achieve free agency and the first collective bargaining agreement.

In February 2019, on the other hand, we learned from ESPN that Colin and Eric's lawsuit had been settled. We have no idea what the terms were or how much money was exchanged because the settlement prohibited them from telling us. The league claimed it donated money to charity, but there's no way to prove that, and *The Wall*

*Street Journal* later reported that making Colin, Eric, and the protests go away cost less than $10 million.

. . .

A FEW MONTHS after the settlement, we heard that the league was organizing a group of team representatives for a private workout that Colin was planning to hold in Atlanta. Roger had been encouraging teams behind the scenes to at least consider scheduling a workout with Colin, and now the commissioner was urging franchises to send scouts to Atlanta.

Colin would conduct football drills and sit for interviews, and the receivers who'd catch Colin's passes would get a tryout of their own. Twenty-five teams arranged travel for scouts, and the league sent a liability waiver in case Colin got injured. Jerry sent no one from the Cowboys.

The league and Colin's lawyers negotiated the particulars for four days, and on the afternoon of the tryout, Colin's team sent new demands. The league said no. I dispatched two NFLPA representatives to the tryout, thinking this would likely be the prelude to another round of warfare. I wanted our own people in attendance.

On the day of the workout, two and a half hours passed with no update from Colin's side. The wide receivers were left to twist in the wind. Late in the day, Lester Archambeau, an NFLPA staffer who oversees certain teams, called me to report that the tryout was moving. It had been scheduled to take place at the Atlanta Falcons' practice complex in Flowery Branch, Georgia. Now?

"He's apparently going to a high school field," Lester told me.

The league heard this from Colin's lawyers.

"Sorry," a member of his legal team texted to a league attorney, according to *USA Today Sports*. "We're going to go in a different direction."

The high school field was sixty miles away. Most teams bailed. Reps from a half-dozen franchises trekked south and watched Colin zip passes to high school players. A documentary crew filmed the showcase. Even Mark Geragos, Colin's attorney, agreed it was nothing more than a publicity stunt. And to no one's surprise, Colin was offered no contract.

A short time later, Michael Rubin, the founder of Fanatics and a close friend of Kraft's, suggested we meet to discuss a resolution to the anthem issue. I wasn't in favor of any rule that threatened players, and though no punishments had been levied, we still had a legal basis to escalate our grievance. Eric Winston and I met Roger and Kraft at a high-end seafood restaurant on Washington's southeast waterfront.

We talked, laughed, negotiated. Kraft offered to have the league kill its anthem rule if we withdrew our lawsuit. Eric and I agreed, and to celebrate, Kraft ordered shots of Don Julio 1942 tequila. When the bartender brought four chilled glasses, Kraft attacked his. Mr. Chardonnay studied his drink before reluctantly sipping it. I raised my glass and looked out the floor-to-ceiling windows toward the Washington Channel. Expensive boats were docked along a stretch that had recently been renamed The Wharf, part of a $2.5 billion revitalization effort that added luxury condos, hotels, and restaurants like this one.

In the 1950s, this was a low-income neighborhood where 70 percent of the residents were Black, not unlike the Ross City community in Arkansas where Jerry Jones grew up. Those families were systematically pushed out, unable to afford to live in their own homes so that people like us could eat charcuterie, drink fifty-dollar-a-glass tequila, and toast victory. I nonetheless downed my shot, realizing that I was sitting at another crossroads. Colin's protest had caused conflict and exposed the league's racism. But in the world beyond these windows, it hadn't done a damn thing. The tequila's burn subsided, but I couldn't chase away a disquieting thought: Money has the power to change things, sure, be it neighborhoods or people.

That doesn't necessarily mean it makes those things better.

# 8

# FRIENDLY FIRE

Most years before the Super Bowl, Roger and I would meet up in advance of our respective news conferences. It was ostensibly a chance to set aside our disagreements, get on the same page, and give each other a heads-up about the topics we may be addressing.

The league never likes negative publicity, but it loathes any surprise or off-field drama during the run-up to the Super Bowl. It's the biggest, most important event on the annual sports calendar, with more than 120 million viewers tuning in. The game is the ultimate showpiece for the NFL and the juxtaposition of capitalism's excess and time for the league to flex its corporate muscles. Estimates suggest that each network pays about $2 billion to air the Super Bowl, and though the game's halftime performers are megastars with global audiences—Usher, Lady Gaga, and Bruce Springsteen, to name a few—the league doesn't pay them a dime. It is a weeklong appreciation of a sport and its best two teams, but it also is a showcase of the league's cultural and financial might.

Months after we came to our agreement on anthem protests, Roger and I were still communicating often. We were, dare I say, getting along better than ever—largely because we were both dealing with dysfunctional caucuses. Or maybe I was finally starting to understand him.

The nation was growing more polarized as Donald Trump's presidential term advanced, and owners seemed desperate to avoid the president's ire. Months after Trump rescinded the Philadelphia Eagles' invitation to the White House following the team's Super Bowl win, Robert Kraft and Los Angeles Rams owner Stan Kroenke attended a dinner with Trump to smooth things over.

On our side, a feeling of disunity was omnipresent. Trust in traditional media had been eroding for decades, and amid a dramatic fragmentation of the industry, our two thousand members were no longer reading and listening to the usual voices. Like many Americans, they were at the mercy of their own echo chambers, with some starting to express not only contempt for me but skepticism of the union itself. Stress was evident within our executive committee, and though Eric had retired from being a player, I could see the exhaustion on his face. I couldn't help wondering if we could effectively communicate our message amid such powerful disinformation.

"We're not getting through to these guys at all," Eric said.

My meeting with Roger in January 2019, therefore, felt less like an inevitable bickering session than a chance to trade war stories. We were just two guys trying to get through the day, even with a formidable showdown on the horizon. Our 2011 collective bargaining agreement was set to expire in two years, and I had already begun trying to educate our new leaders—many of whom were in high school in 2011—about our union's history, the way owners think, and ultimately how they must be negotiated against. It seemed to me that some of our player leadership had checked out. Union work is grueling on its own, and these responsibilities on top of playing football must be exhausting.

Still, the union had begun polling players to identify the key issues for the next collective bargaining agreement, and I planned to tip my hand to Roger. I already knew what the league cared about: adding games to the season, which gives them even more leverage during negotiations with network executives. The regular season had been sixteen games since 1978, and until our 2011 deal, the league had unilateral authority to add games. Now we had veto power, and nearly a decade after Roger boldly predicted that league revenue would reach $25 billion by 2027, I suspected owners would trade plenty for us to turn our key on an expanded season.

Our pre–Super Bowl meeting was cordial, but because Roger is bad at small talk, he immediately got down to business and told me that owners would be insisting on an eighteen-game regular season. That'd be an impossible sell, I told him, at least without a major concession.

Among the issues we cared about were players' overall health and the increasingly irresponsible way teams were dispensing painkillers. Toradol, a high-octane anti-inflammatory, was seen as a badge of courage by many players, not only before games but before practices, too. Some players rarely took the field without boarding the "T-Train," as they called it. But while the medication indeed dulls the sensation of pain, our medical experts feared that its anti-coagulant chemicals could result in brain bleeds following a concussion or subconcussive injury.

I told Roger that injecting players day after day, ignoring the fact that their bodies were crying out for time to heal, was immoral. He nodded. I interpreted this as a signal that he was okay if I went hard on the topic.

Pivoting to my upcoming news conference, I let Roger know that I had recently filmed an interview for a hard-hitting documentary called *A Woman's Work,* about a troubling controversy surrounding the poor pay and toxic treatment of NFL cheerleaders. A 2014 lawsuit claimed that Oakland Raiders cheerleaders were paid below minimum wage, had to buy their own uniforms and pay for them to be cleaned, and were expected to attend charitable events for free. The Raiders settled for $1.25 million in 2017, but that was hardly the end of the scandal.

Staffers in the Washington Redskins' video department had reportedly been instructed to illicitly film cheerleaders while they changed clothes, before marking the videos "For Executive Meeting," which allowed members of the team's front office to leer at topless employees. Daniel Snyder, the team's owner, had been accused of sexual assault and paid one alleged victim $1.6 million to settle out of court. Jerry Jones had been the subject of similar claims, including that he had allegedly impregnated a woman in the 1990s, and Kraft would be accused in 2019 of receiving sexual favors at a Florida massage parlor.

"I'm coming off the top rope," I told Roger, letting him know that I had blasted the league and him during my documentary interview.

He again nodded. Then he blew out a sigh. The league was on track to make $15 billion in 2019, and owners were still pinching pennies by refusing to pay cheerleaders what they deserved and refusing to hold one another to account.

"I get so tired of covering for these guys," Roger said.

■ ■ ■

**AT THE MEETING** of player reps in March 2019, the most important issues ahead were on the lips of almost everyone. Regardless of the union, this is how proposals begin to take shape. Membership articulates the things they care about, and leadership starts ranking them in order of priority. It also helped me understand what guys actually cared about.

Russell Okung, a veteran offensive tackle, had been elected to the executive committee in 2018. I was immediately struck by Russell's intellect and willingness to express an opinion. Before the Seattle Seahawks selected him in the first round of the 2010 draft, Russell played NFL agents against one another to negotiate a lower commission than the typical 3 percent. He later fired the representative he ultimately hired, Peter Schaffer, so Russell could do his own negotiations and save himself millions.

This was someone who clearly cared about social issues, including his position that college athletes should be compensated for the use of their name, image, and likeness, and thought about matters three-dimensionally. He invested in tech companies, bought cryptocurrency, and wrote an essay in *The Players' Tribune* to commend Colin Kaepernick's protest, underscoring it as a moment that proved the immense power of a motivated collective.

This was a person who simply refused to accept things as they had always been, which I found admirable. After a decade of feeling as if I were herding cats, I had hope that Russell Okung was the warrior—the *killer*—I had been waiting for.

Russell had been elected to the executive committee in 2018 on a platform of accountability—to owners and the league, yes, but also the NFLPA and me. He described a kind of economic populism that certainly sounded intriguing, despite the fact that it implied the union itself may have been compromised.

I certainly didn't love that he was putting my integrity in his crosshairs or parroting the league's bullshit talking points. But I kept an open mind. There is always an adjustment when a rank-and-file union member ascends to leadership, and besides, the full collective bargaining agreement and our financial documents are available to everyone on the committee. I told myself this was something I had seen before.

But these weren't the same old times.

The previous years had seen an increasing ubiquity of false claims, a general acceptance that facts and institutions can and should be challenged, and a once-mighty glacier of trust now calving into a zillion icebergs, with each one deeply skeptical of the others. Trump supporters may have been more vocal about their suspicions, but the supposed core Democrat—college-educated, racially diverse, and socially conscious—was by no means immune. Especially when conspiracy websites such as 4Chan and 8Chan were becoming more popular, with mainstream social media platforms emerging as breeding grounds for the once-fringe belief that government, media, and traditional leaders had been installed as pawns in a vast network of lies.

Russell refused to accept our documentation as fact, at first questioning the legitimacy of this evidence before demanding more. He was disruptive during meetings, often haranguing me about my lack of transparency, which resulted in us sending him more evidence that he would summarily disregard.

The misinformation virus was aggressively contagious, in particular among a group of individuals who have spent their lives pushing back against the stereotype that all star athletes are dumb jocks. I could see frustration growing in Eric, who would later wonder aloud about locker rooms becoming impenetrable silos.

Traditional corporations may encourage executives to find win-wins to narrow these philosophical divides. But pro football abides no tradition. The workforce ages out after only a few years, and the danger of the next negotiation isn't just a limitation of potential gains. It is that management is constantly looking to roll back the progress our side has already made and may take for granted. It is an infinite game, with considerable strength and unity on the side of owners. On ours? A bunch of new and younger faces who simultaneously have to learn our past while trying to sketch out a future they won't be around to experience.

All while trying to figure out who to trust.

The worst part was that there seemed to be no right way of handling someone who fully embraces a conspiracy. The very act of reasoning with them reinforces that there *is* conspiracy. We have seen this a thousand times. Facts, statistics, science, and common sense do not matter to a conspiracy theorist. There is some validity to letting it play out, but that assumes that people are willing to be diligent themselves.

*Just let it go,* I told myself. *The leadership will rise to the occasion.* I trusted them completely. What other choice did I have?

■ ■ ■

FEEDING MY STRENGTHENING anxieties, I again studied the National Hockey League's 2004 lockout for exactly how the league and its outside lawyers had publicly and internally battered their union. It had been a bloodbath for players. A yearlong work stoppage ended only when financially strained players agreed to a salary cap, massive pay cuts, and vague and draconian penalties for failed drug tests.

It's fair to suggest that the deal set players back decades. The sport itself never recovered, and I ruminated on the possibility that, for us, a similar fate awaited.

We had fought through a lockout in 2011, but there would be no secret insurance policy this time. That only works once. We had more money in reserve, but accurately appreciating the long-term risks of a work stoppage is my job, as is working to achieve a fair deal without one.

My only solace was that Roger had indicated the league's willingness to discuss an early deal, which gave us the chance to frame the discussion of a renewal. For once, time was on our side. The NFL's obsession with expanding the season meant that our first move should be to submit a proposal that didn't include extra games, and that we should shoot for the moon with our demands: more than 50 percent of all revenue, better benefits and healthcare, and improved rules about working conditions.

This was a simple framework, but doubt and internal discord delayed our proposal to the NFL by more than a month. Outside reports were delivered about the gains in the 2011 deal, but some guys skipped the meeting on those results despite having asked for it.

Owners became aware of our dysfunction, which eroded any leverage we may have had. The sides agreed to a confidential nonbargaining meeting at MetLife Stadium in New Jersey to just gauge interest in trying to get a deal done early. These kinds of meetings are informal, usually with no explicit agenda, but are nonetheless useful to "set the table" for actual bargaining later. Constitutionally, things like this are handled by the executive committee. Shortly before I arrived, our contingent learned that Russell had posted about the meeting on Twitter. To make matters worse, Russell was traveling to New Jersey on Chargers owner Dean Spanos's private jet. Once confronted with this violation of confidentiality, he harrumphed and suggested we should've known that he would post about it because he is active on Twitter.

Actual bargaining sessions with owners tend to be formal, with the rights of each side outlined by the National Labor Relations Act, including an encouragement that meticulous notes be taken in the event of an accusation of unfair labor practices. Russell decided to rant and rave about the antiquated nature of these policies, offering his unsolicited personal thoughts. Again, I was paralyzed, because which outcome is worse for our position: a member of our executive committee hijacking a negotiation, or Eric and me shutting him down in front of owners?

I always love Richard Sherman's passion. At times it ran white hot and could be directed at both me and his fellow members of the executive committee. There was only one moment when I thought that that passion might erupt into a fight with another player, and for reasons I am not allowed to go into, it would have been with good reason. Richard had a fierce loyalty to his fellow union leaders and Okung's actions left me questioning whether his only loyalty was to himself.

. . .

BY FEBRUARY 2020, players and owners had agreed on the framework of a new deal. More high-profile players, such as Patrick Mahomes, Von Miller, and Dak Prescott, had gotten more involved in union activity than ever.

"We're gonna flex some muscle," I texted Tom Brady one afternoon.

More than one hundred player leaders were set to meet in Los Angeles to review the contours of our proposed collective bargaining agreement, the culmination of dozens of negotiation sessions with the league. As expected, the NFL had insisted that every bargaining point be discussed with the expanded regular season in mind, and this allowed us the leverage to demand a 1.5-percentage-point increase in all revenue, and because one or more games would increase revenue league-wide, this would translate into $1.6 billion in player salary and benefits over the deal's term.

Our side had also demanded an increase of salaries to players who earn the league minimum, which applied to more than 60 percent of workers. Media and fans often get preoccupied by the massive salaries that the league's top stars command, but the truth is that the wage gap in the NFL isn't unlike the one that exists more broadly in America: a small number of people pocketing jaw-dropping amounts with a far larger group making dramatically less. Owners had agreed to give those lower earners a $200,000 annual raise, which I saw as small but important progress toward narrowing that gulf in earnings. The rookie league minimum would be $610,000.

We explained these provisions during our meeting, along with increases in pensions, the creation of a new preferred medical services plan targeted at retired players, and an increase to the "salary floor," the minimum amount franchises would be required to spend each year. At the conclusion of the presentation, we distributed cards and asked players to identify the three most important issues to fight for as we finalized negotiations. I reviewed the responses on the flight home, feeling vindicated when I saw that most guys identified matters we had already addressed, negotiated, and won. The guys took it seriously, and I was proud of them. More than one hundred men in the room sat through hours of instruction and debate before thoughtfully writing down their rankings. Only one person didn't.

Our next step was another meeting with players in Indianapolis, set for the same week as the NFL's annual scouting combine. Before we could send the proposal back to the owners, our constitution required a couple of final steps. The executive committee votes first on whether or not to send the document to the thirty player reps for approval. While the executive committee's vote isn't necessarily binding, it acts as a measure of confidence in the proposal and tends to be a bellwether for whether or not the wider membership will support it.

The toughest part of this job is dealing with changing facts. On one day, I could be armed with the knowledge of an executive committee vote to move forward with the process. Only to be surprised the next day when it switches.

For example, the demands of one person created the necessity of me stepping out of a room of players to call Roger Goodell to sheep-ishly ask for one more negotiation meeting with owners.

"Are you kidding?" he asked.

"We're all here," I said. "Let's just do it."

He said he'd call a meeting, and a short while later, a small group of us sat across from owners. Aaron Rodgers started by demanding that the league give us a higher share of all revenue. The owners had to bite their lips to avoid laughing.

"This is our final offer," one of them said.

Then Aaron explained his idea to ban OTAs. Art Rooney II, the Pittsburgh Steelers' owner, looked confused.

"You want us to put a ban on something voluntary?" he asked.

"Guys don't get paid," Aaron shot back, "so we shouldn't have to go."

"So don't go," Rooney said.

We left the room, but I nonetheless heard that some players were whispering that we should've fought for this or that. I knew that we *did* fight: These negotiations had gone on for nearly two years. But I also knew that I could scream that from the rooftops and some guys still wouldn't accept it.

Because in 2020, you could be a player sitting across from the owners, negotiating the deal, wrestling with the issues internally as a group. You could have that documented and still allow people to question what you did for two years. It was a time when facts just didn't matter. I couldn't help but shake my head at the paradox of living during an age in which people have never had greater access to factual information—while more people refuse to believe it.

Aaron, who'd been a player rep in 2011, was never my favorite guy. But this was the first time I actually experienced the antagonistic person I had heard about from other players. Aaron would cut off anyone who dared challenge him and his supposed intelligence, whether it was family, friends, or teammates. In the twilight of Aar-on's NFL career, he would force his way out of Green Bay, peddle bizarre theories about politics, medicine, and science while alternat-ing among being a quarterback, being a prospective *Jeopardy!* host, and being asked to be the presidential running mate of Robert F. Kennedy, Jr., a known vaccine skeptic and conspiracy theorist.

"Hard no on that proposed CBA," Houston defensive lineman J.J. Watt would later post on Twitter.

We were in a debate spiral. I knew I wasn't alone when I wondered how it was even possible to lead a group when high-profile players weren't supportive.

In hindsight, I now understand that some higher earners maybe didn't like the automatic raises in minimum salaries that shrunk the available pie for non-minimum players. But I liked this for the sole reason that it significantly helped the rank-and-file players, guys who have far less bargaining leverage than the stars.

■   ■   ■

AS NIGHT BECAME early morning, the debate turned to the proposed changes to the league's salary structure. The NFLPA and owners had tentatively agreed to add a seventeenth game to the regular season, and to make the math work, we suggested that any player who made less than $5 million per year would receive a prorated additional week tacked onto their existing salary.

Simple. Or so we'd thought.

The proposal to exclude guys who made more than five million was a compromise, but one that recognized that those players had significantly more bargaining leverage to rework their contracts at almost any time.

I heard from some agents who voiced their clients' concern that the extra check should go to their high earners as well.

Adding a prorated payment to top-earning players would mean that owners would have to increase players' revenue share, which was a nonstarter. What followed still bothered me: A collective bargaining agreement that requires the votes of these same reps meant that they decided to decrease the value of their benefits package so that the richest players would get an additional game check.

Guys who made less money, in other words, decided that they

would take less so superstars could get a tiny bit richer. Still, the vote passed. Barely. It was exactly two-thirds, in fact, because one player abstained. Had that player voted against the proposal, we would have been back to square one.

There were many players who made public their disagreement with the seventeenth game and the components of the deal, and some of them were union representatives. I never had a problem with them articulating their particular positions. A union vote is supposed to be messy because democracy is messy. I would be lying if there were some things that bothered me about the comments, however. First, there were several summaries of the deal so that players did not have to read the entire draft document. Dozens of agents requested these summaries, and we sent them so that they could have conversations with their clients. Second, while I am precluded by the NFLPA from referring directly to internal discussions among players, I was proud that players stood up to other players and spoke for the players in their locker rooms who should have had the right to vote on this deal rather than have it scuttled by those in Indianapolis.

■ ■ ■

ON MARCH 9, I traveled to South Florida for the NFLPA's annual board meeting and, I hoped, our chance to put the finishing touches on the new collective bargaining agreement. The NFL league year would end nine days later at precisely 4 P.M., after which point player contracts would officially expire. Free agency would begin, assorted league business would preoccupy franchises and the league office, and the union and owners would lose the chance to ratify an early deal.

The next three days, therefore, were important. But it wasn't the only thing on my mind.

Upon landing, I went to a local bookstore to pick up a copy of *The Great Influenza,* John M. Barry's fascinating but harrowing book about the 1918 Spanish flu. Instead of spending my evening reviewing my executive director's briefing, I immersed myself in the world's most recent pandemic, which had caused more deaths in a single year than the bubonic plague caused in a century. The influenza virus may have killed fifty million people, but Barry suggested that disinformation and a general distrust in the science community had led many of those people to their graves.

"Those in authority must retain the public's trust," Barry warned as he imagined a future pandemic. "The way to do that is to distort nothing, to put the best face on nothing, to try to manipulate no one."

That future was here.

In December 2019, an alarming number of patients in China had begun experiencing symptoms of a pneumonia-like illness. Established treatments were ineffective, leading the World Health Organization to label the pathogen as a novel coronavirus, meaning it was previously undiscovered. The virus, identified as SARS-CoV-2, was spreading remarkably fast. By the time I landed in Florida, at least 539 cases had been detected across thirty-four states, with sick patients beginning to fill hospital rooms in Miami.

Partly because of my reading material, I was terrified. Was the air toxic? Could handshakes lead to death? Was this the apocalypse? No one knew, but I internalized these questions and shared my concerns with no one. We had a deal to finalize, so I summoned *DeMaurice Fitzgerald Smith,* my fearless alter ego, who knew that discussing the coronavirus with anyone, including trusted members of the executive committee, risked that owners would catch wind of it and use the crisis as a scare tactic.

Roger and I were in almost constant communication then, and the terms of a new agreement were basically set. The league's management council executive committee had signed off on the deal's broad strokes, and the next stage was whether players would do the same. We were still dealing with the ramifications of the Indianapolis meeting, and some players had taken to social media to either criticize or support the deal. I was nonetheless confident that our group would recommend passage, bolstered by a video made by Ryan Fitzpatrick, the Harvard-educated Miami Dolphins quarterback, explaining why he would vote in favor of our proposal.

As players checked into the NFLPA hotel, Miami's Ritz-Carlton

Key Biscayne, I showed an outward calmness meant to conceal the crippling anxiety I was feeling. My brain was a congested superhighway of possible obstacles, filled in with a hum of game theory and potential solutions, clouded by the not-so-minor fear that the world might be ending. It was up to me to project confidence during my group presentations and meetings with individual players, many of whom had questions about a 456-page contract written mostly in legalese. To complicate matters a little more, the NFLPA had to also elect a new union president. Eric Winston, who had been in the position since 2014, had been a dedicated and passionate leader. He was also my wingman and friend.

The NFLPA's constitution stipulates that no president may serve longer than two years after his final NFL game, and Eric hadn't suited up since December 2017. The list of possible successors included thoughtful and compassionate men I was eager to work with: New York Giants defensive back Michael Thomas, Cleveland center JC Tretter, and Tampa Bay linebacker Sam Acho. But there was a fourth candidate whose inclusion gave me pause: Russell Okung.

And Russell's platform was intriguing. He wanted the union to be more aggressive, including that the NFLPA receive wider access to the league's financial statements. Other ideas were not rooted in reality. He insisted that union leadership and I were conspiring in a mass campaign meant to hide essential information from players. He produced no proof, of course, but his passion and delivery of these accusations served as a strong enough locker-room speech to get like-minded players fired up.

The NFLPA could audit the league's revenue, but Russell wanted financial documents that would itemize franchises' expenses. This ultimately didn't affect players, considering owners were required to spend a certain amount on salaries each year, and Russell's proposal ran aground when, time and again, he was faced with the inevitable follow-up question: Then what?

What was he planning to do with that detailed financial information? How did it benefit the union? If owners refused to turn over those documents, which they obviously would, then what? Would players strike? Refuse to negotiate? Russell talked in circles before demanding that players spike the collective bargaining agreement and start from scratch the following year.

Okay, but when next year arrives, then what? I am fine with someone demanding more financial information or any other collective bargaining agreement provision, but "then what" ultimately gets to the critical question of whether you are willing to miss games to get it. If so, fine. If you think you aren't, not fine.

Some theories may sound good, but their appeal has no bearing on realistically bringing those theories to life. It would instantly push all leverage toward the league. I knew that if this deal went away, players' only move would be to go on strike. I also knew this was highly unlikely. Much like the real world, management has financial leverage over workers. Strikes work only when they can inflict economic harm on both management and labor. It is a question of whether you are willing to fight, and to date no group of NFL players has ever done a mass skipping of voluntary practices.

"Whether you vote for this deal or not," I told the group, "you have to think about the consequences of that vote."

In other words, reject this proposal all you want.

But then what?

■  ■  ■

VOTING WAS SET to begin on Wednesday, March 11, and continue through Saturday. We emailed every NFL player and their agents the full draft of the collective bargaining agreement and also included a four-page comparison chart between the 2011 deal and this one, along with an eight-page summary of this current proposal.

Eric went through the details of each document with countless players, maintaining a patience I do not possess. But Eric's remarkable communication wasn't enough to avert a wider suggestion that we delay voting in favor of more debate.

This came with obvious risk, and I called a meeting with several colleagues, including NFLPA general counsel Tom DePaso. Among his core beliefs is that players always get it right. It may be frustrating and messy, but they get it right. I had spoken earlier that day with Bob Foose, my counterpart at the Major League Soccer Players Association, which was negotiating its own collective bargaining agreement and had written up a supposedly final proposal. But MLS team owners had tabled their proposal because of the coronavirus, and Bob speculated that owners knew that agreeing to a deal before a potentially cataclysmic economic event would be a mistake. I knew it was a matter of time before NFL owners figured this out and did the same.

To these guys, a global pandemic wasn't a once-a-century health emergency. It was a bargaining chip. Every second that passed was a second closer to Kraft, Jerry, and Giants co-owner John Mara realizing it.

But Tom and Don Davis reminded me that this is the *players* union, and if they were insisting on more time, it was my job to call Roger. So I did, and after issuing a long sigh, he said he would meet with the management council. I rolled the dice and brought up the coronavirus, asking if owners had begun discussing possible protocols for the 2020 season. Roger assured me that the illness was no more serious than a bad cold and that any proposed contingency plans would be indulging in media-driven hysteria.

An hour later, Roger called back and said that owners had approved extending the league year through the following Tuesday to allow players more time to vote. I felt a wave of relief and new worry. Roger clearly didn't believe in the medical impact of Covid-19, but the good news was that he also wasn't predicting an economic calamity. At least he wasn't yet. I alerted our senior staff that players had more time, attempting to tamp down my concerns that, if the union rejected this version of the collective bargaining agreement, the league would soon scuttle the deal before canceling the 2020 season because of the virus, knowing the incredible leverage it would create for players to go unpaid for an entire season. They wouldn't need to threaten a lockout this time. An airborne pathogen was doing the work for them. Owners could offer players 40 percent of all revenue, and players would have to choose between accepting it or spending another year out of work.

The next day, we learned that Russell had filed a formal complaint with the National Labor Relations Board, accusing the NFLPA and me of violating members' rights by restraining discussion about the proposed collective bargaining agreement. He claimed that our lawyers and I had threatened to retaliate against any player who talked about the deal, and while this was all just another figment of Russell's imagination, the timing of the accusations would grant him valuable media attention.

Sure enough *The New York Times* published several stories that included Russell's allegations, and the reporter, Ken Belson, never so much as asked the NFLPA for comment. Belson had written a glowing profile of Russell earlier in 2020, providing pushback on none of the player's more bizarre ideas, and it reminded me of the *Times*'s flawed coverage of Bountygate almost a decade earlier. The publication's editors were again allowing a lead NFL reporter to amplify subjects that simply weren't credible. Russell was intelligent enough to know that he could use this to his advantage, and now the *Times* and Belson were becoming his personal megaphone.

But what the world's most famous media organization *never* wrote was that, two days after our meeting in Miami began, Russell dropped out of the presidential race because of faint support. He later abandoned his post on the executive committee, and while the National Labor Relations Board investigated Russell's complaint, it dismissed it. I told myself that, in an increasingly crowded and splintering media landscape, the *Times* just bet on the long shot, hoping Russell would win the presidency and reward the publication with access—staking its own credibility to a known conspiracy theorist in the process.

Players voted on the presidential candidates actually in attendance. The winner, JC Tretter, had a degree in labor relations from Cornell, and I couldn't have been more impressed with his qualifications. I was a bit more skeptical of his judgment, however, as he had been critical of our collective bargaining agreement proposal during his time as a player rep. Now he was the most influential member of our most powerful bloc, and there was something I needed him—and only him—to understand. So I pulled JC aside.

"I couldn't say this in front of everyone," I said, "but I think this virus is about to shut everything down. As in *everything*."

Just forty-eight hours earlier, the coronavirus seemed too unlikely a threat to be taken seriously. On Wednesday, March 11, 2020, the WHO categorized it as a global pandemic, the first since the Spanish flu, and Trump addressed the nation in an attempt at calming an economic crisis. Tom Hanks and Rita Wilson announced they had tested positive, Utah Jazz player Rudy Gobert did as well, and NBA commissioner Adam Silver announced that his league was shutting down. Tennis and soccer leagues followed, and on Thursday, college basketball conference tournaments were canceled shortly before the NCAA announced it was calling off its men's basketball tournament for the first time since its 1939 inception. College campuses were being emptied, sending my son, Alex, home from the University of Maryland, and shelter-in-place orders were being issued throughout the country.

Von Miller would test positive, telling the media that, because he had asthma, he said that it felt as if his lungs were caving in. But some of his own teammates didn't believe either him or in the virus's power—a dynamic that became all too familiar as the pandemic tore the nation into two camps. There were those who took the pathogen seriously and those who were willing to bet their lives on wishful thinking. Reality was just down the road, in Broward County hospitals where healthcare workers wrapped themselves in trash bags because they didn't have enough protective equipment.

Our guys needed to get home, so we closed the meeting with approval of the budget and, in a side room, assembled the new executive committee. I welcomed the new members and gave them a hurried version of my usual speech to leaders. It centers on the thanklessness of a fight that cannot be fully won, at least not amid the current division of power. Nobody could even know if we were going to have a season, but if we were negotiating a collective bargaining agreement a year from now, it would probably be a hell of a lot worse.

As I studied their faces, I couldn't help but think of John Barry's words: *Society cannot function if it is every man for himself.*

■   ■   ■

**I HAD RETURNED** home by the time voting began. It was to end at midnight Sunday. The Pouncey twins, offensive linemen Mike and Maurkice, threw one last public haymaker to knock the deal out cold. They vowed to put together a strike fund with Russell Okung and others that would cover every player up to $250,000 in the event of a work stoppage. The problem was that players' projected salary in 2021 was estimated at $7 billion, which came to about $600,000 per player and no player had contemplated a canceled season at that time.

Players were casting votes online, and an accounting firm we retained had set up a double authorization system so no one would know who had voted or how. The NFLPA would only receive a final tally.

When Sunday afternoon arrived, Tom Brady proved almost as impatient as I was. He texted me to ask for an update. I didn't have one and wouldn't for hours. Eric, Don, and I spent the evening in the sunroom of my home, with me trying to drown my anxieties with roughly a half gallon of scotch. I kept reminding myself of Tom DePaso's mantra: *Players always get it right.*

Then, at 12:15 A.M. on Monday, my cellphone buzzed. It was one of the lawyers who'd heard from the accounting firm.

Passed
1019 to 959

We won. By sixty votes.

Sixty opinions, life experiences, motivations, and reasons why. Sixty individuals who now received their information from sources that may not have existed a generation earlier, having interpreted facts and feelings before distilling into decisions that were ultimately as unique as they were.

The vote was nerve-rackingly close, but I didn't care. It was done. Whether our guys appreciated all the work that had been done on their behalf, or how frequently truth had come under attack, I could not know. I told myself this was a landmark deal in the history of professional sports and turnout was above 70 percent.

Now it was time for me to call Roger.

"It passed," I said, barely above a whisper.

"That was a slog, wasn't it?" he said. Then he congratulated me.

Eleven years earlier, I took this job and looked at Roger as an oddity and a sellout. I thought he was someone who needed rescuing, and if I modeled following principle often enough, maybe he'd come around. But as I sat here now, my head was spinning. The scotch played a role, but so did a sad conclusion I had been trying for years to disprove.

In this arena, where the combatants are often morality and greed, Roger wasn't trying to change the troublesome population he manages. He accepts them, and regardless of whether they were people he rooted for or were scum, he just took his orders and did his job.

I'd now dedicated a decade to being a defense attorney and crisis manager for an army of 2,500 individuals, many of whom don't understand the point of advocacy work. I had Kevin Mawae and Fox and Brees, but guys like that are in short supply. Now Eric's glass was empty, and as lucky as I felt to work alongside someone who loved players as much he did, he was leaving me, too. Most players trusted me less now than on my first day, and unlike with the 2011 collective bargaining agreement, it wasn't the owners I was battling. My own army had turned on me, and no matter what I did, I would never stop being seen as an outsider and a shyster.

It was time I admitted it: The NFL is no place for an idealist. Not anymore.

Was it ever? Only Roger could answer that. He had never worked a job anywhere else, after all, and the last thought I remember before brown liquor and exhaustion vanquished me was that damned if Charles Goodell's kid didn't have it right all along.

# 9

# FORCE MAJEURE

A few months after I became executive director, I cleaned out the last of Gene Upshaw's things. There was an old checkbook from his personal account, not that of the NFLPA, with a register of probably twenty checks Gene had sent to former players who'd fallen on hard times.

"Rent for the month," Gene had written on one of the checks.

"Graduation gift," read another.

Some of the recipients had publicly criticized Gene over this or that, but this hadn't stopped him from helping these men. I wondered how he had retained his altruistic spirit and why he'd continued in the job after two failed strikes and a generation of former players claiming that neither he nor the NFLPA cared about them. He had built a union that may be the only one in the world that increased pensions of retired workers and worked to guarantee severance, line-of-duty disability payments, and a two-to-one 401(k) match.

Beneath the check register was a handwritten letter. A draft of a speech, I suspected, though it wasn't labeled and I had no idea if he ever delivered it or even planned to. In beautiful cursive, he'd written on the back of a long file folder.

Freedom is coming and we must be ready for the next step. Because if we are not, freedom will be temporary and brief.

At first I thought this was part of a labor parable. But as I kept reading, it seemed almost like a diary of Gene's thoughts on a growing tension in American society. Centuries after enslaved Africans were stripped of their dignity and humanity, Black men were still being conditioned to submit or die. Recourse was fantasy, and state governments instituted "Black Codes" that allowed property ownership and marriage, but these were limited. Many sharecroppers, possibly those I was related to, had been forced to sign contracts that directed some of their earnings toward white landowners.

It had become expected that Blacks accept these new shackles, and many hid in rural poverty because at least that was safe. Those who dared to question authority were risking assault or death, and even in modern times, speaking out felt foreign and dangerous to many of us. Gene seemed unwilling to accept this, and reading his words made me feel connected to a man I had never met.

When someone, or an institution, has had power and control as long as the NFL they will not give it up without a tremendous struggle and each day will try to get it back. . . . As we advance the agenda of freedom on one level we must put in place protections for past, present and future players.

We don't want to look back and say we didn't have the foresight or vision to understand what happens as the slaves leave the plantation.

Not long after we finalized the 2011 collective bargaining agreement, Karen surprised me with a trip to Mont-Tremblant, a resort town nestled among Canada's Laurentian Mountains. I could breathe in the frosty air and defragment my brain while pretending as if my unhealthy habits wouldn't be waiting for me at home.

Sure enough, owners were already disseminating the narrative that I had done a horrible deal. Me personally. Enough reporters and players bought into it that the suggestion that I had been swindled by the league became the drumbeat of my tenure. The truth was that our deal had kept our union alive despite owners' plans of annihilating it by manipulating their man on the inside, Troy Vincent, and I had refused to be controlled or to back down.

I smiled through the attacks, but one morning I woke up and couldn't open my jaw. A doctor diagnosed me with an inflamed temporomandibular joint, or TMJ, because I had been incessantly grinding my teeth.

"The stress is killing you," he told me. But what could I do? He advised that I take time off, but I had no time for that.

Instead, I visited all thirty-two team facilities, explaining over and over that our deal wasn't actually a loss. The doctor injected medicine into my jaw twice a week, hooked me up to an electro-muscular stimulus device, and prescribed muscle relaxers. I stopped exercising, gained weight, drank three martinis and half a bottle of wine just to silence my restless mind. If someone asked how I was doing, I'd either insist I was fine or scream at them. Because look at me: I'm a happy-go-lucky person who gets to be a professional hell-raiser! I get to go to the Super Bowl and meet players! Speak truth to power!

This was one of many lies I told myself, a survival mechanism just as corrosive as the booze. Another was that I couldn't quit or even step away, because that meant owners and the NFL plantation had intimidated and broken me. I vented to Marvin Miller, who had run Major League Baseball's players union, and Brig Owens, the former Washington defensive back and former NFLPA union leader. Sometimes I called Michael Weiner, who'd been named executive director of the MLBPA three months after I joined the NFLPA, because at least he understood what I was going through.

Then Marvin died, and Michael died, and Brig died.

So I kept everything inside, shoveling work duties and new lawsuits and public wars on top of my bubbling emotions. By the time we finished the 2020 collective bargaining agreement, I felt as if my psyche was about to come apart at the seams. But because of Covid-19, Karen and I couldn't travel, forcing me to stay home.

"Put it away," she'd say as I searched my iPad for another problem to solve—my way of avoiding a confrontation with my darker thoughts.

I scheduled endless meetings with medical experts and players, then additional ones with the league. The NFL season was still months away, but it was important for Roger and me to discuss potential protocols. The NBA and its players association had agreed to resume its season in a "bubble," a six-phase plan starting in June that was contingent on players being isolated from everyone but their teammates. They were to be tested every other day, with a confirmed positive diagnosis leading to a nonnegotiable fourteen-day quarantine period. Players were confined to their hotel rooms in Orlando, Florida, with any interaction with friends, family, or strangers resulting in a ten-day quarantine and potential fines.

The plan worked, at least economically, with the NBA avoiding a $1.5 billion revenue shortfall that had been tied to existing broadcast and sponsorship deals. Teams played in an empty arena in front of "virtual" fans, with players, coaches, essential staff, and officials shuttling among their hotel, practice facilities, and the arena before repeating the process the next day. Cut off from society and prohibited from being around their partners and children for more than three months, some players suffered from depression, poor sleep, and persistent fears that relatives might get sick, be hospitalized, or even die. Players could always leave the bubble, of course, so long as they forfeited their paychecks.

MLB made plans to resume its season in July, shortening its 162-game season to 60 games and agreeing to fill stadium seats not with fans but with cardboard cutouts and piped-in crowd noise. Initially without a bubble or strict isolation procedures, the Miami Marlins and St. Louis Cardinals would experience outbreaks just days after the season began. Even when MLB tightened protocols, some players just ignored them.

Kirk Cousins had already publicly declared that he had made

peace with the possibility of dying if he got sick because of football, and this was maddening in part because it told the league that players weren't concerned with safety. After a few of these meetings, colleagues suggested that I sit the next one out. I insisted that wouldn't be necessary, again claiming I was fine, but one day Robert Kraft called after a meeting and left a voicemail.

"I just hope you're okay," he said, "and just thinking about you."

I antagonized co-workers and picked fights with reporters, sniping at ESPN's Adam Schefter one day that he had no right saying pro football is a "necessity" when bodies were stacking up in Florida and New York.

"You know what I mean," Schefter replied.

"I know that you don't know what 'essential' means," I shot back.

If I slept at all, I awoke in the middle of the night and pounded a half bottle of wine before lying back down. I went for long drives through Maryland, the top down in my convertible, wishing the wind would blow away my thoughts. I lifted weights so hard, so irresponsibly, that I tore a muscle in my shoulder, reason to celebrate because the physical pain distracted me from emotional distress.

One morning I got up, packed a bag, and drove to Virginia Beach with our dog, Riley, in the back seat. Karen, Elizabeth, and Alex stayed home, and thank God, because home to me felt like a prison. The actual cell was my mind, which was so cluttered that I was unable to concentrate. I kept driving until the pavement ended and the air smelled of salt.

Riley and I went on long walks as the sun rose, and he'd chase a ball until my arm gave out. I'd return to my rented condo to get on Zooms and strategize with players, and day after day I told myself a new lie: *I'm good now. I just needed to get away.*

If negative thoughts threatened, I'd drown them with a bottle of Harlan Estate as the sun set and sear the porterhouse I'd bought from a nearby butcher. Then another bottle of Melka as I phoned Karen or the kids.

"I'm sorry you have to have dinner by yourself," Karen would tell me.

*Right.*

On May 26, Riley and I went for our usual walk. The air was crisp, the sky a clear blue. It was going to be a beautiful day, its soundtrack the blissful hum of crashing waves and a panting dog. We returned to the condo, Riley found a cool spot on the floor, and I flipped on the television. It was on CNN. The anchors were talking as a cellphone video showed what appeared to be an altercation that had occurred the night before in Minneapolis. I saw a parked police vehicle, and officers had surrounded a man I could hear but not see.

"Please, man!" the gravelly voice shouted. "Please!"

One officer pushed onlookers back. Some of the strained voices pleaded for officers to help the man off the pavement.

"Momma!" the man yelled. For the first time, I could see his face. A Black man of middle age, he was in handcuffs, his nose bleeding as he lay on the pavement. A white policeman pressed a knee into the man's neck, looked directly into the videographer's camera, and smirked. "They're gonna kill me. They're gonna kill me, man."

■    ■    ■

WHEN ELIZABETH WAS born, I held her and hoped she'd never feel the dread that so many young people do. That my parents and their parents did. A baby represents a chance at a better future, and after Alex was born and the two of them grew, I was never anything but certain that their lives would be better than mine.

I believed that their world was inherently good; different from the one that Moses Fitzgerald and his descendants inhabited. The rhythms of my kids' heartbeats were the sounds of a steady march forward.

Now, watching a police officer slowly kill George Floyd, I felt as if my world had shattered. A veil of lifelong denial had been lifted, and I felt something dark and unfamiliar within me. Somewhere deep in my mind, I have always known there's a difference between me and *them*. I knew about racism. Studied it, heard about it, occasionally experienced it. But my parents and uncles and cousins *felt* it. Viscerally. Deep in their bones.

Because of the pandemic, our family paused the annual Homecoming. That was the first time in fifty-six years I had missed it, and I felt so disoriented that I drove to southern Virginia anyway. I wanted to see the property where my father and siblings were born. My uncle Willard, who prayed for my safety all those times, rode with my cousin Lowery—or "Tweet" as everyone called him—to show me the original homestead. We passed a Confederate flag waving in a nearby yard, and when we stopped in the old property's driveway, Willard and Tweet were visibly anxious. A white family resided there now. My uncle and cousin were afraid of what might happen if the family saw cars driven by Black men pulling up unannounced.

Tweet encouraged me to take my pictures and do whatever reminiscing I had come for, but he and Willard weren't staying. At no point did I feel the way they did, and whether that is because my father relocated our bloodline to Maryland or because I became expert at tuning out negativity, I cannot be sure. What I do know is that my steely, dapper, crime-fighting alter ego shielded the real me from those feelings.

As I kept watching the video on CNN, I felt this protective layer dissolve. I had always lived in the same world as George Floyd, one in which a policeman can unilaterally determine which of us lives and dies, often with impunity. I had just shrouded these thoughts, as I had done so many others, in denial. Now I felt everything, and it was overwhelming. I called Elizabeth, then Alex.

"You need to see this," I told each of them. The truth was that, in that quiet condo, I just needed to hear their voices.

I called Karen, friends, colleagues at the NFLPA. I wanted to listen to their reactions, ask what they were feeling. When there was no one left to call, I returned to the beach and went for a run. The warm sea air hurt my lungs, and I listened to the waves as I wondered how my parents, Willard, and Tweet were absorbing the day's news. I love all of them so much, and among the many reasons why is their sheer absence of hate. For all the terrible things they witnessed and experienced, there is no contempt or resignation in them.

Me? I felt a white-hot hate surging through me, something that had been there all along but had never been activated.

A few hours later on that Tuesday, George Atallah called and asked if I wanted to do interviews. I didn't—not because I lacked anything to say but because I was afraid of what I *would* say. There was a question nobody had asked me in a long time, and if someone asked me, I wasn't sure I knew the answer. I had made a career and life out of avoiding it, a house of cards holding on in the stiff coastal breeze.

Then Mike Greenberg, the ESPN personality, texted me. "Your voice is important," he wrote. Mike is empathetic and thoughtful, with the organizational influence to allow nuance. I told George to set it up. I had been alone for weeks, so I hadn't shaved. Trying to look presentable, I put on my glasses and a blue polo, leaned my iPad against a vase, and turned on the camera.

He asked what I was hearing from players and the role athletes can and should play in social change. Then about what action the NFL and its franchise owners could and should take. I answered those questions the way I usually do, with canned responses off the top of my head. Then came his final question.

"If it isn't too personal," he began, "I wonder if I could just ask you to take a moment to speak from the heart . . ."

On live television, I knew he was about to ask the question. I wanted him to. I didn't want him to.

". . . about what we're seeing from our country right now," he continued, "and what it makes you feel."

I opened my mouth, but words didn't come.

How did I feel? I hadn't thought about that in so long. I took in a long, deep breath.

A wave of emotion hit—after forty years of gathering strength. Frustration, doubt, rage. My kids' faces flashed into my mind. Fear, dismay, shame. I paused, trying to choke down the feelings, but with denial gone, they washed over me. Loathing, resentment, and despair.

When I finally looked into the camera and opened my mouth, it was all I could do to avoid bursting into tears.

■ ■ ■

**IN THE DAYS** ahead, these feelings fused into a deep, metastatic anger. I was pissed at the media, furious at the president, mad at police. In the Washington, D.C., Prosecutor's Office, some of my closest friends were cops, and I bought into the belief that they were the thin blue line between civil society and anarchy. The streets of Washington were dangerous in the 1980s and '90s, but it was never a war. Eric Holder and I talked about how there had to be a better way for police: how to arrive at a scene, approach witnesses and persons of interest, the specifics of actual law.

But much of my fury coalesced toward NFL owners. None of them had knelt on George Floyd's neck, but they had stood by Donald Trump as he repeatedly poured gasoline onto the national dialogue and turned football stadiums into political battlegrounds. I truly believe Kraft and Jerry could have stepped in. Or at least tried. And maybe they did.

For nearly a dozen years, I had witnessed countless displays of owners' power, a group of wealthy and influential capitalists allowing nothing to derail the most impressive live entertainment show in history while wrapping itself in all things *America*. The NFL wanted military jets and helicopters to rumble over stadiums before games, so it browbeat the Defense Department into paying for it. Television networks love the spectacle of a giant American flag being stretched from one side of a football field to the other, with no one ever pointing out that this is a direct violation of a statute known as the U.S. Flag Code.

With so much corporate and cultural might, owners were given multiple opportunities to use their power for the greater good. Stand up for the NFL's majority Black workforce amid police brutality and racial attacks? Support players for a silent protest that violated no federal, state, or local law? Tell Trump to keep the NFL's name out of his mouth?

Time and again, they abdicated their duties. Access to the Oval Office was too important, their own anger over kneeling—I personally witnessed Baltimore's Steve Bisciotti and Kansas City's Clark Hunt nearly explode over Colin Kaepernick's refusal to concede—too acute. Denial is a hell of a drug, and the NFL is America's most powerful dealer. When legendary sportscaster Bob Costas dared to criticize the league in 2017 over its epidemic of brain injuries, owners could have listened and used it as a springboard toward progress. Instead, the league ordered NBC to remove Costas from covering the Super Bowl before the network cut ties with him entirely.

As for Trump, Kraft told me he would never engage in a business deal with the man, considering his volatility. But he'd sure as hell placate and make excuses for him during the president's assault on the mighty NFL.

Even in spring 2020, during an unprecedented time in our country, Roger could have whipped the owners into doing the right thing. He could have done it without them, consequences be damned. Instead, he again handed the keys to his bosses, who insisted on threading a needle that attached their own political leanings to America's football and patriotism machine. The NFL didn't encourage players to embrace owners' cultural preferences. The league office mandated it. And if anyone refused or stood their ground or even hesitated, owners directed Roger to punish them.

Players had been left to fight a battle alone, creating a tension between management and labor that felt like a microcosm of a wider system that had become bloated and strained before finally crumbling under the weight.

Into main streets in two thousand American cities and towns, across oceans and into sixty countries, between fifteen million and twenty-six million people marched and chanted, "I can't breathe!" Others set fire to a Minneapolis police station, or fired a gun into a cluster of demonstrators, or killed police officers. I watched with horror, sure, knowing that none of this was new. It was just the blood seeping out of a scab that, for two hundred years, had been picked at and picked at. Just as I had tried denying some of the realities in my life, the nation had done the same.

Roger had done the worst thing he could have done: He remained silent, letting his band of lunatics go unchecked—until he couldn't anymore. With civilization tearing itself apart in front of a global audience, the commissioner recorded a video from the basement of his home, confessing at last that he and the league had screwed up.

"We, the National Football League, admit we were wrong for not listening to NFL players earlier and encourage all to speak out and peacefully protest," he said. "We, the National Football League, believe that Black lives matter."

Two weeks before this, before Floyd's death, Roger and I had met in his office and discussed the national escalation of racial tension. I challenged him to come out in support of players or at least show some humanity during a pandemic and a period of increasing socio-economic and racial strife. It would send a message, I told the commissioner, that the league actually gives a damn about doing the right thing.

But he wouldn't, preferring to remain nothing more than a league-fueled automaton in public and around owners.

"We have to get football back," Roger said during one of our meetings about Covid-19 protocols. "America needs football."

I couldn't take it.

"What does that even mean?" I asked. "We have some duty to distract people? Why?"

"People can't go anywhere," Roger said.

"Maybe people *shouldn't* be distracted," I said.

So when I saw Roger's statement from the basement, I was stunned. We'd had our battles, and I had seen the most dismissive and stubborn sides of him. He *never* threw the train in reverse. Now he was actually admitting that the NFL had gotten something wrong. This wasn't vindication for me. It was just a moment to exhale and feel like I existed in reality again.

And his words were sincere and heartfelt enough that, for once, I suspected that this was Roger actually sticking his neck out. Maybe he called a handful of owners to issue a heads-up, but he couldn't have gotten preapproval from a majority. They are incapable of that, and Roger finally showed he was able and willing to do something besides what was fiscally responsible or legally safe.

At long last, the commissioner did the right thing.

.   .   .

**MY ANGER WAS** so volcanic that its flow reached Tom Brady. It was summer 2020, and the NFLPA was still in discussions with the NFL about the right way to manage Covid. I was consumed with a new problem and the trap players could find themselves in if we made a strategic misstep.

Since mid-February, I had seen almost every obstacle like a level of *Squid Game:* a puzzle to solve just so we could survive for the next one. We had gotten the collective bargaining agreement passed, and its structure and ten-year term gave players leverage. But now facing a pandemic, how could we agree to play football without also having to bear the *cost* of playing football?

I drafted the outline of a letter to Jeff Pash, the league's general counsel, and our top lawyer, Tom DePaso, polished it in a way that would ask an existential question: *Should* we be playing football? The three-page letter raised a series of moral questions, such as whether we should drain already scarce resources from the general public and how we could justify having first responders, who were already strained to their limits, work on game days. These were games we were talking about, after all. If a player opted to sit out the season entirely, what impact would that decision have on his salary? Or his contract status and employment at large?

The purpose was for the letter to immediately put the NFL on the defensive. We didn't yet know the full impact of Covid on the human body or the environments that may strengthen or eliminate the virus. We needed the league to commit to building a work, practice, and game environment so safe that it neutralized the questions we had posed.

We retained doctors at Harvard and organized a Covid task force, led by Thom Mayer, the NFLPA's medical director, and Sean Sansiveri, our lawyer in charge of health and safety. The public had learned that individuals with preexisting conditions, such as diabetes and obesity, were at particular risk. NFL players are almost all in good shape, but many of them also carry excessive weight and have higher body-mass indexes than athletes in any other sport. We needed provisions for players with health conditions so that they would still get paid, even if they didn't play.

It would have been a tough first negotiation for anyone, let alone a new president, and I told JC Tretter I knew that we had no leverage beyond whatever we could create.

Our first conversations with Roger and John Mara, the New York Giants' co-owner and the chairman of the league's management council, were predictable. The league wanted to hold offseason practices, training camps, and preseason games as normal. The NFL proposed putting 30 percent of players' salaries into an escrow account, given the likelihood that stadiums would be forced to limit capacity or prohibit crowds altogether. The league and NFLPA would split the cost of testing, reconfiguration of locker rooms and team facilities, and daily sanitization.

"No," I said.

Mara grimaced and drew in a deep breath. He said that he would therefore cancel training camps.

"Fine," I replied, and the meeting ended.

We had to live and die by the notion that owners needed a football season more than players did. While we were trying to establish this strategy, a report surfaced that Tom, who had left the New England Patriots after twenty seasons and signed with the Tampa Bay Buccaneers, was holding impromptu practices at his home. He had recently told me that his friends back in Foxborough had told him that Patriots coach Bill Belichick actually *hoped* the 2020 season was canceled. Belichick apparently believed his team was going to be "shitty," Tom said.

"He's not motivated to get anything going," he continued.

Still, Tom being Tom, he couldn't just sit still. He invited his new teammates over to run fully padded off-the-books practices. I understood it from a competitive standpoint, especially considering the acrimonious way Tom left a team that he'd led to six Super Bowl championships. But after Deflategate, I expected more from him and let Tom know that I intended to bust his ass in the media.

"Come on, man," I said. "Practices? Not helpful. Until we have a deal that gets our guys paid and protected, we shouldn't be doing a damn thing."

By then, training camps were scheduled to begin in a few weeks. Our legal team knew that the escrow idea, which NBA players had agreed to before they entered the bubble, was a nonstarter. Escrow incentivizes the account holder to find costs to count against the earmarked amount, essentially reasons you shouldn't receive the full share.

We pored over the new collective bargaining agreement, all 439 pages, 69 articles, and 29 appendixes of it. Then I read it again. There had to be *something* in the language that would grant us leverage. I needed there to be. Running out of ideas, my mind couldn't just accept that we held a mediocre hand. If we tried to bluff, the league would immediately call us on it.

So, to try to feed my brain *something*, I started reading the collective bargaining agreements of other leagues—the National Hockey League, Major League Baseball, then the NBA. On page 467 of the NBA's deal, which had been finalized in December 2016, I noticed something interesting.

Article 34, Section 5: Termination by NBA/*Force Majeure*.

[T]he occurrence of any of the following events or conditions . . . makes it economically impracticable for the NBA to perform its obligations under this Agreement: wars or war-like action (whether actual or threatened and whether conventional or other, including, but not limited to, chemical or biological wars or war-like action); sabotage, terrorism or threats of sabotage or terrorism; explosions; epidemics; weather or natural disasters, including, but not limited to, fires, floods, droughts, hurricanes, tornados, storms or earthquakes; and any governmental order or action (civil or military) . . . the Compensation payable to each player who was on the roster of a Team that was unable to play one or more games during the *Force Majeure* Period shall be reduced by 1/92.6th of the player's Compensation for the Season(s) covering the *Force Majeure* Period.

In layman's terms, the definition of that obscure Latin phrase means that if something unforeseen happens—like, say, a global pandemic—the NBA was under no obligation to pay players for games they missed. Don't play, don't get paid. It was as simple as that. That at least explained why players had been willing to take pay cuts and agree to a 10 percent escrow. It was that or nothing, at least in theory, and force majeure made it so Covid represented an impediment to a service being performed or completed in a timely fashion, so owners were therefore absolved of their contractual responsibility.

Lawyers have been putting that language in contracts since the Magna Carta, making it one of the most important legal principles in history.

But the NFL's most important edict is that, no matter what, the show goes on. Games are played in rain, snow, or monsoon. The league doesn't cancel games. In fact, before Damar Hamlin's heart stopped on the field in early 2022, no game had been called off since 1935. Multiple games were postponed in the immediate aftermath of the terrorist attacks of 9/11, but those contests were rescheduled. The league wanted to play on, but former NFLPA president Kevin Mawae, who was the New York Jets' center in 2001, told me that players had refused to suit up.

Fog, blizzard, flood—there will be football. During a Texas heat wave in 2000, the temperature on the field reached an astonishing 130 degrees before a scheduled game between the Philadelphia Eagles and Dallas Cowboys. There wasn't so much as a delay. Eagles players resorted to drinking pickle juice to stay hydrated and their 41–14 walloping of Jerry's team became a badge of honor, and this underscored the fact that owners believe that there is no scenario in which a game cannot be played.

A force majeure provision, therefore, is antithetical to the league's business model and was never added to our collective bargaining agreement. I read through our 2020 contract yet again, and sure enough, there was no language whatsoever that would let NFL owners off the hook the way NBA owners had been.

This was it. Finally.

During our next call, Mara again threatened to cancel training camps and the preseason. Hell, the league was contemplating calling off the regular season, too. So, like in 2011, it was time to play our trump card.

"That's fine, John," I said. "But if you shut down football, it's not Covid or an earthquake or a tornado shutting it down. It's John Mara shutting down football."

I pointed out that we have no force majeure provision that says otherwise, and then I listed off the NFLPA's next moves if the league kept wanting to play coronavirus chess.

"You say we have to play, we'll say no," I said. "So we sue you, and it may take forever, but you will have to pay players despite having no games. And that'll be, let's say, six or seven billion dollars."

Mara grimaced again. We had just taken his queen.

"Or," I continued, "we can figure out a way to have a full season and get players paid their full projected salary, according to the collective bargaining agreement, regardless of any downturn in revenue."

I had learned to love that moment, years earlier, when a witness crumbles during cross-examination. There's a look of defeat that spreads across their face, and the blood seems to drain from their skin. It was the same look Mara had now.

Roger had known and understood the implications of not having force majeure language in our contract. He knew this was checkmate. But Mara just glared at me. Movies make you think there are moments of capitulation, when the evil empire admits defeat. That never happens in real life.

The conversations just end.

The league nonetheless folded on the escrow suggestion and on splitting the cost of protective equipment. Tom and other quarterbacks publicly backed the elimination of preseason games, and the NFL finally capitulated. He, Ryan Fitzpatrick, and a few others had urged guys to stick together as a way to force the league's hand.

Owners were welcome to carry on with preseason games, but no team would have a quarterback in uniform. As we approached the end of July, the league capitulated. Owners agreed to play the season and cover the full cost of Covid-related health and safety measures, and players would receive their full salaries. We constructed an amendment to our new collective bargaining agreement, outlining provisions that would allow us to leverage the length of the contract to borrow against and manage benefit costs so that every dime a player expected to get before the pandemic was what he'd be paid during the pandemic.

Behind the scenes, I believe it was Roger who brought us to the finish line. Unlike most deals, we never went through the time-wasting marathon of meetings. That's what I know.

But I suspect the guy was, like most of us, at the end of his rope during a highly stressful period in American history. I like to think that Roger just wanted to move on, so at least in my imagination, it was the commissioner who called owners and told them, if only this once, to cut the crap.

■  ■  ■

AMONG THE ONLY things that kept me going in 2020 was the promise of 2021. It had to be better. America's healthcare system didn't collapse, and neither did the economy.

December 2020 saw the Food and Drug Administration grant emergency approval to distribute two new Covid vaccines, the final hurdle of an incredible achievement in the vast history of science and medicine. Planning for an NFL season with a vaccine was almost guaranteed to be easier than somehow forging a season without one.

Our staff had weekly calls with players, who were growing impatient with the constant testing, tracking, and monitoring of their activities at the team facility and beyond. Some guys even suggested deliberately contracting the virus to "be done with it." This was just vocalized frustration and dwindling impulse control, I told myself, because surely grown men weren't actually advocating for exposing themselves to a disease that, by the end of 2020, had killed nearly two million people worldwide and continued straining hospitals beyond capacity.

Every year we have dozens of players who are hospitalized for injuries sustained during practices and games. Our collective goal had always been to *reduce* potential hospitalizations, not to engage in behavior that could increase them. Other players relayed fears of how the virus would affect their family members, some of whom were elderly and who lived with their son the NFL player. The union secured extra housing or reserved hotel rooms in some cases and, in a few, delivered private medical care to those who couldn't get to a hospital. We hadn't offered a potential timeline for a vaccine, considering the structure players depend on and how literally many of them take what they're told.

So when the vaccines were approved, it felt like a miracle. Development of a flu vaccine a century earlier had taken decades—a monumental achievement, to be sure, but too late for the fifty million people that virus had killed. The mumps vaccine, which had been the fastest ever developed, had taken four years. I was at once awestruck and inspired by the fact that, in the face of a catastrophe, some of the world's best and brightest minds had come together to unlock the genetic code for SARS-CoV-2 before building an injectable mRNA sequence to be distributed by Moderna and Pfizer. From initial detection to shipment of those first vials, it took thirteen months.

Amid the most disastrous economic collapse since 2008, NFL players received every dollar of their salaries despite the fact that the league's revenue was down $4 billion. The only thing we had conceded was the league's 401(k) match, but we later got reimbursed for that, too.

The worst year of my professional life was over.

I was proud that, on our respective sides, Roger and I had risen to the occasion. Our conversations were constructive because we both seemed motivated to accomplish something. The best example? The flu shot.

While Covid vaccines remained in clinical trials, Roger and I talked about how and when they would be distributed. The league suggested mandating the flu shot, which, in theory, sounded fine. Teams would have their medical experts administer the vaccines at their facilities, and because Covid symptoms resembled those of the flu, it would both serve as a warm-up act and establish a precedent.

Then again, a precedent was precisely the problem. Mandating anything, I explained, was a legal and political mess. First, I believe that no union should sign off on workers being required to take medication in order to keep their jobs. It is a worker choice issue, and while I wouldn't sign off on a mandate, we would strongly encourage players to get vaccinated against the flu and issue reminders of the two viruses' effects.

Still, an owner called me one day and explained that a friend was researching an early treatment for Covid. It hadn't been vetted by the FDA, but the friend was confident in the treatment, and who better to try out an experimental drug than a group of elite athletes in fantastic condition?

"Love the passion," I told this owner. "But you ever hear of the Tuskegee experiments?"

For four decades during the twentieth century, scientists at the U.S. Public Health Service had intentionally injected Black men with syphilis so that they could study the bacteria's effect on humans. The subjects weren't told what was being unleashed into their bodies, and 128 of the men died of syphilis or related complications.

"This isn't like that," the owner shot back.

"I'm afraid we'll have to pass," I said.

Later I called Roger to let him know about the call.

"I told him it was a really bad idea," he said. "He said he was going to call you, and I told him that was a bad idea, as well."

We later learned that some owners were telling their employees that the league was planning to mandate the Covid vaccine, and as I had predicted, this wasn't going over well. The virus had cost owners money the year before, and a handful were sending word through their organizations that players would be expected to perform the next season. George and I went out of our way to overmessage about the vaccine and the processes for the coming year. Players would not be forced to take the vaccine. For those who did not want it, they would be subject to the previous year's protocols. The message was the same for everyone, be they NFL agents, players, or the general public.

For much of the previous year, I had started to feel myself becoming indifferent to remaining executive director and fighting for players who, by and large, refused to be helped. As it had been so often, the NFLPA wasn't just trying to move the ball against a single opponent. They were attacking from all sides.

And, like with the collective bargaining agreement, it didn't seem to matter what we told them. This was now a country where experts were seen as conspirators, science was being questioned, and facts convinced skeptics of nothing and seemed to add kerosene to some individuals' urges to mislead. Then, one morning in February, George called me. Two well-known ESPN reporters had been working on a long-form profile of me, and it had been published earlier that day.

"It's a hit job," George said. "A brutal fucking hit job."

I had known these reporters for years, holding numerous background conversations with them for context about Ray Rice, Deflategate, or negotiations with the league during anthem protests. The reporters, Don Van Natta and Seth Wickersham, receive information; the NFLPA gets its side of the story into the wider conversation. It's a tried-and-true political maneuver that helped us quietly push back on the league's massive PR apparatus.

Now, as I read the ESPN piece, I couldn't understand why the reporters had framed the story as they had. It suggested that owners had manipulated and exploited me while negotiating a collective bargaining agreement that expanded the season to seventeen games, going so far as to indicate that I was in the pocket of certain owners. Significant parts of the narrative were flatly untrue, and George and I had handed over documented evidence that proved it. The reporters had ignored that material and jammed forward a story that the public wasn't exactly clamoring to read.

I knew some owners were bitter after the collective bargaining agreement and Covid deals. I had attended a lunch with Carolina Panthers owner David Tepper, who announced to the table that players had gotten far too good a deal, especially heading into a pandemic. Tepper wanted me to know that he'd urged the league to pull the deal off the table. It was true that a crisis was coming and that the NFL bought an extra regular-season game for nearly $2 billion after having the right to expand the season for free before 2011. But was Tepper implying that owners had been hoodwinked? And that was somehow my fault?

Regardless, George reminded me that ESPN pays the NFL $2.7 billion per year for broadcast rights. And when I first met Jimmy Pitaro in 2018, shortly after he became president of the network, he told me that his first order of business was to stop antagonizing "our most important business partner." It was an about-face of the company's strategy under John Skipper, Pitaro's hard-charging predecessor who built his organization on a foundation of hard-hitting and accurate pieces of investigative sports journalism.

Whatever ESPN's motivations had been, I couldn't shake the belief that the reporters each had important ownership sources they wanted to serve. We had conducted a nearly two-and-a-half-hour interview with them in October 2020, and George and I both believed they had a predetermined story premise long before reaching out to us. Despite that 154-minute interview and the fact that the story published at 10,378 words, my quotations—in a story about me—came to a mere 130 words. Even before our call, it seemed as if the deck was stacked against me.

"They care more about getting a rise out of you," George had told me, "than they care about the facts."

He urged me to avoid getting angry, no matter what the reporters claimed. He cited the racially charged environment and my profile against that of a group of owners who resent being held accountable and especially being called out by an aggressive and confident Black man. Both of the reporters are white, neither having walked a step in a Black man's shoes, but I don't hold those blind spots against them.

What did rub me wrong was that both reporters lobbed question after question about the harsh, occasionally ridiculous allegations of anonymous owners and league officials—shots that had been fired by Cyrus Mehri, a lawyer who was never considered for my job, and Russell Okung, who actually admitted to the ESPN reporters that he'd violated the NFLPA constitution by illicitly recording our confidential meetings. But the worst was an allegation, again made anonymously, that the union had bribed Drew Brees to the tune of $10 million so he would publicly and privately support me and criticize Roger.

It was absurd, offensive, and just flat-out untrue.

Drew was paid royalties, just like everyone whose jersey sales and appearances for Players Inc. earn money. Hundreds of players receive similar payments. We had produced a formula that calculates how much players get paid for each jersey sold, and audited accounting records of fees paid to Drew and everyone else are handed over each year to the executive committee. George sent the reporters those internal documents, including LM-2 forms that, under penalty of perjury, were submitted each year to the U.S. Department of Labor. He sent evidence from audits, after which everything had come back clean.

The story glossed over these facts, favoring a their-word-against-mine situation that implied that we—*I*—had illegally funneled payments to Drew so he'd have my back. And I was supposed to sit there and calmly defend myself for lies in a story whose primary sources wanted their identities protected, men who are paid billions directly by the same company that employs these reporters? I'm meant to shrug off that the unsubstantiated opinions of white billionaires, all of whom make it clear at every instance that they have disproportionately more power than I do, are weighted more heavily than my written evidence?

With apologies to George, my days of repressing emotions were over.

"I'm on the record, onscreen, and you're challenging me with *some* owner at *some* bargaining session at *some* time that's completely out of context to anything," I said a half hour into what felt a lot like a sham interview, which we had transcribed and a copy of which I still have. "I don't spend a whole heck of a lot of time . . . trying to clean up misunderstandings because it has become clear to me that there are people that just want to facilitate the misunderstanding.

"If I show someone that the sky is blue and they want to continue to engage in misinformation or disinformation that the sky is yellow, I've come to the conclusion that I can only show so many pictures of the sky."

This, to me, was a highly personal display of a trend I had been noticing for years: NFL reporters who seem to have been asked to holster their ethics, nuance, and common sense to keep their place under the league's tent. Many of the people who cover America's most popular league, our unofficial sports historians, have come to the same crossroads as so many in and around the NFL: Doing what's right or greed? Speaking truth to power or bowing to it?

Resistance is a moral, thankless duty. Pushback is harder, and more discouraged, than ever. That's also why it's so damned necessary. It was Teddy Roosevelt who juxtaposed the critic against the person who's actually in the arena; who strives and errs; and who, to put it a slightly different way, gives enough of a damn to try.

"Who, at the worst," Roosevelt said during a speech in Paris in 1910, "if he fails, at least fails while daring greatly."

These two ESPN reporters knew better. They *know* better. And yet they did the league's bidding anyway. They came to the crossroads and made a choice. They are the same kinds of people who undermined Gene Upshaw, and it didn't hurt Gene or me as much as it sold out the players. To truly represent workers is to decide that you will never be an owner's apologist, friend, or ally.

It just so happens that our arena is a plantation, and the workers are supposed to keep their damn mouths shut if they want to retain the privilege of existing.

I reject this, I'm afraid, just as I rejected the advice to conceal my anger. I can't. Not anymore. I have chosen, even now, to believe in things like oaths, standards, and facts. I trust them. They are, and will remain, my North Stars. These things must be defended—angrily, if necessary.

So, with that in mind, here are a couple of related facts.

Just months after that ESPN piece, Wickersham published a tell-all book about the Patriots' dynasty. Belichick and Tom were painted as cold-blooded savages who cared about nothing but victory. Kraft, curiously, came off as the organization's noble and wise leader, clearly the book's protagonist.

In 2024, it was announced that Van Natta had his own book deal: a blockbuster biography of Jerry Jones. The publisher announced this "unauthorized" project despite pointing out that the author had conducted "dozens of interviews" with Jerry. Van Natta also promoted the book with a photo he posted to social media, of him and Jerry hamming it up in what appeared to be Jerry's private jet.

Nothing more than a series of interesting coincidences, I'm sure.

■　■　■

IN AUGUST 2021, my phone chirped with a text from Aaron Rodgers. "Can you call me?" it read. Could I not run into traffic instead?

Aaron would later become a full-blown conspiracy theorist and vaccine skeptic, going on shows hosted by Joe Rogan and Pat McAfee to spread his unsubstantiated opinions about the news media's supposed business relationship with pharmaceutical companies, lament the actions of "woke culture," and attack Kansas City tight end Travis Kelce because he appeared in an ad for Pfizer.

"As more research comes out," Aaron claimed during one such appearance on Rogan, "there's more papers published in very reputable scientific publications that talk about all of the things I was stumping for and talking about."

Of course, none of it was true. I had pulled together some of the best medical researchers in the world to advise us, and I simply left it up to him and whatever he could prove about his immunization. A few days later, a Green Bay Packers reporter asked Aaron if he had been vaccinated. He claimed to have been "immunized," which even he would admit later was a lie, and suggested he was appealing the NFLPA's vaccine protocols. No such appeals process exists.

Several media outlets would report that Aaron Rodgers tested positive for Covid-19 after his self-asserted homeopathic remedies failed to immunize him. It was not the first time I had heard of such a remedy. Rodgers is far from a shrinking violet, and he has one of the best agents in the business. He publicly stated that he was immunized, and that obviously turned out to not be true. A different player, Buffalo Bills wide receiver Cole Beasley, publicly announced he would rather retire than be vaccinated against Covid. Players started openly suggesting that vaccines contained microchips and had been engineered for government espionage. As much as we tried educating and reasoning with these men, nothing was getting through. These were many of the same men who lined up every week to get a shot of Toradol and whose exact job description is to hurl their bodies into harm's way.

This went on day after day, another microcosm of an exhausting national conversation. I was spent, and with my term as executive director set to expire after the 2021 season, I wasn't sure I wanted to stay on. Richard Sherman and Lorenzo Alexander spoke openly about being interested in new leadership at the union.

Once the season began, we risked missing more games than we'd missed the year we *didn't* have a Covid vaccine. Rodgers and Beasley each tested positive, forcing them to miss games, and Beasley racked up about $100,000 in fines for openly flouting the league's guidelines and claiming in a social media post that a teammate was hospitalized *because* he had received the vaccine. As hard as I had fought to make sure every player got paid, healthy or not, it drove me crazy that Cole Beasley was actively spreading disinformation and a virus while collecting his full paycheck.

And he was by no means alone. One player insisted that an undercover agent for the Drug Enforcement Administration had warned him that Covid vaccines were instruments meant to enable government control. Three Tampa Bay players were suspended for presenting fake vaccine cards, and the Baltimore Ravens just openly refused to comply with protocols. Players violated curfews, went to restaurants and clubs with sick teammates, and worked alongside a strength and conditioning coach who had just flat-out refused to participate in mandatory contact tracing.

Covid was running rampant, and because the league was financially on the hook for testing, it threw its hands up and stopped paying for daily tests. With testing now occurring at random, we warned players that Covid might now infiltrate their locker rooms without their knowledge. The overwhelming majority didn't care.

Roger and I spoke by phone almost every day, discussing the possibility of canceling or moving games. If a team's roster was dramatically reduced, should it forfeit? Play anyway?

One afternoon before our weekly call with another group of players to discuss the in-season protocol, explain best practices, and answer questions, Don and JC came into my office. It was clear they had previously discussed whatever they were about to tell me.

"Don't worry about getting on the player calls," Don said.

Dealing with players was my job, I told them. I hated the calls, but I couldn't just blow them off. I explained that I had a responsibility to answer questions.

Don took a deep breath.

"De," he said, "you're done."

JC laid a hand on my shoulder.

"We got this," he said.

■ ■ ■

SITTING OUT THE player calls gave me time to think and work on my personal evaluation statement, which was due by the end of the sea-

son. It was all I could do to avoid writing, in bold letters: FIND SOME-
ONE ELSE. Instead, I took a breath, started typing, and . . .

> The years 2020 and 2021 represent a period in our history
> during which we have confronted a global pandemic, racial
> unrest and upheaval, a President who made us the subject of
> his campaign, and a new CBA.

I paused. Why was I doing this? I had no interest in negotiating a
third collective bargaining agreement in 2030. The first two nearly
killed me. Even one more term, which would amount to three more
years in the job, seemed like an eternity.

> There has never been a period of economic, public health, and
> cultural turmoil like the one we are experiencing . . .

The cursor flashed, waiting for me to find a reason to continue.
Then it hit me. I hadn't just taken a job in 2009. I took an oath. I had
promised players that I would never put the union in a situation like
the one I had inherited when Gene died.

The NFLPA had been so close to falling into Troy Vincent's hands,
allowing the league to manipulate the union from the inside. I'm not
even sure he understood the leverage owners had over him. Perhaps
they knew that Troy had been sued over a sexual assault that occurred at a beauty parlor he owned, or that he was in over his head
on a number of investments, or that he had shared confidential documents without authorization.

This is how many large corporations behave, and the NFL is willing to take on a short-term loss if it means a long-term gain. Billionaires want to destroy the opposition and eliminate oversight. If I
walked away now, they would surely try to cripple the union again. I
told myself there was still good I could do, including a joint venture
with other professional sports labor unions that, if all went right,
would be worth billions that players could access in the event of a

strike or lockout—a measure of financial power that would prevent generations of players from being crushed like NHL players had been in 2007.

> . . . and I am proud to note that the NFLPA staff has continued to fulfill the vision and values of this union and provide world class service to its membership.

The words came easier now. I reminded players of our broad economic gains, the protections and benefits we had made accessible to all former players. I outlined our office's gradual weakening of Roger as the league's one and only disciplinary czar, the evolution of our revenue split, and improvements made to health and safety since I joined the NFLPA.

At the end of the 2011 lockout, the union's war chest of savings was approximately $250 million. A decade later, it exceeded $700 million, with hundreds of millions more invested in companies such as Whoop and Fanatics. Players' annual royalty checks grew from a few thousand to $32,000 each.

I wanted my statement to tell a twelve-year story to a group of executive committee members who may not have known about the full trajectory of their union. In a sports industry that is overwhelmingly white and male, nearly half of our office was staffed by women, and 50 percent of senior leadership was diverse. We had a positive net operating revenue for nearly ten years, and since the lockout, we had never used any money from player dues.

Yes, I wanted one last term. But did players want me?

I submitted my self-evaluation and scheduled a two-hour Zoom with the executive committee. After my presentation, I opened the floor to questions. Nobody asked a single one.

"Anyone," I said. "Fire away."

After a couple of awkward minutes, I logged off to allow the executive committee to deliberate and vote. If all eleven guys plus the two most senior player reps vote for you unanimously, you win another term. If there's a split, the ballot moves to all thirty-two player reps, which can become a bit dicier because those guys don't know me as well. I'd need twenty-two of those thirty-two votes, and if I got fewer than sixteen, I wouldn't even be among the candidate pool the next March when my replacement was chosen.

JC called to let me know that the executive committee vote wasn't unanimous. So, sure enough, the vote would move to the next stage. Two days later, George alerted me that a reporter from *The Wall Street Journal* needed to speak with me. The reporter, Andrew Beaton, claimed to be in possession of portions of emails that had been written by Jon Gruden, the coach of the Las Vegas Raiders. One of the emails, Beaton would tell me, included racist language. He didn't have the entire email, so I withheld comment for the moment.

The story was set to run the same day as player reps were scheduled to vote, so I asked Beaton if he could hold the story until after the weekend. Though I had no idea how a story like this would be interpreted, I preferred to avoid the implication that I had leaked information to garner sympathy. Beaton said a competing news outlet had access to the same information, so holding the story was impossible. The *Journal* would be publishing later that day.

I walked directly to my car, left the office, and drove to Kensington, Maryland. My dad was ninety-two, my mother eighty-eight. I hated the fact that, at this stage of their lives, I was about to let them know that some jerk-off coach had called me "Dumboriss Smith" and used a racist trope about the size of my lips. As I drove, I called Elizabeth and Alex so they wouldn't learn about the story on social media.

As I pulled into my parents' driveway, my phone rang. "Roger Goodell," the display read. Maybe he was calling to apologize on the league's behalf.

"How you doing, Roger?" I asked.

"Just wondering what's going to happen with your vote," he said. I rolled my eyes.

"Who knows?" I told him. "It's in the players' hands."

He wished me luck.

"Oh, hey," he continued. "I know there's this email and that the *Journal* is going to write a story about it. I just want you to know that apparently that guy said some awful things about me, too."

Not an apology on the league's behalf. Not that he felt bad for me because it was racial. Or that he was sorry that guys like Gruden continue to permeate the league, feeling completely comfortable to say whatever they wish, just as owners did. That was as close as Roger and I ever got to being kindred spirits sharing a tough time.

Two days later, Gruden was coaching the Raiders as if nothing had ever happened. Then *The New York Times* published the contents of more emails, including one in which he referred to Roger as a "f——t" and another calling him a "pussy." Gruden resigned the next day. In this world, there's using racist language, and there's calling the NFL commissioner names. One is worse than the other.

In my parents' driveway, I turned off my car and headed toward their front door. I was prepared to tell them about the emails, the *Journal* story, the fact that if I wound up winning another term, it was going to be my last.

After the previous two years, the time had come to save myself. With or without me, the NFLPA would live on, continuing the march forward. My job was to set it up for that march. I walked in and sat on my parents' sofa.

Arthur Smith, the ex-Marine, listened to my words and processed what I was saying. As he'd done long ago on that bus in North Carolina, he kept his cool.

"I know you can handle this," he said. "It's going to be fine."

But my mother, Mildred, all five feet six of her, filled with so much beautiful intensity, looked as if she were ready to pop.

"Yeah, well," she began, "I'll kick Jon Gruden's cracker ass, I swear to God."

When I took the job in 2009, I had taken over the union following Gene Upshaw's death. I promised myself that no person should ever come in as I did, with less than two years to prepare for a major collective bargaining battle. It is unfair to membership and certainly is not in the best interests of the union, which was and is the only major check on the NFL's power.

Upon being reelected in 2021, I decided this term would be my last. It was necessary for me and the right thing to do. It would provide the union stability while allowing me to do something Gene never got the chance to do: step out of the executive director's office willingly.

Signing my last contract felt amazing. The beauty of running track or playing football is that the competition always ends. There's always a finish line or final whistle. A murder trial ends with a verdict. But my responsibilities for the NFLPA never concluded or weakened, and neither did the stress. I was so relieved that I felt like crying.

The Jon Gruden controversy broke me. And not only because his casual racism confirmed what I always suspected was said about me and other Black leaders. More hurtful was that virtually nobody had my back. Neither Mike Tirico, Tony Dungy, nor James Brown said a word in my defense. In fact, all three went on national television to defend *Gruden*. James and I grew up together in Maryland's Prince George's County, and had a head coach said that about James, I would have publicly called out the perpetrator and demanded his ouster.

James? He just threw his hands up.

This was as good a representation as any about life in the NFL ecosystem. A terrible thing is exposed, but almost everyone scurries to protect their own skin. It's safer and easier to shut up or defend the status quo.

Dungy disappointed me most. A former Super Bowl champion head coach himself, he knows the discrimination Black players face. He has surely experienced it. But he chose to give cover to billionaires while continuing to wrap himself in his Christian faith. In which book of the New Testament does Jesus recommend being an apologist for the powerful? I don't believe you can lead with your faith while refusing to hold bullies to account.

But that's just me.

The whole episode was enough to convince me that this final term should be treated as nothing more than a victory lap. My intention was to lay down my saber, seek out the things that brought me fulfillment and joy, and coast.

I should've known that was never going to happen.

■ ■ ■

FOR A MOMENT, let us cross time and space to the National Basketball Association in March 1983. NBA players were threatening to strike as they tried to retain their right to free agency, and owners were desperate to curb skyrocketing salaries.

In 1979, Moses Malone and Bill Walton had become the first players to make $1 million per season, and Julius Erving and Kareem Abdul-Jabbar joined the seven-figures club a year later. This compelled every superstar to demand to be paid just as much. The Los

Angeles Lakers got creative by signing Earvin "Magic" Johnson to a contract that, starting in 1984, would pay Johnson $1 million per year for twenty-five years.

Malone was named most valuable player in 1982, and with details of Johnson's megadeal having been reported, Malone was a restricted free agent and wound up signing with Philadelphia. His $1.8 million base salary could reach at least $2 million annually if he reached certain incentives.

This turned every offseason into a bidding war for elite players, and owners knew this was unsustainable. By the 1983 labor impasse, owners were so determined to establish a salary cap that, in exchange, they agreed to hand over a majority of what they labeled "basketball-related income." This was the first time owners in any team sport divided the pie with players, and when the 1984–85 season began, each franchise's payroll could not exceed $3.6 million.

Still, that gave both sides a few months to explore loopholes. Among them was that, before the cap went into effect, teams could spend as much or as little as they wanted. Whatever the amount spent would be their organization's cap number the next season.

Larry Bird, the Boston Celtics' star, demanded a new contract that guaranteed him more than what Moses Malone was paid. Bird threatened to negotiate with every team but the Celtics if the team waited until he became a free agent.

So to retain Larry Legend while also avoiding the ire of fellow owners, the Celtics made an intriguing counteroffer: a seven-year contract that, at $2.1 million per season, would make Bird the NBA's second-highest-paid player, just below Malone. The news media reported that Malone remained at the league's financial mountaintop, but the truth was that his deal contained numerous bonuses for making the all-star team, leading Philadelphia to the playoffs, and merchandise sales.

Bird's contract contained none of those incentives. His $2.1 million salary was fully guaranteed the moment he signed the deal, making him the NBA's richest player while also giving owners a public relations victory.

A few months later, Bird and the Celtics won the NBA championship. This arcane provision became known as "The Larry Bird Exception," and from then on, every major free agent demanded their contracts be fully guaranteed, too. If the player was injured or forgot how to rebound or shoot, or if the team's plane got rerouted to Jupiter, the franchise is on the hook for every penny stipulated by the contract.

After Bird's landmark deal, every other major sports league followed the NBA in providing fully guaranteed contracts to players, a dramatic change that would shift the balance of power away from owners and toward players.

Every league, that is, except one.

■   ■   ■

IN 2012, THE Philadelphia Eagles signed star wide receiver DeSean Jackson to a five-year extension worth a staggering $51 million. It was a huge deal that rewarded a free-spirited and lightning-quick young receiver who had grown up in Los Angeles's infamous Crenshaw neighborhood before becoming a breakout player at the University of California.

"I'm able to focus and be comfortable and be confident that I'm at a place where I'm wanted," he told reporters two months after signing the deal. "I just really want to be able to bring a championship to the city."

Then Jackson broke several ribs during a game in November 2012, the Eagles fired coach Andy Reid after a twelve-loss season, and Reid's replacement, Chip Kelly, butted heads with several players—none more than Jackson. After the 2013 season, a New Jersey newspaper reported that Jackson had maintained "gang connections" from his youth in Los Angeles and had been loosely connected to two murders. The Eagles cut him, and despite the fact that Jackson had a clean criminal record and had done nothing wrong, there wasn't a damn thing he could do.

That $51 million contract? Only $18 million of it was guaranteed, so the Eagles didn't just get rid of a player Kelly viewed as a pain in the ass. The $33 million that remained on Jackson's deal went back into the salary cap and to the discretion of the GM.

A generation after Larry Bird, during a time in which fully guaranteed contracts are seen as the cost of doing business, NFL owners have insulated themselves from financial loss by refusing to even entertain the possibility of signing players to fully guaranteed deals. They claim that it's because rosters are huge, injuries are often catastrophic, and player decline happens unexpectedly. Some also suggest it's because of an obscure provision in the collective bargaining agreement that requires guarantees to be put into escrow, antiquated language that, decades ago, shielded the league from being sued if one owner fell into financial default.

The real reason that NFL players don't have fully guaranteed deals is that owners just don't want them. They're not against the rules, and nothing in our collective bargaining agreement prevents them. The league has historically protected its own interests, and despite the fact that many owners hate one another, they unite during an attack.

Owners have been so consistent in their unwillingness to discuss a fully guaranteed contract that players and their agents don't even ask for them. Nobody skips out of training camp or practices over this, because everyone knows what the answer will be. So, year after year and decade after decade, players have accepted that this is a nonstarter and settle for lopsided deals that, like Jackson's, sound better than they really are.

In 2018, Kirk Cousins actually gave it a shot. Because of the changes we made to the franchise tag in 2011, Kirk had earned a combined $44 million when Washington franchised him in 2016 and 2017. So Kirk's agent, Mike McCartney, worked with the union and clearly understood that if teams could fully fund the franchise tag, they could also fully fund a free-agent deal. Kirk therefore signed a three-year contract with the Minnesota Vikings that, for all intents and purposes, was worth a fully guaranteed $84 million. That agreement still contained $6 million in incentives, making it not *fully* fully guaranteed.

During the 2020 season, Houston Texans quarterback Deshaun Watson led the NFL in passing yards and set a team record for touchdowns, announcing loud and clear that a new superstar had emerged. The Texans stank and, like the Eagles had done eight years earlier, fired their coach and shepherded in an era of considerable dysfunction. The team's owner, Cal McNair, hired a self-described "character coach" as the team's executive vice president, who then traded away star wide receiver DeAndre Hopkins.

Watson, who signed a four-year extension worth a maximum of $156 million (with $110 million guaranteed), offered input on the Texans' searches for a general manager and head coach. The front office ignored him, leading Watson to demand that he be traded.

A standoff ensued, Watson held strong and refused to so much as meet with team executives, and a few weeks later, a Houston attorney filed a civil lawsuit against Watson that alleged sexual misconduct. An avalanche of lawsuits would follow, outlining a pattern of behavior in which Watson allegedly propositioned massage therapists for sexual favors. One of the suits called him a "serial predator."

Police and the league kicked off investigations, and legal filings and public pressure ballooned. One therapist told a television reporter that Watson had exposed himself and touched her with his penis without consent.

"Your charitable work and good-guy persona," another therapist wrote in an open letter, "are nothing more than a meticulously designed façade to keep your victims silent."

The accusations were sickening. Two decades after I stopped being a prosecutor, I hadn't lost my contempt for anyone who uses their power and status to intimidate and inflict pain on others. In my old world, the math was simple: I would find and prosecute you, laying bare your abusive tactics for all to see, before you disappeared into a prison sentence. I will never understand the mind of a predator, and I used to go to work every day excited about the possibility of locking another one away.

Then again, this was Ray Rice all over again. I didn't know Watson at all, but appalled as I was by the things I was reading, the NFLPA had an obligation to defend members. I wasn't a prosecutor anymore. I was closer to being a public defender, with no control over the people or cases that crossed my desk, just a responsibility to make certain I worked as hard as I could on their behalf, regardless of how offensive and disgusting the allegations.

Watson wasn't yet facing discipline from the league, but sponsors were dropping him as twenty-two lawsuits stacked up. We made contact with Watson's agent, David Mulugheta, a smart and brash young representative whose approach I liked and who seemed committed to building a client portfolio primarily with players of color. Months passed, and as the 2021 season approached, Watson's public stance was that he wouldn't play for the Texans, who were openly demanding three first-round picks in exchange for their franchise quarterback.

When training camp opened, ten women had filed criminal charges against Watson, and a grand jury was considering an indictment. The Texans benched him, ruling him inactive week after week for "non-injury" reasons. He didn't take a snap all season, Houston went 4–12, and the team fired coach David Culley after one season.

In March 2021, the historically underachieving Cleveland Browns reached out with a huge trade offer: five draft picks total, including each of the Browns' first-round choices for the next three years. It was precisely what Houston had asked for, and the team's front office quickly accepted.

In the quarterback-obsessed NFL, the trade wasn't necessarily a shock considering the Browns, who, since returning to the league in 1999 after suspending operations the year prior, had started thirty-four different players at the game's most important position. Watson was set to be number thirty-five.

Cleveland seemed content to ignore Watson's problematic status off the field and immediately offered him a contract extension. This was during a burgeoning era of quarterback megadeals, so the Browns' five-year offer for a maximum value of $230 million wasn't unusual, either. No, what got everyone's attention was something else entirely.

Because Jimmy Haslam, the Browns' owner, had defied the league's bro code. The contract he authorized for Watson was, for the first time ever, just like Larry Bird's. Every single dollar—all 230 million—was fully guaranteed.

■ ■ ■

**WHEN THE REST** of the owners heard what Haslam had done, they went berserk. General managers and owners had insisted to talented players for decades that *nobody* was worthy of a fully guaranteed deal. Not Joe Montana, Dan Marino, or Troy Aikman. That was enough for Peyton Manning, Tom Brady, and Drew Brees to not even ask.

Now Deshaun Watson, of all people, had broken the seal.

And with a slew of star quarterbacks contemplating their own contracts, owners knew what this meant for their own payrolls.

"It's like, 'Damn, I wish they hadn't guaranteed the whole contract,'" Ravens owner Steve Bisciotti told reporters in March 2022. "I don't know that he should've been the first guy to get a fully guaranteed contract."

And with that, Bisciotti said the quiet part out loud. His words finally unmasked the fact that owners had merely refused to entertain the possibility of fully guaranteed deals, and the truth is that such contracts were antithetical to owners' preferred business model and that they had collectively chosen to avoid them. Which is in conflict with the federal laws that allow the NFL to exist.

More than a century earlier, Congress overwhelmingly passed the Sherman Antitrust Act. Politicians from both sides of the aisle realized that the country's economy was in peril, not by some foreign actor or unseen pathogen but by greed. The richest and most powerful businessmen who owned railways, coal mines, oil refineries, and steel mills transferred their holdings to a trust, which in effect became a collective legal entity for all of these companies. This dramatically increased these individuals' wealth and destroyed competing businesses because, in short, the trust only did business with its own members.

To put it a different way, this was, in effect, a private club of rich industrialists who colluded among themselves to control prices and eliminate competition. Why? Because competing companies weren't part of the trust. Without alternatives, consumers had no choice but to purchase their train tickets, energy, and metal from those providers.

John Sherman, an Ohio senator, believed this practice was suffocating the free market and curbing broader capitalism, so he introduced a bill that suggested these trusts be declared unlawful and therefore broken up. "Every contract, combination in the form of trust or otherwise, or conspiracy, in restraint of trade or commerce among the several States, or with foreign nations, is hereby declared to be illegal," the bill read, and it passed both houses of Congress with little dissent before President Benjamin Harrison signed it into law.

From then on, it was considered a felony if companies attempted to conspire or collude to restrict competition, manipulate wages, or suppress worker mobility.

Almost by definition, the NFL is precisely the type of organization the Sherman Antitrust Act was meant to eradicate. It is an exclusive business, owners are admitted by invitation only, it operates across state lines, and it engages in interstate commerce. It has a rigid system of minimum and maximum wages and its largest source of revenue is a singular television contract that everyone shares equally. The overwhelming majority of workers aren't free to choose their employer. They are assigned to a company through the NFL draft, and the best players are sent to the worst team in order to improve the overall product through competitive balance.

All of those actions are textbook antitrust violations. But through a combination of special legislation afforded to the NFL by Congress and permissions granted by the collective bargaining agreement, the league's business structure is allowed to exist despite the Sherman Antitrust Act. The most important reason why is the existence of a players union that, at least in theory, has the same power as management.

Still, any collusion beyond permitted instances—the draft is among those because our collective bargaining agreement sets the associated salaries and benefits—doesn't just violate our collective bargaining agreement. It is a federal crime.

Bisciotti's admission regarding Watson's contract suggested that owners had been colluding for decades in order to prevent fully guaranteed deals and that a player facing criminal charges and an increasing number of lawsuits wasn't the guy to set that precedent.

I imagine that owners were so angry at Jimmy Haslam that they wanted his head on a platter. But because all franchise owners are equal, at least in the league's eyes, Roger couldn't punish Haslam. He hadn't broken a rule, after all, at least not a written rule.

But the commissioner could punish Watson.

As loathsome as I found the allegations surrounding Watson, I knew the public's desire for frontier justice gave Roger no legal right to issue discipline. Almost from the moment I became executive director, we started chipping away at Roger's enforcement power; be it neutral arbitrators to hear appeals for on-field fines, suspensions, and drug punishments, this was one of our key points of emphasis. The holy grail was to remove the commissioner's unfettered authority to punish players for what the league called conduct detrimental to the league or team, the NFL's catchall for any act that supposedly stained the league's reputation.

A small but important provision we added to the 2020 collective bargaining agreement was that Roger could no longer be judge, jury, and executioner on matters of personal conduct. Owners had gotten tired of the NFLPA continually humiliating the league (and Roger) in cases such as Bountygate, Ray Rice, and Deflategate. Kraft and Jerry were surprisingly keen to skip over the part in which Roger made a decision before having it overturned, so we all agreed that the first step would be to appoint a neutral arbitrator to determine punishment.

It wasn't perfect. The owners and Roger still insisted that we allow the commissioner to reserve the right to overturn the arbitrator's decision. We essentially traded this final veto power for our increased share of revenue and the automatic raises to minimum salaries.

In August 2022, the league and union agreed that Sue L. Robinson, a retired federal judge, could hear the Watson case and recommend potential penalties. Following an investigation, Robinson recommended a six-game suspension without pay. I thought that was overkill, considering Houston had kept Watson off the field the entire previous season. He hadn't been formally charged for a criminal offense, after all. But this was the deal we had agreed to in the collective bargaining agreement.

Immediately after Robinson announced her decision, pointing out that Watson had committed "nonviolent sexual conduct," the public went crazy. Watson had settled with twenty-three of his twenty-four accusers by that point, and while the settlement terms weren't disclosed, it didn't exactly make Watson look *less* guilty.

I have to imagine that owners were still incensed over Watson's contract, and a six-game suspension wasn't enough to soothe them. I began calling a few owners, knowing there would be pressure on Roger to exercise his power to overturn Robinson's decision. But these owners' worst nightmare was that Cleveland might somehow win the Super Bowl with a problematic quarterback on a fully guaranteed contract.

So, with the ink barely dry on our collective bargaining agreement, Roger used his veto power on the first case we had under the new system. He went against his own deal and defied common sense, because six games were already a longer suspension than Ben Roethlisberger wound up getting after being accused of sexual assault in 2009. It was three times as many games as Roger had initially given Rice. And it was a hell of a lot more robust than anything Roger had ever handed down to any owner for similarly credible accusations of sexual harassment or assault.

Based on my conversations, owners' anger was only tangentially about what had or hadn't occurred in those massage rooms. It seemed they just wanted to send a message to Haslam and everyone else that the NFL doesn't do guaranteed contracts. And because Roger answers to owners, and they answer to no one, he had to appease them.

The commissioner spoke to reporters about Watson's "predatory behavior" and pointed out that the quarterback's repeated instances of misconduct had been "egregious." Roger had again clipped on his sheriff's badge, and in our conversations, I didn't get the feeling that this time he was doing so because he enjoyed it—though, in general, he does—but because owners couldn't stomach having an outsider, Robinson, telling them what to do.

No matter how tired the public gets of Roger's authoritarianism, I had learned something after more than a dozen years of fighting him: Whatever the guy rules, he rules, and then we all argue about it before everyone just moves on. Then the union and league cut some deal that allows everyone to just get back to football.

So, with gritted teeth, I began to gear up for another fight if Roger suspended Watson for the season. At the last minute, Watson and the NFLPA agreed with the league on an eleven-game suspension with an additional fine of $5 million. Because it looked good, the league kicked in another million that would be donated to various nonprofits that educate young people on healthy relationships and the prevention of sexual misconduct.

It was a savvy PR move, and it placated owners because the Browns weren't going to the Super Bowl with Watson sidelined and Jacoby Brissett starting at quarterback. By the time Watson returned in December 2022, Haslam had been forced to watch his team—with its $185.5 million payroll—trudge to a 4–7 record. Cleveland didn't make the playoffs that year.

Mission accomplished?

Not for us. I wanted this to be just the beginning of a larger conversation, especially if we were to encourage players to shift the paradigm, as Larry Bird had done a generation earlier. Haslam and Watson had given players the opportunity for an economic breakthrough, and owners were so desperate to kill the precedent of fully guaranteed contracts that they'd kept Watson off the field for nearly two years.

After the 2022 season, three star quarterbacks were scheduled to become free agents. Strange and infuriating as it was, Deshaun Watson had kicked down the door that Kirk Cousins had cracked in 2018. Now it was up to Russell Wilson, Kyler Murray, or Lamar Jackson to walk through it. All three were deserving of the same or better deals as the one Watson had received, and my job was to make sure they understood that full guarantees became the norm in other sports not because of those leagues' collective bargaining agreements but because free agents merely demanded them.

If one or more of those players reached the open market, I told myself, it was inevitable. Now it was a question of whether clubs would actually choose any of those guys to become free agents and whether owners could restrain their instincts to collude.

Bisciotti's words echoed in my mind as the 2022 league year ended, ushering in a potentially historic process. "I don't know that *he* should've been the first," the Ravens' owner had said of Watson.

Okay, then, smartass: If Watson isn't the right guy, then who is? I'll give you three guesses and spot you a hint: He's already in your building.

■ ■ ■

THE MOMENT I saw Bisciotti's comment, I sent it to Don Davis. Raven quarterback Lamar Jackson was careful, emotionally intelligent, and guarded almost to a fault. Almost nobody knew what happened during Lamar's childhood in South Florida beyond that his father had died unexpectedly at age thirty-one. He never discussed it, whether during interviews or among teammates at the University of Louisville, where Lamar had bet on himself by refusing to play any position but quarterback, before winning the Heisman Trophy in 2016.

Lamar kept his personal business to himself in a way that I had never witnessed, confiding in a small number of friends from Pompano Beach, his hometown, and defying almost every established football norm. Before the Ravens drafted him in 2018, Lamar refused to even meet with or return calls to teams that suggested he play any position besides quarterback. He didn't hire an agent to negotiate his rookie contract, doing it himself with guidance from his mother, Felicia, who is neither a financial adviser nor a lawyer. Lamar simply didn't trust a stranger to work in his best interests.

I made sure that Bisciotti's words would reach Lamar, who is smart enough to realize that the timing of his free agency, once-in-a-generation talent, and personal brand in Baltimore gave him incredible leverage as he began negotiations for a contract extension. He also has a spotless reputation and, in 2019, was unanimously voted as the NFL's most valuable player.

In other words, he could become pro football's Larry Bird, clearing the way for fellow star quarterbacks Josh Allen, Joe Burrow, and Jalen Hurts to forever shift the sport's balance of power.

It could have been Patrick Mahomes, a once-in-a-lifetime player and person who would almost single-handedly transform the Kansas City organization from perennial loser to winners of three Super Bowl championships in five years. He is the rare player with more power than his coach, general manager, and owner. But when Patrick signed a ten-year extension in 2020, he relinquished this incredible leverage. On the surface, his deal looked astonishing: a maximum of $450 million and a decade of job security. The truth was that it was a good deal only for the Chiefs, because it guaranteed their franchise quarterback only about a third of that maximum amount. It was loaded with incentives and contingencies, giving the team the ability to get out of the contract at any time.

It also could have been Kyler Murray, but apparently rather than maximizing his own leverage, he agreed in July 2022 to an extension of his rookie deal—supposedly worth $230 million but guaranteeing him less than half that amount. Russell Wilson, a likely Hall of Famer, might have gotten every dollar guaranteed when he signed a five-year contract extension with the Denver Broncos that guaranteed him $124 million of the deal's maximum of $242.6 million.

I kept telling the Bird story every chance I got, attempting to use it to grow support among Lamar's fellow quarterbacks. We communicated occasionally with Felicia, Lamar's mother, and our salary cap department provided her with contract language and financial breakdowns about other players' deals. Often through Don, colleagues and I advised Lamar on how to say the right things publicly to not only create pressure on the Ravens but avoid handing leverage to Bisciotti and Baltimore's general manager, Eric DeCosta.

We told Lamar to just keep saying the same things: "I want to be a Raven. But I want a fair deal."

It was important that he stay as boring as could be, largely because history told us that franchises often push a public narrative that helps themselves during negotiations. When we were working with the agent for Joey Bosa, the dynamic edge rusher for the Los Angeles Chargers, our people made Joey's agent aware that other Chargers players had agreed to contracts with team-friendly language. When Joey turned down the team's initial offers, suddenly NFL media members were reporting supposed whispers circulating throughout the league about Joey's selfishness.

I expected the Ravens to similarly attempt to tarnish Lamar, but his squeaky-clean image and Bisciotti's comments about Watson had put the franchise in a corner. Instead, reports suggested that the team was concerned with Lamar's six-foot-two, 215-pound frame, fearing that he was more susceptible to injuries than other top quarterbacks. ESPN promoted the lie that Lamar "turned down" the Ravens' offer of $200 million guaranteed, but that offer actually guaranteed $70 million less than that.

Besides, the point all along was to get a *fully* guaranteed deal. Watson had set the precedent and shattered the glass ceiling, and regardless of the talking points teams push in the media, deals like Watson's and Bird's have little to do with future performance. The jobs of owners, coaches, and executives are supposed to be about selecting and maximizing talent, so why should the player bear all of the risk? The contracts of coaches and executives, after all, are fully guaranteed.

The system was fighting back against Lamar's demands, so the

NFLPA had to join the fight. In October 2022, I decided to file a lawsuit in the form of a grievance that accused owners of conspiring to prevent guaranteed contracts league-wide. There were people inside our building who thought it was a waste of time, but internally, our office had evidence of collusion, including hearing from multiple sources that the league and teams were discussing their avoidance of fully guaranteed contracts like Watson's.

On top of that, why *wouldn't* I be aggressive? The NFL is insulated from legal scrutiny and has been allowed to engage in business practices that would otherwise run afoul of antitrust laws. If there were no union, there could be no draft or price fixing. The truth is that the league couldn't operate without a players' union. They merely take umbrage at the fact that the NFLPA is neither compliant, ignorant of labor history, nor as blindly consumed by greed as owners. Instead, I pointed out that the NFL has run and thrived because it is the largest unregulated socialistic system in the history of the United States, and it cannot seem to abide by the conditions that actually make it lawful. There are organizations and agencies that could hold it to account, but they just don't. Nothing has ever stopped the Justice Department from launching an investigation into the league's handshake agreement to create an artificial salary cap in 2010, even after I delivered the secret spreadsheet that demonstrated collusion.

There was no concern about the document's authenticity, as it had been sent directly to me by an NFL owner. Federal and state authorities have the power to investigate allegations of sexual harassment, racial discrimination, and failures to follow workplace safety guidelines. All they would have to do is open a case file or send a letter.

It's just that . . . nobody does.

The only people who dare hold the mighty NFL to account is the NFLPA. We enforce the rules and at least try throwing our bodies between a cabal of corrupt billionaires and the financial malpractice that, because it is merely sports, we're just supposed to ignore.

Also, this was shaping up to be my last crusade as executive director. And with time running out to alter the league's abusive business model or at least be a pain in owners' asses, I didn't plan on ignoring a damn thing.

.   .   .

WHEN THE CALENDAR switched to 2023, I was already counting down the months. My term ran through the year, but I wanted the executive committee to hire a search firm and establish a list of potential successors so that players could vote in March. That way, the next leader of the NFLPA could take office with me still around to help ensure a smooth transition.

Karen and I booked a trip for late summer to Australia and New Zealand, where we would attend the women's World Cup, tour the countries, and ignore our phones. For me, it was the promise of sweet, blissful escape. With the clock therefore ticking, it was becoming clear that Lamar's contract situation was transforming into a merry game of chicken.

Lamar had sprained his knee during a game late in the 2022 season, and with hundreds of millions potentially at stake, he decided to sit out, playoff contests included. It was highly controversial, and fans questioned his work ethic and commitment to the team, his teammates, and the sport itself. But Lamar's choice was the right one. No player should risk his personal health and financial future because of the long-perpetuated myth that team comes before individual. The true reason for fans' discontent was because Lamar Jackson wouldn't dance for them.

Our staff had worked hard to help players shed the "gladiator" image that had produced a small number of legendary characters but had created several generations of chronically damaged brains and bodies. The days of guys getting their "bell rung," which is what coaches used to call concussions, or experiencing a "stinger," the old term for compressed or severed nerves in the spine, were over. It's not selfish for players to get as much out of football as the game gets out of them. Isn't that how most people approach their jobs?

NFL media assisted the Ravens in their smear campaign by repeatedly pointing to Lamar's knee sprain as proof that he was selfish and soft. Reporters and talking heads wondered aloud about his questionable knees and deteriorating judgment and losing playoff record, spinning a narrative that suggested Lamar might not even *want* to play football.

Gone, or at least on life support, was the belief that quarterbacks were aloof and indifferent. Setting guys like Aaron Rodgers aside, we repeatedly pointed to the commonality that quarterbacks shared with their teammates.

I made it clear to the top quarterbacks in the league at the time that this was their fight, too. And the only way I know how to convey that message is directly to them. When I want to talk to them all at once, I just set up a call. They heard the Bird story about guaranteed contracts.

But even on this issue, there was dissension. The league *wants* players to believe that a fully guaranteed contract is a nonstarter, and that turning down an otherwise strong offer is a mistake. That's precisely how the NFL gets you: Its preferred message soaks into your brain via various channels, reaching someone whose opinion you may trust, and soon you're questioning whether you made a mistake in even asking for a guaranteed deal—that it's selfish and potentially a mistake to pursue financial security at the height of your earning potential while playing a brutal game.

The NFL loves to paint itself as a "family," especially when that sentiment serves owners. And historically, players in Lamar's position second-guess their methods and eventually crack. Plenty of guys would grow weary of the endless back-and-forth, deciding to sign a franchise's supposed best offer before limping back to a hero's welcome.

But Lamar? He didn't waver.

I don't recall him saying anything during the call, nor did I expect him to.

He held strong while the Ravens' offense, a glimmer of itself without one of the most exciting players to ever suit up, lost in the first round of the playoffs. Whatever leverage the team had created vanished within the chatter of Lamar compared to his backup, Tyler Huntley.

"When you have something good, you don't play with it," Lamar wrote on social media shortly after that playoff loss. "You don't take chances losing it. You don't neglect it. When you have something good, you pour into it. You appreciate it. Because when you take care of something good, that good thing takes care of you too."

The dance was on.

Still trying to neutralize the league's media strategy, I penned an open letter to explain the "Larry Bird Exception," reminding our members and fans that we knew owners weren't above collusion. NFL loyalists trumped the power of supposed free enterprise, but when owners act in concert to manipulate that market, it should be obvious to the public that they're being lied to. Winning may be fun, and owners enjoy hoisting championship trophies and showing up rival owners, but that's not what these guys get into this for. I had personally seen repeated evidence of teams not spending up to their own salary cap, a signal that owners of those franchises would prefer to take profits over playoff appearances.

Then, in March 2023, owners finally committed what I thought was their second-most-brazen act of collusion ever. Baltimore used the nonexclusive franchise tag on Lamar, which would have guaranteed him $32.5 million for the coming season. The nonexclusive tag allowed other organizations to make offers to Lamar, and if the Ravens failed to match those offers, he was free to join another team. Lamar followed by announcing his desire to be traded, essentially begging other franchises to come and get one of the best players to ever line up at the game's most important position.

It's possible that the Ravens opened lines of communication with other teams, but the fact is that no calls came in. Zero. This during a pending collusion case. Not one NFL team made an inquiry. A parade of coaches, executives, and owners publicly claimed that they didn't *want* Lamar Jackson on their team because whoever their quarterback was gave them a better chance to win than Lamar.

"That's just something that never felt suited to what we wanted to do," Washington Commanders coach Ron Rivera would tell reporters, explaining his franchise's choice to pass on Lamar and stick with Sam Howell. A few months later, Washington went 4–13, and Rivera was fired.

"I'd say there's some concern over how long he can play his style of game," Atlanta Falcons owner Arthur Blank said, redoubling his commitment to young quarterback Desmond Ridder and refusing to pursue Lamar. During the 2023 season, Ridder was benched and later traded after the Falcons went 7–10.

"We have a quarterback," Detroit Lions coach Dan Campbell said. As for Lamar? "Man, he's a heck of a talent."

Campbell, a real-life Ted Lasso, came closest to letting the truth slip. You could hear in his voice how much he wanted the former MVP as Lamar was just beginning the prime of his career. The Lions deploy a similar power-rushing attack as the Ravens, and the addition of such a player would have almost handed Detroit an NFC championship.

Around and around it went, the reasons becoming more baffling by the day. Kraft claimed that Meek Mill, the rapper who'd performed at Kraft's wedding, had encouraged the Patriots to pursue Lamar. But Kraft deferred to Bill Belichick on personnel matters, and Belichick didn't want Lamar. This is the same organization that would start Mac Jones at quarterback in 2023 before going 4–13, trading Jones to Jacksonville, and parting ways with Belichick after almost a quarter century.

George Atallah sent me some of the more amusing media chatter, including the insistence by former Green Bay executive-turned-agent Andrew Brandt that our collective bargaining agreement gave management too much power with the franchise tag.

Those are the lengths owners are willing to go to, racking up losses and public humiliations as they contort themselves into unnatural positions to avoid paying a superstar quarterback what he deserves. The publicly available facts supported our collusion claim. We would win or lose in front of a neutral arbitrator, but not before the league was forced to turn over internal documents.

I hoped the owners, as they did with the rigged television contract that gave them ammunition before the 2011 lockout, would continue to write down their unlawful actions and intents in emails and PowerPoint slides.

By April 2023, it was open season for trades. There's no more valuable currency than draft choices, as franchises often load up on the possibility of acquiring game-changing players as they bid fare-well to aging, established ones. Supposedly without an interested trade partner, the Ravens had nowhere to shop Lamar. It was sit out or play, and as different as Lamar is, he's still a football player.

He couldn't just bring himself to miss a season of his career and potentially lose a year of earnings.

So, with the sides at a stalemate, Baltimore and its quarterback agreed on a new contract: five years, worth a maximum of $260 million. Three of the years were fully guaranteed at $135 million, mak-ing it an incredible coup for a young star who had dug in his heels and stood his ground more than anyone before him. The bummer for me was that the contract wasn't fully guaranteed. The owners had done what they do by forming a united front to create the illusion of lever-age where there was none.

I wonder what would have happened if Lamar had stretched his negotiation into training camp, or played the 2023 season on the franchise tag before hitting the open market. The Ravens were never going to let Lamar Jackson walk away, and under those dire circum-stances, I believe they would have caved.

Alas, owners know players. They actually know them better than I do. The most important factor in the league's economic formula is that the average playing career is three and a half years. No one, not even the amazing Lamar Jackson, has convincingly shown a willing-ness to forfeit one of those years.

The contract Lamar ultimately signed wasn't perfect but also wasn't a white flag. He had fought the good fight, working language into the deal that benefited him and squeezed more out of the Ravens than he would have probably received. But like many players, Lamar had more leverage than even he realized, largely because football players have been conditioned from childhood to believe things that simply are not true. That all choices are binary. That they're either tough or soft. In the lineup or not. Willing to sacrifice for the team or selfish.

It is a perfect lie, a silver bullet, the only thing in the NFL that has ever gone undefeated.

$$\blacksquare \quad \blacksquare \quad \blacksquare$$

OVER MY FINAL few months as executive director, I wondered how I could possibly prepare a successor for the job. There's no instruction manual, and much of its responsibilities are often too outrageous to be believed.

Considering the messes that accompanied the 2020 collective bargaining agreement, the agreement on the Covid-19 protocols, and my reelection, absurdities were the norm and a new conspiracy seemed to lurk around every corner. So, for starters, I decided to completely remove myself from the search process. After the executive committee retained the search firm, I spoke with its leaders and suggested they read *A Whole Different Ball Game,* the autobiography of former MLB union chief Marvin Miller. I also recommended that they educate themselves about the NFLPA's history and find someone who's open to learning. I have my doubts that they did either.

And that was it. Until the executive committee elected someone new, I would have nothing to do with the process. Like me, the next leader would learn more on the job than they possibly could beforehand. The job would be different from mine, anyway, as new storm clouds were gathering around the NFL: the increasing pervasiveness of gambling, including television networks' cozy relationships with online sports books, and private-equity investment into franchises.

There were strong internal candidates, including George and

Don, who, depending on the day, took turns being my right-hand man. George understands messaging and strategy like few people I have been around, and Don used to be a player representative and had spent a decade in our office. Teri Smith, our union's chief operating officer, was a savvy mix of experience and fresh eyes. It wasn't my job to anoint or even openly support anyone, though, and looking back, I may have overcorrected.

I believed strongly that, armed with enough information, players will make the right choice. Our executive committee was full of intelligent and thoughtful football players, and they had been around good and bad leaders most of their lives. Coaches, unlike most corporate heads, must think beyond profitability and be more in tune with assembling a team, establishing chemistry, and running a machine that works to the best of its potential.

At least in my mind, an ideal union leader possesses many of the same attributes as a winning coach: an ethical North Star, driven by doing not only what's best but also what's right.

Tom DePaso would be staying on as general counsel, and his more than forty years of experience had been the best resource I could have asked for. I later heard that our internal candidates had been passed over by the search firm, which appeared to be looking for another outsider, and those colleagues had also pledged to remain on staff.

That was encouraging.

On the final Saturday of June 2023, I came into our mostly empty office to tag everything that was mine in the executive director's suite. As the movers boxed up some of my things, I thought of an old drinking game that's popular among lawyers in a trial's postmortem. Usually over shots, attorneys from both sides of the case would name someone who had surprised or impressed them.

Who had I been most surprised by? Even I couldn't believe the answer.

It was Roger.

Just as I experienced my own transformation, mostly centering on my exhaustion and the erosion of my idealism, so did the commissioner. The shift in him was subtle. It's not as if the man changed, and it wasn't anything he explicitly said or did. But I did sense a gradual acceptance that he was limited in his own ability to protect owners from themselves. He remained the league's ultimate protector, but there's no shield strong enough to keep most of these guys in line.

It was during our meetings over anthem protests that, for the first time, I detected embarrassment from Roger over the owners' position. In 2017, after Colin Kaepernick had sued the league, owners just couldn't let it go that a small number of players continued to protest. Roger visibly disagreed that this was a battle worth fighting, but his control-freak bosses wouldn't let him off the hook. After that, he stopped defending owners when they said or did something stupid. He'd just let Kraft or Jerry or Art Rooney talk, digging themselves and the league into a deeper hole. He never told me this, but if you're Roger and Bisciotti says what he did about Deshaun Watson, wouldn't you just love to take Bisciotti aside and tell him to shut up?

I believe Roger finally realized what Paul Tagliabue had: that owners are his bosses, sure, but there's no changing them. There's damn sure no controlling them. On his best day, all the commissioner can do is corral his herd of billionaires and, when it's necessary, play one against the other to achieve what the NFL actually needs. Or at least prevent it from caving in on itself.

When I took this job, I thought Roger lacked depth. I learned that he did not. He is his father's son, just a far better politician, and he has never deviated from his job description. I wanted to change the world and modernize pro football. Roger just wanted to keep the league alive and the owners happy, and he'd come into his position with a kind of fulsome understanding I wish I'd had.

I may have lost some of my optimism and swagger, but I never stopped believing this job was, at its core, a mission. Players had to understand their power, and I kept thinking—at times foolishly—that they would rise to the occasion, stop being selfish, and fall into line like warriors. Most times, they were more complicated, shortsighted, and interested far more in self-preservation than in advancing the collective. I cannot imagine that Roger held on to this kind of aspirational mythology, but then again, how could he? He had known and worked with many of his bosses since he was a teenager.

The guy takes every arrow, shovels pile after pile of shit, and keeps coming back for more. Is he overpaid? Hell, I think it's the opposite. The fact that NFL fans never learn of some of the colossally stupid things Cincinnati's Mike Brown and Indianapolis's Jim Irsay have said or done is almost breathtaking. Each owner pays Roger $2 million per year to ride into some unwinnable war, get his ass kicked publicly, and help increase the value of each franchise and net worth of each owner.

In 2006, when Roger became commissioner, five NFL teams were worth $1 billion or more. Today, the *least* valuable club is worth $4.1 billion, and Jerry's Cowboys are valued at more than $10 billion—the most of any sports team in the world. That's more than seventy-two times the $140 million he paid in 1989 and is nearly $3 billion more than the estimated value of Kraft's Patriots.

Then again, Kraft has those six Super Bowl trophies, and the things Jerry and Kraft *don't* have are the true source of a hatred for each other that'll continue until one or both of them are gone. In 2017, Jerry became the fifteenth team owner elected to the Pro Football Hall of Fame. No disagreement here. But if you want to know how petty these guys are, all you need to know is that Kraft badly wants to be enshrined in Canton, Ohio, and has been on the ballot thirteen consecutive years. He has been shut out every time.

Surely just another interesting coincidence.

I have noticed signs that Roger is growing weary of these never-ending feuds. But the owners know he's a wartime general, and because the league cannot seem to avoid starting pointless and self-defeating battles, I wonder how many more times Prince Valiant will keep charging into enemy fire before he hangs up his armor.

He outlasted me, and it took nearly fifteen years and endless squabbles that turned Roger's face red for me to realize that he was the yin to my yang. Even after all this time, I'm not sure which of us had the more difficult job. Is it harder to manage a group of alpha males, most of whom are younger than twenty-seven? Or being in charge of thirty-one billionaires who answer to and respect no one—overgrown children who are constantly trying to lie, cheat, and steal, and will throw a tantrum if you catch them?

The limitations and peculiarities of my job were immense, and I hoped my successor would whip up support, rally players, and accomplish more than I did. Still, during that summer day packing up my office, I thought about the day President Barack Obama sent a note on White House stationery that congratulated me on the completion of the 2011 collective bargaining agreement. And when Larry Probst, the former chief executive of EA Sports, left me a hilariously unhinged message after I threatened to move players away from the Madden video game. Or the day I called Tom Brady from my desk, telling him the district court overturned his suspension.

I'll forever hold on to the feeling when Richard Sherman approached me after my last rep meeting, when players actually applauded me. Richard wrapped me in a hug and said something I'll never forget: "I know sometimes we didn't get along, especially in this room. But I hope you always knew that's how we treat people we love."

I knew, then, that I would leave the job feeling satisfied but not necessarily good. So when I finished packing, including carefully boxing up the photo of Grandmother Mary I kept on my desk for years, I sat down and started writing. The vote for my successor was scheduled in three days, and the executive committee would elect Lloyd W. Howell, Jr., a veteran businessman who had been chief financial officer of Booz Allen.

I wanted him to know that, if Gene Upshaw hadn't fought the league in 1993, it might have taken players twenty more years to achieve free agency. He'd stood up to the owners, refusing to be controlled or seen as anyone's property, and as easy as it might have been for Gene to concede, he never did. He fought. And that's what you do in this job: You fight.

You cannot give in or be intimidated, I wrote, no matter the power or wealth of your opponent. You make them learn your name. The only way to do this job right is for it to be the most difficult, unrewarding position you ever have. Doing it right, and therefore doing right by the players, sometimes means burning every bridge, nuking every relationship, and driving yourself crazy. You are not running a business. You are running a labor union, and you will have to make a choice of whether you will be consistent with the principles that have made labor unions strong or fall victim to some belief that this organization is somehow unique. It is not. Our guys might get paid better than those descending into a coal mine, but the reality for both is that there is always someone taking the risk and someone benefiting from it. You can never be friends with the latter.

I wanted him to understand that NFL owners evolve and they are far more clever now than they had been when I took the job. They will go overboard to seduce you into believing that you are a lot more like them than I was, and if you believe it for a second, you will be behind the curve. The men and their families will be worse off for it.

If this is a springboard job, then walk away now. Because if you are in this to become personally successful, we will be institutionally worse.

This business, and any in professional sports, is designed to use people who do the work and empower those who make the most money. It is a plantation on which some owners view the people you represent as machinery, not as human. If you do the job the right way, it should come with an acceptance that it will eat away at your emotional health, and I learned that the hard way.

Show up, be there for the guys, and congratulations. And, oh yeah: In the words of that noted sage, Mike Vrabel, don't fuck it up.

My plan was to set the note on the center of Gene's desk, and on top I would leave a small gift. Nothing expensive or fancy, just something that comes in handy when you're in this office. It was a bottle of extra-strength heartburn medicine, from De with love.

The guy is going to need them. Players should hope he does, anyway.

# THE QUESTION

Not long after discovering the draft of Gene Upshaw's speech, I made two important decisions. The first was to have the folder laminated and placed in the lobby of our offices at NFLPA headquarters, which, in 2009, we had renamed 63 Upshaw Place.

The idea was for visitors to consider the display, remember Gene, and think of a warning he'd never gotten a chance to deliver. He knew a pivotal moment was coming, and with owners signaling their plans for a lockout, this struck me as a rallying cry.

[W]e must never forget that freedom can be hollow. . . .
Change is taking place in the NFL and the clock will never be turned back.

My second decision was more personal. I vowed that, unlike Gene and Michael Weiner, my first counterpart at the Major League Baseball Players Association, I would not die in the job. Or, put a different way, I wouldn't let it kill me.

And damned if it didn't try.

So when I walked away, handing over the reins to Lloyd Howell in July 2023, part of me felt defeated. But I reminded myself that I had fulfilled my oaths, to both the union and myself. We had fought, trading blows with some of the wealthiest and therefore most powerful people on Earth, and survived. Time marches on. So could we.

I have spent much of the last two years as a teacher, lecturing to business and law students at the University of Virginia, Harvard, Yale, and Pepperdine. In my classes, I tell a version of the story you just read. It is my interpretation of a proverb about how truth, as it approaches a fire whose brutality scared off others, sees the fire's totality: potential destruction, yes, but also beauty and warmth and light.

Truth doesn't run away. It persists, continuing onward.

I had no interest, then, in writing this as a *football book,* just as my classes are only tangentially about sports. I have always seen the NFL as a reflection of America, revealing as much about its grandeur and promise as its shortcomings and illusory realities. Our most popular and powerful sports league has so much in common with our wider society: racial disparity, a vast economic divide, a political gulf that grows wider through misinformation and by each side's poor understanding of the other. White men largely control the nation's wealth and power, minorities keep the labor machine running, and we all pretend this is sustainable beneath banners of red, white, and blue.

There has been much talk in recent years of where we are in the lifespans of these parallel experiments. Brain injuries have threatened the long-term viability of tackle football, albeit with twin trend lines showing a decline in youth participation alongside the continued increase in television ratings and revenue. Some suggest players have more influence than ever, while others insist owners have never had it better.

Like the fire metaphor, multiple things can be true. When I became executive director in 2009, Stephen Ross bought a controlling stake of the Miami Dolphins, and with a net worth of $7.7 billion, he became the league's second-wealthiest owner, behind only Paul Allen, the Microsoft co-founder who'd purchased the Seattle Seahawks a dozen years earlier. In 2022, the year before I left the union, Walmart heir Rob Walton—worth more than $110 billion—bought the Denver Broncos. *Forbes* now estimates that the twelve richest owners and their families control more than $312 billion, or about 7 percent of the entire U.S. economy. It is an investment that has tempted no less than Tom Brady, the ultimate team guy and union man, who bought into the Las Vegas Raiders and who I fear may begin to lose his connection with the rank-and-file men with whom he shared locker rooms. But if anyone is capable of maintaining both his focus and his soul, it's Tom.

Still, owners have never been wealthier, and the temptation to join them is powerful. The billionaire class has recently been granted unprecedented access to the levers of American government. Their ticket to such influence, of course, came when one of their own was granted a return to the White House.

■　■　■

**SIXTEEN YEARS AGO**, I spent Barack Obama's first Inauguration Day in transit. It was my first job interview with the executive committee, and for both sides, it felt like a fact-finding mission—a chance to understand.

So, as 2025 began, I was again craving more information. Not about football, my future, or even Donald Trump's second term as president. But about us.

Just hours after Trump's inauguration, where he was surrounded not by average Americans but by billionaires, I traveled to Jekyll Island, Georgia. This tiny outpost is where, more than a century ago, a secret cabal of the nation's wealthiest individuals came together to shape policy. The Jekyll Island Club Resort is a historic landmark and tourist attraction now, with a coffee house, a museum, and massive live oaks that loom over the 240-acre property. Its lavish "cottages," with Victorian architecture and some 8,000 square feet of living space, still stand, named after some of the famous families who owned them: Goodyear, Macy, Pulitzer.

"The richest, the most exclusive, the most inaccessible club in the world," a lifestyle magazine declared at the time.

In November 1910, Senator Nelson Aldrich invited a few of the country's most powerful bankers to join him on the island to go duck hunting. In actuality, the purpose was a secret meeting to discuss a central bank, which was widely unpopular because this would give the private sector—the country's wealthiest individuals—financial might equal to or greater than the federal government's.

Over six days, the men referred to each other only by their first names and sketched out a proposal whose contours would be nearly identical to what became the highly controversial Federal Reserve Act in 1913. American currency would be elastic, with its value capable of rising and falling at any time, putting an end to the gold and silver whose values remained static.

Sixteen years later, the Fed attempted to restrain the stock market boom that led to the economic growth and exuberant culture of the Roaring Twenties. America's wealthiest people didn't like that their little club wasn't so little anymore. After the Fed raised its target rate, industry cratered, the dollar suffocated, and banks failed. In panic, it then raised interest rates, which caused a global panic and sent the world economy into steep debt.

Put more plainly: The last time America allowed its richest, most self-serving individuals to strong-arm the government, it directly led to the Great Depression.

A quarter of the labor force was out of work, one in five banks went under, and Americans were reduced to living in shanties made of cardboard and tin. It took World War II, which resulted in eighty-five million deaths, to reinvigorate the world economy.

Members of the Jekyll Island Club? The guys who lit this fuse? They just pretended it never happened, abandoning their cottages, letting the vines grow and limbs fall as they ignored their part in the

Federal Reserve's genesis, as a once-pristine resort—and the economy they'd unilaterally commandeered—was left to decay.

■  ■  ■

THROUGHOUT MY TENURE with the NFLPA, I sometimes felt as if I had a front-row seat in a theater run by oligarchs. So, as we enter what seems like a new era in American politics, I feel not only compelled to issue this warning but qualified.

The parallels from what I experienced with owners to what played out on Inauguration Day are almost breathtaking. There, seated and smiling immediately behind Trump, were a small group of men worth a combined $1.2 trillion, men who are so used to getting what they want that they expect it. Who, when pushed back on, use their economic scythe to force the movement of markets, the reduction of workforces, and the fluctuation of the dollar's value.

Trump won the 2024 election by promising to curb inflation, lower gas prices, and restore the economy to one that empowers everyday Americans. But when Trump's inauguration was moved inside the Capitol rotunda because of freezing temperatures, it wasn't the billionaires who were left out in the cold. It was the tens of thousands of working-class voters, many of them struggling, who'd traveled to Washington to celebrate after Trump had his power restored.

It was a ruse, no different from the bait-and-switch I saw time and again from NFL owners. When a David Tepper, Terry Pegula, or Clark Hunt wants an upgraded stadium, the public narrative isn't that a billionaire wants the public to pay for yet another massive asset and monument to his ego. It is that the current stadium is old, worn out, even dangerous. The *fans* deserve a better, more state-of-the-art game-day experience.

This used to help voters ignore the fact that they'll be the ones footing the bill for a renovated or new building that, at least from a legal standpoint, is publicly owned. In 2024, Jackson County, Missouri, home of the Kansas City Chiefs' Arrowhead Stadium, added a ballot initiative in which three-eighths of a cent would be added to the local sales tax, generating the $500 million needed to improve the facility. The politics were clever, considering the vote would be held just months after the Chiefs won their third Super Bowl in five years. The franchise also contracted an army of consultants and lobbyists to "educate" the public about the issue.

But despite the team's popularity and cultural resonance, nearly two-thirds of locals voted against the tax increase. That accomplished two things. It infuriated the Hunt family, who own the Chiefs and aren't used to being told no, and proved that Americans hate taxes more than they love football.

Billionaires don't just take the hint, so what did the Hunts do? They followed the recent trend of owners bypassing a public vote and ramming through their desired solution. A few years before the Chiefs' ballot measure, Buffalo Bills owner Pegula wanted a new building and took his demands directly to lawmakers, and whatever Pegula said compelled Gov. Kathy Hochul of New York to announce that the state legislature would cover $600 million of the estimated $1.4 billion cost. Hochul didn't ask taxpayers to consider an increase. She told them one was coming. Erie County kicked in $250 million after legislators voted 10–0, and just like that, the majority of Pegula's eye-popping new stadium was paid for.

Pegula, whose net worth is nearly $8 billion, didn't need to win the support of millions of voters because he'd learned from other owners that you can get what you want by convincing just a couple dozen elected officials. So what did the Hunt family do? They created leverage by crossing the state line to neighboring Kansas, and two months after the failed vote, Gov. Laura Kelly signed a new bill into law that would combine a tax increase with revenue bonds, simultaneously finding an avenue for funding while also putting pressure on Missouri to keep the franchise on its side of the state line. Either way, taxpayers are *going* to pay for the Chiefs' new construction.

This is billionaires' new strategy: Socialize costs and privatize wealth. We pay for things, in other words, that they get to keep. Owners get to lease out the space, sell tickets and ad space, and charge for concessions and parking. Think Pegula reimburses the state and county for that revenue? Quite the opposite. His government deals actually entitle him to $3 million per year in tax deductions, earmarked for programs geared toward social justice, affordable housing, and feeding the hungry—but with no actual obligation to spend a dime. You read that right: Neither Pegula nor the Bills have to spend that $3 million a year to *claim* that amount as a tax write-off. Over the life of the thirty-year contract, Pegula can do whatever he'd like with his combined $100 million in savings.

As written, it's perfectly legal, a glimpse not only into nearly fifteen years of my life and the kinds of bullshit the NFLPA had to undo with the 2011 collective bargaining agreement. It's a look at America, and I can't definitively say that the NFL wrote the playbook for how to get what you want in this country. I just know that tech billionaires, empowered by the unlimited political contributions made possible by the Supreme Court's 2010 ruling on *Citizens United,* are following it to the letter. Create a ruse, make a convincing public case that a strategy is good for everyone, then maximize profits while turning all of us into fungible parts in their revenue machine.

So what do we do? What *can* we do?

The answer is a version of what I teach my classes. Since the days of John Steinbeck's *The Grapes of Wrath,* set during the billionaire-created Great Depression, unions have known that management always wants more control. The same is true now. Business leaders will try to convince workers of a populist message: that we're all in this together. But the first step is to recognize that this is a lie and redouble a willingness to fight.

Maybe this seems overly simple. It's not. The preceding pages of this book should be evidence enough that the mega-wealthy believe that everyday people, be they NFL players or autoworkers or journalists, are happy to merely exist and will never push back on C-suite edicts. That the kindly billionaire just wants to win, and the responsibility of labor is conciliation. Owners didn't overreact because the NFLPA was demanding unreasonable outcomes. They did so because we wouldn't fall into line and accept their unilateral doctrines.

The very act of resisting is enough to draw the wealthy to the bargaining table. You may not get everything you demand, but neither will they. They may not respect you as an equal, but they must respect you. We are not batteries, born and breathing just to power their greed. That's a colonialist's viewpoint, not terribly different from the one my ancestors were born into.

It's imperative we realize what they did: We are human beings, and we must not be deceived or bamboozled or bought. We must not forget and we must not stand in awe. We damn sure can't wait for politicians to save us, because money and politics don't mix. Neither do billionaires and media.

Those of us curious enough to seek truth have no choice but to seek out reliable messengers. That's harder to do than ever before. Don't just believe what you watch or read. Ask why something is believable, then question the root source. Upon reaching a conclusion, question *that*. This doesn't make you indecisive. It makes you thoughtful.

It means you want to understand. And that you're unwilling to accept something just because someone in power endorses it. Instead of being afraid that our elected officials and business leaders can make our lives harder, let's turn the tables, making theirs more difficult than they've ever been.

Most of all, let's stop idolizing billionaires and trusting them to save us or at least do what's right. Because, after living in their world for nearly decades, take it from me.

They never fucking will, and they must be pressed to accomplish only the things we, the collective, allow.

■  ■  ■

AT THE BEGINNING of this book, I asked a question: If you could commit a crime and knew that you would get away with it, would you do it?

Well? Now you know most of what I do. You've seen behind the curtain and, hopefully, considered the motivations and values of thirty-one of our country's most influential men. Not only is it possible to skirt laws and face no consequences. In some cases this can be handsomely rewarded. Me? I still believe in the oath I took so many years ago.

But billionaires, tasked time and again with morality pitted against greed, seem to make a consistent choice. Maybe that's part of the neurological wiring that makes it possible to be a billionaire. To devote your life to the singular objective of accumulating as much money as possible is to embrace the sacrifice of everything else: relationships and joy, sure, but also virtue.

Today's would-be oligarchs have chosen their paths, and by and large, they are far more intelligent, manipulative, and cutthroat than even the most powerful NFL owners. I believe it is why they have hitched themselves to Trump, because nearly a decade after Colin Kaepernick's protest, the league is no longer a reflection of America. The country has become a reflection of the NFL.

Trump, after all, is an entertainer. He is a master of stagecraft and misdirection—look *here*, not there—and captivates us with tales of illegal immigrants eating pets, the purchase and annexation of Greenland and Canada, the "Gulf of America," all while boldly and unapologetically dismantling the controls of our democracy.

The president was never allowed entry into the NFL owners' club, but it took me years to realize what Jerry and Kraft immediately knew: Trump is one of them. He may not own a team, but he is an owner: someone who distracts us with a dazzling spectacle, appointment television, a continuous flow of dopamine. We are so thoroughly entertained that it obscures what's happening behind the scenes, and as we're so busy picking a side and staking everything to our desired outcome, suddenly a whistle blows and we're pulled back to reality.

As I write this, it's too early to know if Trump's people will be or can be as good at this as the NFL. The league is successful because Roger projects incredible discipline, even if that's just another mirage. There was nothing disciplined about Trump's first term. Only time will tell if that changes in his second; if, either in his cabinet or in his cadre of sycophantic billionaires, there can be his commissioner. Or, for that matter, someone who will succeed Roger when he finally steps away. I cannot imagine that it will be Troy Vincent, who remains a mouthpiece for the league but, having been relegated to crisis management in the years after Deflategate, seems to have allowed his blind ambition to be exposed. And it will not be Jeff Pash, for so long the league's Merlin, who retired in 2024. Is Roger settling all family business? After decades of taking arrows, I like to think he's firing a few of his own.

．　．　．

ON A FEROCIOUSLY cold Wednesday, I walked among the oaks of a rebuilt Jekyll Island just hours after a winter storm. Ice had glazed roads and broken limbs, littering the club's grounds with debris. Decades after the state of Georgia condemned the abandoned site before a long and expensive revitalization, the property remained beautiful, and it's hard not to be charmed by the glamour and history that once existed here. Men stepped off yachts, into the clubhouse, behind long tables to decide what was best for *their* America.

It never occurred to them to weaponize entertainment, because in their day, relentless force was enough. Though the public had grown suspicious of these men, no one dared push back, and it took a worldwide collapse to prove them selfish and hapless. Politicians from both parties eventually stood up to them, ushering in legislation that curtailed their ability to collude and gave workers the ability to fight back.

These were among the first unions, a revolution born of failure and necessity, and the mega-wealthy would spend decades experimenting with ways to weaken or even cripple the notion of a labor uprising. It wasn't until the 1950s that a handful of new robber barons struck gold, taking over rivals to establish a monopoly and, in 1961, successfully convincing Congress to declare this business a nonprofit enterprise and therefore immune from antitrust laws.

And thus, the modern NFL was born, giving rise to what would become the largest, most successful socialistic monopoly in our nation's history. Its leaders would answer to no board of directors, shareholders, or federal authorities. Until the most recent Inauguration Day, they ran the richest, most exclusive, most inaccessible club in the world. With the White House emerging as the new billionaires' playground, I suspect that owners will try to reassert themselves and continue the WWE-ization of pro football, sinking deeper into the lusty embrace of satisfying fans' most primitive impulses—gambling, dehumanization of modern-day gladiators, the further intertwining of sports with alcohol and drugs—at the expense of sophistication.

As we stand on the craggy precipice of a new era, we're again faced with a choice. What would you do? What *will* you do? Allow billionaires to unilaterally remake our economy once more? Or fight for yourself? For the collective?

I was blessed to live long enough to speak the words Gene Upshaw never did, and because it's apt, I paraphrase him here: Change is taking place in America, and the clock must never be turned back.

The flames of truth mustn't be suffocated. We must not fall victim to the temptations of entertainment and distraction. I may have stepped away from the front lines of this war, but I'll spend my remaining days standing where I belong: between billionaires and America, a version of which my ancestors could have only imagined but which they would have wanted me to protect.

To persist and avoid running away, to carry on speaking the truth and continuing to push onward.

—*DeMaurice F. Smith, January 2025*

# ACKNOWLEDGMENTS

I am deeply grateful to the many people who have supported me throughout this journey. Your time, friendship, instruction, criticism, and love have been invaluable.

The idea for this book was born shortly before we signed the 2011 collective bargaining agreement. I remember the core members of the NFL's bargaining team—including Robert Kraft, who had recently buried his wife—and the NFLPA executive committee members were in our D.C. office for the signing. I walked into the players' conference room with two John Mackey jerseys, honoring the first president of the union, who had recently passed away. I told them that we were signing this before finalizing the new deal between the players and the league and that one would go to Mackey's widow. I have the other, and it is my most prized possession from my years at the NFLPA. Looking around that room, I realized that the past eighteen months had been about more than football. Young men had elected a new leader after Gene Upshaw passed away, embraced the idea that players were more than gladiators, used their share of revenue to improve the pensions of former players, and successfully wrestled the power to control their work away from owners who had held it for decades. I had witnessed the power that comes from a collective belief in fairness and the duty of sacrifice.

This story goes beyond the game and business. I will never be able to thank all the players who trusted me and fought for principle. Today, many of us could learn from a group of people in their twenties fighting billionaires in their sixties.

This book would not have come to fruition without my agent, Howard Yoon, who believed in it from the start. You have given me brilliant advice and exhibited more patience than anyone can ask for in the ten years this project has taken. I owe a special debt of gratitude to my dear friend Kent Babb. You are my fellow barbecue connoisseur and occasional partaker of bourbon who never failed to deliver your passion, skill, wit, candor, and brilliance. Thank you both for your unyielding friendship.

I have been blessed to work with the best team at Penguin Random House. My editors, Ben Greenberg and Marie Pantojan, understood the vision and worked with me to make this book special and something I am very proud to have produced with you. The rest of the team—Azraf Khan, Dan Novak, Greg Kubie, Ayelet Durantt, Victoria Hernandez, and Nithya Rajendran—provided expert advice and diligence. I owe a special thanks to Mark Warren, who was the first person on this project and to whom I connected and continue to consult for his wisdom. Thank you all.

*Turf Wars* is not only about what happened but also about my journey as a man of color, a lawyer, and a student of history and ethics. Gary Percesepe, my favorite professor and friend, your classes in philosophy, religion, and ethics shaped my worldview and helped me maintain my faith. To all my friends, fellow lawyers, and union leaders who contributed to this worldview, thank you for your instruction, wise counsel, and friendship.

My friendships are for life, and for all of you who have taken the time and love to seal this relationship, I am deeply indebted to you and your help on this book. I have known many of you for decades, some of you work for the league, some of you have been colleagues, some of you have been on opposite sides, and all of you have provided me with valuable insights for this book. Almost all of you have answered a call without many details when I just needed a word or two to know that I was doing the right thing or headed in the right direction. Thank you all: Heather McPhee, Teri Smith, Stephanie Linehan, Ira Fishman, George Atallah, Tom DePaso, Ahmad Nassar, Don Davis, Sandra Hanna, Mark Bucher, Michael Rubin, the Barretts, Jim Barker, Jim Atkinson, Sherri Toomb, Catherine Ramsdell, Dave Zirin, and, of course, the Sports Junkies. A special thanks to Robert Kraft. Early on, you told me, "This is not a straight-line business." This book provides a small window into how prescient that advice (and warning) was when you gave it. Despite our occasional fights and disagreements, you have been a good friend and provided wise and indispensable counsel.

We live in challenging times when the greatest failure will be the lack of will to fight for what is right. The NFL is a microcosm of America and brings with it her politics, benefits, excesses, and prejudices; and more often than not, positive change usually comes from the people most impacted. In this case, it is the players. I have had the privilege of learning from some of the best who stood on the shoulders of Bill Radovich, John Mackey, Freeman McNeil, Justice Alan Page, Reggie White, the great Gene Upshaw, and many others who made the thankless decision to sue the NFL for decades. Their courage mirrored others like Oscar Robertson and Curt Flood. Much like our democracy, the successes of our union fall to a small group of people who are willing to make sacrifices for the future and for people they likely will never know. While I will forget some, I have served with the best: Kevin Mawae, Tom Brady, Drew Brees, Eric Winston, Brian Dawkins, Mike Vrabel, Kevin Carter, Tony Richardson, Brian Waters, Ryan Wendell, Ryan Clark, Shaun Suisham, Cornelius Bennett, Floyd Little, Brig Owens, Desmond Howard, Eric Reid, Domonique Foxworth, Mark Bruener, Donovin Darius, Keenan McCardell, Sean Morey, Ernie Conwell, Tom Carter, Vincent Jackson, Colin Kaepernick, Matt Hasselback, Don Hasselback, Richard Sherman, Michael Thomas, Scott Turner, Andy Studebaker, Jason Belser, Adam Vinatieri, Zak DeOssie, Lee Smith, Matt Slater, Calais Campbell,

Wesley Woodyard, Pat Richter, John Riggins, Sam McCullum, Tyson Clabo, Thomas Davis, Frostee Rucker, Mason Crosby, Jordy Nelson, Nick Sundberg, Ramon Foster, Andy Goldberg, Ben Garland, Steve Smith, Sr., Johnson Bademosi, Von Miller, Kyle Williams, Dhani Jones, Chester Pitts, Mike Pouncey, Brandon Chubb, Zamir Cobb, Dwayne Allen, Maurkice Pouncey, Martellus Bennett, Bobby Wagner, Malcolm Jenkins, Kelvin Beachum, Josh McCown, Drew Bledsoe, Scott Fujita, Charlie Batch, Kenny Stills, Osi Umenyiora, Jason Baker, Patrick Mahomes, Lester Archambeau, and Clark Gaines, just to name a few. Thank you all.

To the small group of people whose time was more valuable than any precious metal, you taught me how to be a union leader and appreciate the struggle to validate the humanity of work and the rights of those who perform it. Thank you, Marvin Miller, Michael Weiner, John Wilhelm, Rich Trumka, Liz Shuler, Ed Garvey, Tony Clark, Terri Jackson, Becca Roux, Meghann Burke, Bob Foose, and Don Fehr. *Turf Wars* is a union book and blessed be the fight. The generations of Smiths, Fitzgeralds, Motleys, and Scandretts endured, survived, and thrived despite a legal bondage system. They could never predict the comfort of my life, but they could imagine the benefits of their children's freedom and they were willing to die for it.

Finally, my wife, Karen, makes everything possible, including this book. I look back on nearly fifteen years of over one-hundred flights annually and countless emergencies and realize that this all came after ten years as a prosecutor who received death threats, and then another dozen years of being on call for clients. I have been gone for an exceptionally long time, and you managed to raise our two beautiful children, Elizabeth and Alex, and keep our lives in some sense of normalcy. Thank you and I love you. My parents, Mildred and Arthur Smith, celebrated their sixty-fourth wedding anniversary around the time we finished *Turf Wars*. They provided me with an unshakable faith in family, true love, and resilience. I love you and our entire family with every fiber of my being.

# SOURCES

In addition to my firsthand experience as the Executive Director for the NFLPA, this book draws from additional primary sources, which will be linked to on my social media and websites.

# INDEX

## ABOUT THE AUTHOR

DeMaurice Smith is the former executive director of the National Football League Players Association. Prior to the NFLPA, Smith was an Assistant United States Attorney and counsel to the U.S. deputy attorney general and a partner in major law firms. Smith is currently a law and business professor in residence.

X: @demauricesmith